Academic Tribes and Territories

Other titles recently published under the SRHE/Open University Press imprint:

Michael Allen: *The Goals of Universities*
William Birch: *The Challenge to Higher Education*
David Bond: *Teaching in Laboratories*
Heather Eggins: *Restructuring Higher Education*
Colin Evans: *Language People*
Derek Gardiner: *The Anatomy of Supervision*
Gunnar Handal and Per Lauvås: *Promoting Reflective Teaching*
Vivien Hodgson *et al.: Beyond Distance Teaching, Towards Open Learning*
Peter Linklater: *Education and the World of Work*
Graeme Moodie: *Standards and Criteria in Higher Education*
John Pratt and Suzanne Silverman: *Responding to Constraint*
Marjorie E. Reeves: *The Crisis in Higher Education*
John T. E. Richardson *et al.: Student Learning*
Derek Robbins: *The Rise of Independent Study*
Gordon Taylor *et al.: Literacy by Degrees*
Malcolm Tight: *Academic Freedom and Responsibility*
David Watson: *Managing the Modular Course*
Susan Warner Weil and Ian McGill: *Making Sense of Experiential Learning*
Alan Woodley *et al.: Choosing to Learn*

Academic Tribes and Territories

Intellectual enquiry and the cultures of disciplines

Tony Becher

The Society for Research into Higher Education &
Open University Press

Published by SRHE and
Open University Press
12 Cofferidge Close
Stony Stratford
Milton Keynes MK11 1BY

and
1900 Frost Road, Suite 101
Bristol, PA 19007, USA

First Published 1989

British Library Cataloguing in Publication Data
Becher, Tony
    Academic tribes and territories: intellectual
    enquiry and the cultures of disciplines.
    1. Higher education
    I. Title
    378

    ISBN 0–335–09221–7
    ISBN 0–335–09220–9 pbk

Library of Congress Cataloging-in-Publication Data
Becher, Tony.
    Academic tribes and territories: intellectual enquiry and the
    cultures of disciplines/by Tony Becher.
        p.   cm.
    Bibliography: p.
    ISBN 0–335–09221–7   ISBN 0–335–09220–9 (pbk.)
    1. Universities and colleges – Great Britain – Faculty.
    2. Universities and colleges – United States – Faculty.
    3. Universities and colleges – Great Britain – Curricula.
    4. Universities and colleges – United States – Curricula.   I. Title.
    LB2331.74.G7B43   1989
    378.1'2'0941 – dc20   89–34087
                                                                    CIP

Typeset by Scarborough Typesetting Services
Printed in Great Britain by St Edmundsbury Press,
Bury St Edmunds

Each tribe has a name and a territory, settles its own affairs, goes to war with the others, has a distinct language or at least a distinct dialect and a variety of ways of demonstrating its apartness from others.

F. G. Bailey (1977)

Contents

Preface

This book began with a mild obsession. In 1959, I read – and, in common with a number of others, was profoundly irritated by – C. P. Snow's *The Two Cultures and the Scientific Revolution* (1959). Having myself been trained in philosophy, I took the view then, as I do now, that it offered a superficial and conceptually flawed polarization between the worlds of the sciences and the humanities. That experience triggered off a concern to establish that there are many more numerous and more subtle boundaries than Snow's polemic allowed within the world of scholarly enquiry, and many bridges across what he chose to depict as a grand canyon of the intellect.

It was not, however, until a further 20 years had passed that I found a way to develop more actively my interest in mapping the variegated territory of academic knowledge and in exploring the diverse characteristics of those who inhabit and cultivate it. If I owe the physicist who wrote *The Two Cultures* the debt of making me think about the question, I owe the anthropologist Clifford Geertz, more than anyone else, the inspiration of how to get to grips with it. It was his unpublished paper, 'Towards an ethnography of the disciplines' (Geertz 1976, partly reproduced in Geertz 1983), that set me off on the investigation on which the present study is based.

Having once identified the means, the opportunity followed closely. I am beholden to the University of Sussex, where I was by then teaching, for giving me 9 months' study leave in 1980, and to the University of California for awarding me a Visiting Fellowship to the Center for Studies in Higher Education at its Berkeley campus for 3 of those months. I was able during that period to undertake a substantial part of the fieldwork for my investigation. I was not, however, in a position to follow it up more than sporadically for the subsequent 6 years, until another period of study leave and another Visiting Fellowship to Berkeley allowed me to complete my data collection and to do a great deal of relevant background reading. The wide range of sources listed in my bibliography is a tribute to the excellence of the University of California's multi-campus library system. During both periods of active research, I was also indebted to the Nuffield Foundation for awards under its Social Sciences Small Grants Scheme which contributed towards the costs of travel, typing and other research expenses. In the intervening years, two colleagues in particular – Burton R. Clark of the University of California at Los Angeles and Eskil Björklund of the Swedish National Board of Universities and Colleges – encouraged me to develop my emergent ideas and sponsored me to write about them. Their support helped significantly to sustain my commitment to the enterprise.

I have always found dialogue a more congenial mode than soliloquy of generating and shaping ideas, so I am in the habit of asking the more indulgent and long-suffering of my friends to comment on the drafts of most of what I write. On this occasion, no less than 10 of them were prevailed upon to read critically through the whole of the book in draft: Michael Black, Roger Blin-Stoyle, Barry Cooper, Mary Henkel, Eric Hewton, Dorothy Jerrome, Robert Murray, Trevor Pateman, Sheldon Rothblatt and Martin Trow. Their comments, individually and collectively, led not only to numerous improvements in style and clarity but also to my recognition that a sizeable part of the original text needed to be jettisoned and another substantial element restructured. I am deeply grateful to them for the trouble they took and the help they gave me – and so ought any reader to be, for a much improved exposition.

The plan of the book, as it now exists, differs significantly from the one I had in mind when I first embarked on my systematic study of the cultures of academic disciplines. At the time, I saw myself as putting together a series of perhaps six to a dozen different ethnographic accounts, each attempting to portray those who worked in a particular field and the particular field they worked in. But as the enquiry proceeded and the piles of data accumulated, it became clear that some of the most interesting features of the investigation lay in the comparisons and contrasts between different groups, and that the process of marking these demanded an analytic approach, as against successive portrayal.

The decision to focus on recurrent and apparently significant themes across disciplines brought a major change in its wake. When they key issues began to emerge and to become more clearly identifiable, it was obvious that my data were not sufficiently exhaustive to allow me to pronounce on every theme with equal conviction or with comparably persuasive supporting evidence. This was especially the case when I came to consider in detail those aspects relating to the nature of knowledge, as against those concerned with the workings of the academic community. To do the argument proper justice, it was clear that I could not rely on my own field material alone, but would have to draw extensively on the research findings of others.

In consequence, my exposition now rests on a combination of two main categories of testimony: that drawn from my first-hand enquiries into different disciplines, and that which derives at second hand from a diversity of written sources. I hope I have made the distinctions between them evident enough in the process of quoting them: but the reader will soon be as aware as I am that the balance between the two shifts quite markedly from place to place in the text. The interview material comes most strongly into its own in Chapters 4, 5, 6 and 8; Chapters 1, 2, 3 and 7 call more extensively on the relevant research literature. The majority of previous enquiry has focused on the natural sciences (on my rough estimate, science-related investigations outnumber by about two to one those in the humanities, social sciences and applied fields taken together). A subsidiary consequence is that they also seem at times to dominate my account. I have tried as far as I can to offset this bias, but the material available has not always allowed me to do so.

For those with a taste for methodological issues, the way in which I collected my field data and the longer-term research implications of the study are reviewed in the Appendix. Here it is only necessary to mention that I built up my understanding of the different subjects in my chosen sample by asking practitioners in each of the relevant fields to share with me their own ideas, perceptions and experiences. Altogether, I interviewed just over 220 academics, spanning 12 disciplines and 18 institutions in two countries (Britain and the USA). I owe my largest debt of all to those colleagues, for so willingly giving their time and so generously contributing their thoughts to my enquiry.

Tony Becher

1

Points of Departure

Relating tribes and territories

The central thesis of the pages which follow is the relationship between people and ideas. The people are the practitioners in a dozen varied disciplines whose livelihood it is to work with ideas; the ideas are those which lend themselves to sustained exploration, and which form the subject matter of the disciplines in question.

The contention I advance, and here set out to substantiate, is that the ways in which particular groups of academics organize their professional lives are intimately related to the intellectual tasks on which they are engaged. In practice, the two would seem to be inseparably intertwined; but in attempting to explore the characteristic features of their relationship it is necessary to separate the first analytically from the second. I therefore seek to draw a distinction between the social aspects of knowledge communities and the epistemological properties of knowledge forms, and also to look closely at how the two influence one another.

I do not claim that the pattern is a simple one, or that the connections are unconditional. In many cases, both individual and group behaviour can be seen to be affected by factors outside the field of knowledge itself – and sometimes outside the academic world broadly defined. In other cases, the most appropriate explanation for a particular cultural phenomenon may be in terms of apparently arbitrary convention. But my concern is to highlight a significant number of situations in which disciplinary practices can be closely matched with the characteristics of the relevant domains of enquiry.

In the process of identifying the interconnections between academic cultures and the nature of knowledge, a number of subsidiary themes are developed. The first is about how knowledge itself can usefully be categorized and characterized for the purposes of the present argument. Other topics relate to the properties of disciplines, individually and collectively, and to their subsidiary specialisms; others again to the people who inhabit the academic world, their careers, their interactions and the rules which govern their behaviour.

The source material

The subject areas on which the study is based cover a deliberately wide variety: biology, chemistry and physics are from the pure sciences; mechanical engineering and pharmacy are from applied science; economics and sociology are normally classified as social sciences; history and modern languages are located among the humanities; academic law may be described as a humanities-related profession; and geography and mathematics are not easily categorized, though the former is sometimes included among the social and the latter among the pure sciences.

The content and structure of the book derives in the first instance from the testimony of practising academics in each of these 12 fields, as conveyed in the individual interviews I conducted with them. Wherever assertions or quotations remain unattributed in the text, they should be taken as based directly on this source material. But I have also drawn extensively on the published – and more rarely the unpublished – writings of other researchers interested in this general area of enquiry. My references to their work are acknowledged through the normal conventions of citation.

The questions which I raised in my interviews fell into five main categories. The first concerned the characteristics of the discipline: its overall nature and content, its internal and external boundaries, its degree of unity across specialisms, its nearest intellectual neighbours, the extent to which its profile varied from one country to another, and so on. The second group concerned epistemological issues: the role of theory, the importance of specialized techniques, the extent of quantification and modelling, the degree to which findings could be generalized, the way conclusions were established, and the like. The third concerned career patterns, including questions about the recruitment of new members and their induction into the discipline, how their specialisms were chosen, how they established independence and gained tenure, how much mobility there was between specialisms, and whether it was common to experience a 'mid-career crisis' in one's research. A fourth, closely related cluster of issues concentrated on reputations and rewards, such as the criteria for professional recognition, the existence and characteristics of disciplinary heroes, terms of praise and blame, and prizes and other marks of distinction. The fifth category explored questions about professional activity: the nature of communication patterns, forms and rates of publication, the structure of personal networks, competition and priority, plagiarism and sharp practice, grantsmanship and fashion, the extent of teamwork, and the incidence of jargon. A final set of questions sought, without intruding too far into respondents' private lives, to explore their value systems: the extent of their involvement in their work, the aspects of their jobs which they considered particularly rewarding or unrewarding, the degree to which, as professionals, they were concerned with contemporary social and environmental issues, the wider benefits of their academic training, their stereotypes of fellow practitioners, and their stereotypes of practitioners in a variety of other disciplines.

As a matter of policy, I confined my attention to members of those departments which were viewed as reasonably prestigious within their disciplinary communities.[1]* With more time and resources, it might have been useful to explore the whole spectrum from leading research departments to ones whose activity focuses largely if not entirely on undergraduate teaching. However, it is the former which most clearly delineate and embody the central values of the discipline. As Clifford Geertz (1983), among others, has pointed out:

> Induction into the [disciplinary] community takes place at or near the top or center. But most people are not settled at or near the top or center but at some region lower down, further out. . . . The majority of people follow a career pattern in which they are for several years at the perceived heart of things and then, in differing degrees and with different speeds are, in the jargon, 'downwardly mobile'.

Most academics will have taken their own first and higher degrees in élite institutions, even if they currently hold posts in non-élite ones. The disciplinary values with which they are first inculcated are therefore the values of the leading departments in their fields. Although these values might become modified by the demands of their present jobs, the definitive pattern is the one which is to be found 'at the perceived heart of things'. So it seemed sensible to concentrate on the pacemakers rather than those that follow behind them.

The interviews were designed to encourage reasonably open-ended discussion about professional issues, but not specifically about the academic's role as a teacher. A limited number of respondents – particularly in the more vocationally oriented disciplines – did choose to talk about undergraduate courses and students, but the large majority preferred to focus on their activities as seekers after knowledge rather than as communicators of it.[2] The reason for this, it might be inferred, is that membership of the academic profession – at least in élite departments – is defined in terms of excellence in scholarship and originality in research, and not to any significant degree in terms of teaching capability. Had the programme of interviews included non-élite institutions, the pattern of responses might have been different. However, if it is indeed the leaders in the field who set the norms, those norms do not for the most part appear to include pedagogic considerations. In consequence, there is relatively little

---

* Superscript numerals refer to numbered notes at the end of each chapter.

in this book about the transmission of knowledge, as against its creation, development and communication to fellow specialists.

Limitations of perspective

Any piece of research which does not aspire to be encyclopaedic and all-embracing must start from a particular perspective. In addition to its concentration on research rather than on teaching and learning, there are two other limitations of the approach adopted in this book about which the reader should be forewarned. First, it adopts an internalist rather than an externalist standpoint, deferring until its last two chapters even a limited consideration of contextual issues and influences. Much has already been written, particularly by sociologists of knowledge, about the extent to which human enquiry is shaped by the environment in which it is conducted, with the strong implication that academic activity cannot be separated from the broader political and economic structures in which it takes place. It is not my concern here to contest this view, although I seek in the course of my analysis to establish that an alternative starting-point can highlight different, but none the less comparably revealing, aspects of the academic enterprise. My own focus is on the way in which those engaged in research perceive their own activities, rather than on how such activities can be interpreted by others who choose to set them in a wider canvas and to discern in them meanings of a less straightforward (and sometimes a more deterministic) kind.

The second assumption is related, albeit indirectly, to the first. If the choice has to be posed between a realist and a relativist view of knowledge, my inclination is towards the former. It is not essential to my line of argument to contend that truth is somehow 'out there'. Nor would I want to maintain the characteristics of knowledge to be immutable: it is evident that people look at the same phenomenon in different ways at different times and, more generally, that the nature of a field of enquiry may change as our apprehension of it increases. However, it is crucial to my argument that, once such a field becomes identified in terms of certain characteristics (once it is defined, for example, as dealing in generalities rather than particularities), a whole set of properties inherent in that identification come into play – properties which can profoundly affect the way of life of those engaged in the exploration of the field. The cultural consequences in these instances have to be seen as closely derived from epistemological considerations.

This is not the place to go into the realist–relativist controversy in any detail. But to claim that every aspect of intellectual life can ultimately be explained in sociological terms seems to me to constitute an extreme form of reductionism, if not of disciplinary imperialism. If questions of truth and falsity owe nothing to phenomena outside the socially constructed interpretations of members of contemporary society, it would seem no more than a matter of arbitrary consensus that Newton's laws of motion were held to be valid, or that the atomic bombing of Hiroshima foreshadowed the end of the Second World War. Again, any sense of progress, any claim that our understanding of the natural or the human world has advanced over time, must presumably be attributed to no more than an intersubjective strengthening of our confidence in our current criteria of intelligibility.

In considering the progressive development of understanding – a possibility which relativism would seem to disallow – it may be relevant to ask why the notion of discovery is crucially important in some fields of enquiry and less important, or perhaps important in a different way, in others. For example, in solid-state physics and molecular biology, discovery is a central theme. It is less obviously so in taxonomic studies of plant and animal life, while in mechanical engineering the concept is largely replaced by that of invention. Moving further afield, the term seems out of place in academic law; and in history, the discovery of new primary material, though significant when it occurs, is not the central feature of the historian's interpretive task. These differences do not, I want to suggest, lie merely in the differing social norms that mark off the members of one academic culture from another; they derive in part at least from the epistemological characteristics of the types of enterprise on which the academics in question are engaged.

Some landmarks in the argument

It is in the final chapter that a systematic attempt will be made to identify the linkages between the social and the cognitive – between academic tribes and the territories they inhabit. The patterns of interconnection will be built up gradually throughout the text, rather than presented initially as a matter on which the reader is offered no evidential base to exercise his or her own critical judgement. However, it may be helpful to identify in advance some of the main considerations which support the concluding analysis, and to draw attention to some particular features which differentiate my argument from the accounts which have been advanced by others.

The first point to be established is how academic knowledge may usefully be categorized for the purposes of the study as a whole. The consideration of that issue will occupy the concluding part of the present chapter, and will provide a base from which to embark on a survey of the nature of disciplines and their constituent specialisms. It will be seen that the proposed classification is a well-established one, based on the two independent dimensions of hard and soft, pure and applied, knowledge.

The dimensions used to categorize the social features of knowledge communities are, however, less familiar. The first, which denotes the spectrum between convergent, tightly knit disciplinary configurations and those which are divergent and loosely knit, is first adumbrated in Chapter 3, but is developed further in the subsequent discussion. The second, marking the continuum from urban to rural modes of research activity, is introduced in Chapter 5, as a prelude to the scrutiny of the distinctive patterns of communication associated with different types of academic networks.[3]

Another dichotomy worth highlighting at this point, in that it plays a significant, if sporadic, part in the discussion, is one between contextual imperatives and contextual associations. These opposing notions derive from the the antithesis between hard and soft knowledge areas. Contextual imperatives denote closely patterned sequences of explanation, with each new finding fitting neatly into place as the whole picture is pieced together. Contextual associations signify loosely knit clusters of ideas, with no clearly articulated framework of development. Both have clearly identifiable social correlates.

The characteristics attributable to the various levels of aggregation of knowledge – from broad subject groupings to small segments within specialized subdisciplinary areas – form another, and more important, subsidiary theme in the exposition. In particular, it transpired in the course of the study that specialisms display certain structural features which distinguish them from other specialisms within the same discipline, but which they share with comparable specialisms in other disciplines. As a result, the specialism rather than its parent discipline not only emerges as the fundamental unit of analysis but also comprises the domain in which the interrelationships between the cognitive and social aspects of the academic enterprise are most clearly manifested.

If the book as a whole has something new to say, it is perhaps because its theme straddles the little-explored border zone between the sociology of knowledge and social studies of science on the one hand, and the study of higher education on the other. The first has tended to concentrate almost exclusively on highly articulated areas of enquiry – the physical as against the biological sciences, physics as against chemistry, and high-energy physics as against more applied specialisms such as optics. It has had relatively little to say about technology, the social sciences or the humanities, except in so far as it represents them as less perfect manifestations of the orderly and relatively easily depicted ideal of hard pure knowledge. Writers on higher education have focused largely on structural and organizational issues, playing down what Trow (1976a) has called the 'private life' of higher education. My own prime concern has been with the latter, and in particular with the range of disciplines and disciplinary communities outside as well as within the domain of 'big science'.

A fitting way to begin mapping this relatively uncharted territory is by recognizing the diversity and range of its topology and attempting to bring some order into the apparently chaotic configuration of features which constitute the landscape of academic knowledge.

The pieces of the patchwork

Knowledge has many metaphors. The image of a landscape is only one: another favoured candidate is a seamless cloak. That, however, has implications of continuity and coherence which bear poor comparison with the current state of human understanding. From the perspective of those engaged in its creation, knowledge would appear more closely comparable with a badly made patchwork quilt, some of whose constituent scraps of material are only loosely tacked together, while others untidily overlap, and yet others seem inadvertently to have been omitted, leaving large and shapeless gaps in the fabric of the whole.

This claim may be readily illustrated from the accounts of witnesses who are themselves involved in the enterprise. The brief bulletins which follow on the current state of awareness in four different subject areas are based directly on the evidence of my interviews with researchers in each field in question. Their individual statements may not of course be representative, but, taken together, they indicate a series of idiosyncratic approaches towards the definition of relevant knowledge on the part of their own disciplinary groups. None matches closely the stereotype of hard pure knowledge adopted by many writers on the subject.

Let us start with biology: it is a field in which 'the living organism is the centre of gravity'; but 'the biological sciences are more wide-ranging than other scientific disciplines – and the extremes are further apart from one another'. Besides being 'very heterogeneous', biology is also 'an inexact science': 'the evidence is incomplete and scrappy, and in many cases the observations can't be repeated'. Although 'biologists are attracted by the idea of generalisation, [they are] very conscious of the variability of the material with which they deal'; 'virtually every generalisation is suspect'. In their turn, 'the variations in nature give rise to interpretation – there is a greater degree of subjectivity than most of us like to admit'. But even so, 'there is not much room for ideology . . . whatever your own beliefs, eventually someone will be able to demonstrate that results caused by personal bias are invalid'.

Mechanical engineering is also said by its proponents to be a 'very wide-ranging subject'. It is centrally concerned with 'the application of mechanical principles to technical devices', but it is about 'hardware for people' as well – and is thus 'concerned with economics, environment and the social situation'. Because it is 'a professional discipline . . . the problems are in a sense externally defined'. Moreover, 'the problems usually have no unique solutions'. Knowledge is cumulative, in the sense that 'it follows the development of understanding and technique'; but 'the relevance and implications of particular results are less clear than they are implicit'.

The core of sociology lies in 'exploring the action of social forces', and 'understanding the principles of change in society'. This involves 'looking for generalities', 'seeking causal explanations', and leads to a concern with 'the development of theory' and 'choices between hypotheses' – with 'knowledge that has explanatory power'. But the material for investigation is held to be too complex to allow for 'immutable social laws': there are 'very few axioms'. So a more realistic aim is to seek 'common patterns and processes in particular contexts'. There is a sense of 'progression in ideas' – 'both the subject-matter and the theoretical emphasis change over time'. Sociology is 'closer to history than to physics', in that 'it's more a matter of revising the existing corpus than building a new one'; of 'refutation and reformulation' – there is 'no sense of superseded knowledge'. The discipline embraces 'a spectrum from hard to soft data' – there are 'no tight, clear boundaries'. Theories are 'always contested – there are no consensual judgements'. But there are none the less 'perennial issues and problems', certain 'basic continuities and perennial concerns' which give the subject its definition and its shape.

In academic law, 'the centre of the subject is a body of rules'. The concern of its proponents is 'mainly with ordering a corpus of knowledge: it is a largely descriptive pursuit'. Law, one respondent observed, 'is the object, not the method of study – it can only be the method of practice'. There is a constantly changing body of material arising from new legislation – 'everything is always in a state of flux'. There is 'a tradition that law is value-free'; it is arguable that 'it is more resistant to ideology than some subjects'. Nevertheless, 'it leaves open the possibility of a critical, ideological function'. The subject allows 'room for shades of opinion', 'an absence of certainty, no clear-cut rules'. However, 'some aspects are un-contentious'; there are 'shared criteria of judgement'; 'a substantial consensus – at least until recently'; and 'validity in some areas within the existing norms'.

These very diverse accounts seem at first glance to point towards an unmanageable variety of knowledge forms. To be able to discuss them in any coherent manner, the next step must be to find a suitable means of grouping and classifying them.

Restrictions and paradigms

Taxonomies of knowledge fields have been generated in a wide variety of ways, and have yielded a multiplicity of different structures. Two examples are worth quoting at the outset, because of their particular contributions to the understanding of forms and communities of knowledge. The accounts of their originators (Pantin and Kuhn) share certain superficial similarities: both advance a simple, two-fold categorization; both are ostensibly concerned with the sciences to the exclusion of other disciplinary groups. However, it should be remarked that the basic distinctions that are made in each case can be extended to apply across the whole realm of academic knowledge, rather than being confined to one part of it; and that the import of the two is different in significant respects. Pantin's classification bears primarily on knowledge structures and relates to individual special-isms within disciplines, while Kuhn's is primarily concerned with academic communities and applies to the disciplinary rather than subdisciplinary level of research activity.

In marking the contrasts between what he calls the restricted and the unrestricted sciences, Pantin (1968) writes:

> There is one real, and graded, distinction between sciences like the biologies and the physical sciences. The former are *unrestricted* sciences and their investigator must be prepared to follow their problems into any other science whatsoever. The physical sciences, as they are understood, are restricted in the field of phenomena to which they are devoted. They do not require the investigator to traverse all other sciences. But while this restriction is the basis of their success, because of the introduction of this restricted simplicity of their field we cannot necessarily take them or their methods as typical of all the sciences.

Earlier in the same chapter, he elaborates on the point:

> The more we restrict the class of phenomena we observe and the number of its variables, the more far-reaching are the possible deductive consequences of our hypotheses. But in doing so, much of the grand variety of natural phenomena is systematically excluded from study. Very clever men are answering the relatively easy questions of the natural examination paper. In contrast, in biology such problems as 'What will be the ecological consequences of a general increase in nuclear radiation?' are so difficult that our answers seem paltry and emotional.

He does not attempt, in discussing the application of this dichotomy to 'the relations between the sciences', to draw out its implications to any significant extent (though Whitley 1977 argues that restricted sciences are also characterized by an esoteric theoretical structure and the need for elaborate technical facilities, while unrestricted fields are less theoretically specific). Moreover, it is less clear how current developments in unrestric-ted fields should be evaluated, and what directions future work should take. The more 'narrowly and specifically conceptual closure is made', the more clearly the domain boundaries are drawn.

The stratagem which Pantin's analysis exposes is that of defining out the messy problems in order to maintain the clarity and coherence of the physical sciences. To the extent that this is successful, one might say that the disciplines concerned depend on an artefactual definition of their bounda-ries. But it also has to be recognized that the territory so bounded has certain inherent characteristics which make such a definition possible (these will be further explored below, in the process of marking the distinctions between hard and soft knowledge). In contrast, other areas of science – those which span 'the grand variety of natural phenomena', but also those which embrace practical applications are less tidy. And in the social sciences and humanities many of the problems seem, as one historian I interviewed vividly put it, 'inherently lumpy'.

Kuhn is concerned with exploring a different distinction. His starting point (Kuhn 1962) was in the study of revolutionary phases in the development of physics, which led him to develop the notion of a paradigm. This is central to his differentiation of disciplinary groupings: on the one side the 'mature' sciences with clearly established paradigms, on the other those areas of research which are still at a pre-paradigmatic stage of development.

The contrast Kuhn marks is predominantly a social one: it is more akin to that between convergent, tightly knit and divergent, loosely knit academic communities than it is to that differentiating hard from soft knowledge domains. Its attraction to those who have subsequently adopted it seems, however, to have rested at least in part on the malleability of the underlying concept of a paradigm. The term is variously used and variously defined.[4] In some contexts it appears to denote the particular constellation of ideas and techniques, beliefs and values which serves to define a disciplinary culture (a sense that it is 'global, embracing all the shared commitments of a scientific group'; Kuhn 1977). In others, it is given the narrower sense of a 'disciplinary matrix', a compilation of the symbolic generalizations, models and exemplars which form 'the common possession of the practitioners of a professional discipline' (Kuhn 1977).

Clear and unambiguous paradigms denote disciplinary consensus; competing, formless, or non-existent ones are ascribed to communities in which there is a significant level of internal disagreement in both general ways of seeing the world and specific ways of tackling research issues. Scientific progress stems from working in a context in which there is close agreement on theories, methods of inquiry and the training of newcomers to the discipline. Where there is pluralism and dissension, as in many of the humanities and social sciences, systematic advances in knowledge must await the onset of maturity and the emergence of a developed paradigm. The implication here – which Kuhn does not develop in any detail – is that in the course of time preparadigmatic subjects will evolve towards mature paradigmatic status. As things now stand, there are a number of key distinctions, such as the demands for solutions to problems in the mature sciences to be unique, though this is not required or necessarily expected in other fields; the extent to which past knowledge is superseded, as against its maintaining some relevance over long periods of time; and the 'radically different value placed on innovation for innovation's sake' (Kuhn 1977).

It is tempting at this point to ask whether it is right to interpret Kuhn's analysis as suggesting that the differences in degree of consensus which a disciplinary community is able to command are the result of no more than historical or social circumstance. Can it be nothing at all to do with the nature of their subject matter that physicists are able to identify 'shared commitments' in a way that, say, sociologists and modern linguists seem incapable of doing? The answer will, I hope, become evident as the argument proceeds.

Knowledge as portrayed by the knower

Both Pantin and Kuhn base their taxonomies on the detached observation of how researchers operate in their exploration of different domains. From the standpoint of this study, another useful approach to categorizing and characterizing knowledge forms derives from an examination of how the actors themselves perceive the particular arenas in which they are engaged. This type of phenomenological analysis can be illustrated by the contributions of Biglan and Kolb.

Biglan (1973a) based his discussion of 'the characteristics of subject matter in different academic areas' on questionnaire data from academics. His sample was relatively small (168 faculty members at the University of Illinois and 54 at a small western college), but his findings were detailed. On the basis of the judgements he had solicited about similarities and differences among 36 subject areas, he was able to derive three main dimensions against which to map the responses: hard *vs* soft, pure *vs* applied and life system *vs* non-life system. He associates the first with 'the degree to which a paradigm exists' (though it would in my view be more aptly identified with Pantin's restricted–unrestricted dichotomy); the second is related to 'the degree of concern with application'; and the third serves to differentiate 'biological and social areas from those that deal with inanimate objects'. His mappings of subject areas on to pairs of these dimensions help to underline the diversity of epistemological characteristics of different academic disciplines. While the data suggest some close affinities between particular groups of knowledge fields across any two of the three mappings, only relatively few (such as chemistry and physics or the various subspecialisms of engineering) form a stable cluster across the whole range.

Where Biglan – in common with other writers such as Lodahl and Gordon (1972) – concerned himself with how academics themselves perceive the characteristics of knowledge fields, using survey techniques, Kolb (1981) adopted a contrasting approach. His data were derived from students' learning strategies rather than from the judgements of faculty members and involved the application, not of a questionnaire, but of a psychometric test – the Kolb Learning Style Inventory (LSI). It would seem all the more remarkable that his findings were quite closely consistent with those of Biglan. Kolb set out to measure 'learning styles along two basic dimensions of abstract–concrete and active–reflective' (the former contrasting a bias towards conceptualization with a domination by immediate experience, and the latter a preference for active experimentation over detached observation). In a study of 800 practitioners and students of management, who came from a wide variety of disciplinary backgrounds,

Kolb found that 'variations in learning style . . . were strongly associated with
. . . undergraduate educational experience'. When the average LSI scores
for various undergraduate majors were charted against the abstract–
concrete and active–reflective axes, the subject mappings overlapped to a
significant extent with Biglan's. To be more specific, using the latter's
'dimensions accounting for the most variance . . . hard–soft and
pure–applied' (i.e. dropping the life system–non-life system category), Kolb
was able to show that 'of the twelve disciplines common to the two studies,
nine are in identical quadrants'. When the exercise was repeated on a much
larger and wider database, the results were again 'highly consistent' between
Kolb's classifications and Biglan's. Kolb concluded that:

> the commonly accepted division of academic fields into two camps, the
> scientific and artistic, or abstract and concrete . . . might be usefully
> enriched by the addition of a second dimension, namely active–
> reflective or applied–basic. When academic fields are mapped on this
> two-dimensional space, a four-fold typology of disciplines emerges. In
> the abstract reflective [hard pure] quadrant are clustered the *natural
> sciences and mathematics*, while the abstract–active [hard applied]
> quadrant includes the *science-based professions*, most notably the
> engineering fields. The concrete–active [soft applied] quadrant
> encompasses what might be called the *social professions*, such as
> education, social work, and law. The concrete–reflective quadrant [soft
> pure] includes the *humanities and social sciences*.

The Kolb–Biglan classification of academic knowledge seems to me a
particularly apposite one for the purposes of this enquiry, though I prefer
Biglan's more familiar contrasts between hard and soft, pure and applied, to
the more esoteric terminology used by Kolb. It has a number of advantages
over its competitors. It is capable of making more subtle distinctions than are
the unidimensional scales adopted by Kuhn, Pantin and many other writers,
but is not so complex as to become unfunctional – a defect from which
Whitley's (1984) scheme would appear to suffer. It is more directly related to
established disciplinary groupings than are such abstract categorizations as
that developed by Hirst (1974), but departs from the well-worn clustering of
the natural sciences, social sciences and humanities to elide the division
between the latter two and to include relevant areas of application. In
contrast with the organizationally based taxonomy of Collins (1975), it
directs attention to the epistemological properties of knowledge fields as
much as to the social characteristics of research groups. Accordingly, it is the
system I propose to adopt in the subsequent discussion.

Characteristics of subject matter

So far, the emphasis has been on categories rather than contents. While
consideration has been given to the broad areas into which knowledge might

conveniently be classified, relatively little has been said about the epistemological features of any given category. That calls for a somewhat different
exercise, drawing on a related but not identical tradition of analysis. In
discussing it, I will limit the references to previous contributions on the
subject to eight sources in particular, three of which have already been cited
in the earlier discussion: Bazerman (1981), Becher (1987a), Bulik (1982),
Crick (1976), Kolb (1981), Kuhn (1970), Pantin (1968), and Storer and
Parsons (1968). To avoid tedious repetition, I will attribute sources in an
abbreviated form in the analysis which follows, using only the first two
letters of the relevant author's name (thus Ba will stand for Bazerman, Be
for Becher, and so on). The overall framework within which characteristics
will be assigned will be the one already identified, comprising four
domains: hard pure, soft pure, hard applied and soft applied.

Hard pure knowledge – the favoured domain of the natural sciences –
has almost invariably enjoyed the major share of the discussion of different
forms of intellectual enquiry. Since it is the best surveyed and most fully
charted of the four areas in question, it forms a natural starting point, with
soft pure knowledge as its most appropriate foil. There seems to be a
number of rough-and-ready groupings among the typical properties of
each area, though the connections are often too tenuous to allow such
clusters of characteristics to be identified by a common descriptor.

One dominant feature of hard pure knowledge is its relatively steady
cumulative growth (Be, Ku). One might say that new findings here are
typically generated by a linear development from the existing state of
awareness (scientists are prone to visualize themselves as standing on the
shoulders of their predecessors and to locate themselves with reference to a
moving frontier of knowledge). This process of accretion may be contrasted with the predominantly recursive or reiterative pattern of development which characterizes soft knowledge (Be, Ku). In the latter domain,
academic work often traverses ground already explored by others. Basic
issues maintain their currency from one generation to the next. Where,
metaphorically, hard pure knowledge grows like a crystal or branches out
like a tree, its soft pure counterpart evolves like an organism or meanders
like a river.

The accumulation of hard pure knowledge is, in a manner not easy to pin
down, connected with a variety of other features. Among these is the
apparent clarity of the criteria for establishing or refuting claims to new
knowledge (Ku). Major claims, if accepted, are regarded as discoveries, and
may result in novel types of explanation (Be). The mirror image in soft
pure knowledge can be seen in the diversity of criteria for, and the lack of
consensus about, what constitutes an authentic contribution to a particular
field. Widely recognized contributions commonly take the form of
interpretations, resulting in an enhanced insight into, or an understanding
of, familiar objects of knowledge (Be, Ku).[5]

Steady growth can also be associated with 'channels of implication' (St),
i.e. the predictability of problems which have direct relevance to future

advances. Scientists in hard pure fields seem able at any given time to identify what questions they should attempt to answer next. Perhaps this is because the boundaries within which they work are both clearly defined and circumscribed (Bu, Pa). In soft pure areas, the lack of such well-marked boundaries, and the greater apparent permeability of the loosely defined border zones which exist between neighbouring territories, may contribute to the *laissez-faire* manner in which new issues are selected and taken up at any particular point (Bu, Pa). It may be noted that the implications of present knowledge can relate to the past as well as the future, in that hard pure areas would appear to allow for the assimilation (and, in that sense, the supersession) of previous findings, while the notion of ideas becoming obsolete fits less comfortably into a soft pure context (Bu).

A number of these juxtapositions can be caught in the dichotomy, mentioned earlier in this chapter, between contextual imperatives and contextual associations. Yet another cluster of contrasting hard pure/soft pure properties is dominated by the opposition between analysis and synthesis. Where the natural sciences and mathematics might be said to break down complex ideas into simpler components, this process of reduction and atomization is repudiated in most of the humanities, and to some extent – if not so emphatically – in the social sciences as well (Ko, St). In the soft pure domain, complexity is regarded as a legitimate aspect of knowledge, to be recognized and appreciated as a holistic feature rather than served up as a candidate for reductionism.

The quantitative–qualitative dichotomy forms a grouping not far removed from this last. The humanities and social sciences, it has been argued, deal with 'minute conceptual delineation', as against the 'precision of measurement' demanded in physical science (Cr). Scientists learn about nature by seeking regularities and framing mathematical models (Cr, Ko, Pa). There is in contrast little scope for patterning and reproducibility within the soft pure domain. To make the point another way, scientific knowledge is concerned predominantly with universals; non-scientific knowledge tends to be focused on particulars (Ba, Be).

A further group of considerations links the differing degrees to which variability can be limited with the distinctive procedures for argument in the two domains. In hard pure disciplines, it may be conjectured, explanations appear 'strong', because they derive from the systematic scrutiny of relationships between a few carefully controlled variables; in soft pure subjects, where variables are more numerous and less amenable, researchers 'must often settle for weaker [explanations]' (Bu). Causal connections are relatively easier to establish in the natural world; 'human data' demand complex forms of reasoning in which judgement and persuasion play a more prominent role (Ba, Cr).

There is also what appears to be an important distinction between the impersonal, value-free nature of scientific knowledge and the personal, overtly value-laden domain of the humanities and social sciences (Ba, Ko,

St). It is relevant here that the notion of intentionality plays an important part in the study of human thought and action but has no such role in scientific and mathematical enquiry (Cr).

It would be rash to claim that such considerations exhaust the constituent properties of, and mutual contrasts between, hard pure and soft pure knowledge. None the less, they are perhaps numerous and familiar enough to provide an acceptable characterization and comparison. No such ready wealth of detail can be found when one attempts to carry out a similar analysis in relation to hard applied and soft applied knowledge fields, whether they be set off against one another or against their respective pure counterparts. Those authors who have provided an abundance of relevant ideas on arts, science and social science have had little to say about the social- or science-based professions, and other sources are hard to find: the intellectual territory here remains largely uncharted.

Two related reasons for this state of affairs come to mind. The first is that applied areas are by definition concerned with practical as well as theoretical knowledge, and that the former is the less easy to pin down and analyse (see the comparative neglect, among philosophers, of 'knowing how' as against 'knowing that'). The second is that, if it is easier, more attractive and more rewarding to dissect and display the prestigious world of the hard sciences than it is to grope one's way through the tangled undergrowth of the soft pure disciplines, it is less inviting still to try to illuminate the obscure and ill-favoured hinterland of application. But whether one, both or neither of these are the occasion of it, the dearth of material is evident enough.

One can at least observe, however, that hard applied knowledge is amenable to heuristic, trial-and-error approaches (Ko). It is not necessarily cumulative, though it may from time to time and area to area depend substantially on the techniques and findings of cumulative knowledge. It is not altogether quantitative, since application will always involve some element of qualitative judgement (consider, for example, the function of design in engineering or diagnosis in medicine). Because hard applied subjects are concerned with ways of mastering the physical world, the activities to which they give rise are typically directed towards some practical end and judged by the effectiveness with which they work, i.e. by purposive and functional criteria. Their primary outcomes, one might say, are products and techniques (Be).

Soft applied knowledge, in contrast, is built up to a sizeable extent on case law (Ko). It draws on soft pure knowledge as a means of understanding and coming to terms with the complexity of human situations, but does so with a view to enhancing the quality of personal and social life. It is not as stable as, and has a less evident sense of progression than, hard applied knowledge, since its intellectual roots are in the frequently reformulated interpretations of the humanities and social sciences rather than in the steady growth of the natural sciences (in academic law, as one of my respondents pointed out, 'there isn't much building on someone else's work'). For most subjects in this category, such as education, social administration and the humanistic aspects of medicine, the primary outcomes are protocols and procedures, whose functions are judged mainly in pragmatic and utilitarian terms.

Some concluding reservations

The result of using such broad and sweeping brush strokes to depict the four knowledge domains which have formed the subject of this portrayal must inevitably be closer to a sketch in rough outline than to a fully formed and faithful likeness. The qualifying detail and the particularities of feature and expression remain to be filled in, and must form the subject of further representation. But for the present, two particular caveats must be entered against the account that has been given: the one concerns the effects of temporal change and the other the oversimplification of categories.

The steadily changing (and, in the long term, transient) nature of knowledge makes it difficult to claim that any attempt at categorizing it can be permanent and enduring. It is not only that what counts as present understanding quite obviously differs with the passage of time: as Hirst (1974) allows, it is also possible that quite new forms of knowledge could emerge and – one might add – existing ones become defunct, or drastically modified.[6] Taxonomies of the kind discussed in this chapter can do no more than take account, more or less effectively, of our existing state of intellectual awareness. Accordingly, they can at best be seen as convenient but contingent devices for ordering our understanding of what knowledge is like in all its various forms.

The usefulness of knowledge categorization systems has to be further qualified by noting that they do not comprise neat and regular pigeonholes; nor do they, in practice, contain perfectly formed and pure-bred pigeons. To put it more plainly, the boundaries between the hard/soft, pure/applied knowledge domains cannot be located with much precision, and even when they have been staked out, several of the established disciplines fail to fit comfortably within them. It is all very well to group together, say, the social sciences and humanities, as one more or less homogeneous category of soft pure knowledge; but to do so is to brush aside the evident differences between and within their constituent subjects. Economics, one might argue, is closer to a hard pure than a soft pure discipline, especially if contrasted with, for example, anthropology; and there are quite fundamental distinctions too in methods, concepts and forms of argument between history and psychology. Moreover, most individual subject areas themselves turn out on examination to contain a diversity of research styles and epistemological characteristics. Physical geography has to be placed on the hard, and human geography the soft, side of the dividing line between science and social science; some of the more theoretical aspects of engineering are purer in character than some of the more practical aspects of physics. To allocate disciplines to domains in the apparently straightforward way that Biglan and Kolb have done – alongside the exponents of other taxonomic systems – may be acceptable at a broad general level of analysis, but could prove seriously misleading when subjected to closer and more detailed examination.

Classificatory exercises of this kind nevertheless serve a useful purpose. As Kolb (1981) points out, they 'cannot do justice to the complexity and variation of inquiry processes and knowledge structures in various disciplines', but they do 'identify useful dimensions for describing [disciplinary] variations'. They also help to show up continuities and interconnections which more minute and localized scrutiny could obscure, or at best, fail to bring to light. The Kolb–Biglan framework, as subsequent discussion will show, can provide a workmanlike set of categories and a useful basic terminology for exploring knowledge in all its variety (as evidenced in the diverse subject fields) and in all its particularity (as exemplified in their constituent specialisms).

Notes

1 The selection of departments in Britain was in most cases based on advice from members of the disciplines concerned in my own university.
2 Compare the observation by Sanford (1971) that:

> teachers at distinguished institutions are orientated not to their institutions but to their disciplines. . . . Such professors, when they assemble informally or formally, almost never discuss teaching; this is not the 'shop' they talk.

3 It is interesting to note that, although urban research (typically involving densely populated problem areas, close interaction, intense competition, high budgets and large teams) occupies a relatively small part of the whole scenario, it tends to be singled out for attention by most social scientists concerned with the study of research activity. This undue weight of concentration on one particular mode of enquiry may perhaps reflect the predominance accorded to the positivistic world-view, even by those who profess to be out of sympathy with it.
4 Masterman (1970) was able to distinguish no less than 21 different senses of the term in Kuhn's exposition.
5 The point has been aptly developed, in relation to history, by Weber (1977):

> essentially . . . the study of history is the re-reading of the past . . . in the beginning because one wants to discover it for oneself and assimilate it, and later because what one looks for (hence sees) in familiar territory may be quite different from what one has discerned before or learned from others.

In a different disciplinary context, Becker (1982) makes the closely related observation that, as a general rule:

> Sociology does not discover what no one ever knew before, in this differing from the natural sciences. Rather, good social science produces a deeper understanding of things that people are pretty much aware of.

6 The candidates for mortality identified by my respondents were all at the subdisciplinary level: geometrical optics in physics as 'a subject that has died'; comparative anatomy in biology as 'played through'; the classification of finite groups in mathematics as 'pretty well moribund'; and human capital theory in economics, 'once a lively area, now virtually defunct'.

2
Academic Disciplines

The nature of a discipline

The concept of an academic discipline is not altogether straightforward, in that, as is true of many concepts, it allows room for some uncertainties of application. There may be doubts, for example, whether statistics is now sufficiently separate from its parent discipline, mathematics, to constitute a discipline on its own. The answer will depend on the extent to which leading academic institutions recognize the hiving off in terms of their organizational structures (whether, that is, they number statistics among their fully-fledged departments), and also on the degree to which a free-standing international community has emerged, with its own professional associations and specialist journals. In some of the typical instances of dispute, certain institutions may have decided to establish departments in a particular field but may find that the intellectual validity of those departments is under challenge from established academic opinion (as has happened in the case of black studies, viniculture and parapsychology). Disciplines are thus in part identified by the existence of relevant departments; but it does not follow that every department represents a discipline. International currency is an important criterion, as is a general though not sharply-defined set of notions of academic credibility, intellectual substance, and appropriateness of subject matter. Despite such apparent complications, however, people with any interest and involvement in academic affairs seem to have little difficulty in understanding what a discipline is, or in taking a confident part in discussions about borderline or dubious cases.

One way of looking at disciplines is through a structural framework, noting how they are manifested in the basic organizational components of the higher education system (e.g. Becher and Kogan 1980, and Clark 1983). Such a perspective tends to highlight one particular set of issues: the variation in how academic institutions elect to draw the map of knowledge; what operational distinctions need to be made between traditional established disciplines (such as history or physics) and interdisciplinary fields (urban studies, peace studies and the like); the organizational complexities of combining autonomous, self-generating units within a single managerial structure; the mechanisms for accommodating newly defined intellectual groupings and phasing out those which are no longer regarded as viable. However, in attempting to explore the relationship between disciplines and the knowledge fields with which they are concerned – as against the organizations in which they are made manifest – a more abstract approach is called for.

A wide-ranging representation of what a discipline is can be found in King and Brownell (1966). Their account embraces several different aspects: a community, a network of communications, a tradition, a particular set of values and beliefs, a domain, a mode of enquiry, and a conceptual structure. Other analyses are more parsimonious. Some writers focus on epistemological considerations, presenting disciplines as 'each characterized by its own body of concepts, methods and fundamental aims' (Toulmin 1972);[1] others define them unequivocally as organized social groupings (Whitley 1976, 1984). For the most part, however, commentators on the subject give equal emphasis to both aspects. Thus Price (1970) admonishes: 'we cannot and should not artificially separate the matter of substantive content from that of social behaviour'. Lodahl and Gordon (1972) conclude their study by remarking on 'the intimate relations between the structure of knowledge in different fields and the vastly different styles with which university departments operate'. Jacobsen (1981) refers to knowledge and social organization as 'equally important, mutually determining'.[2] On the basis of a careful empirical study of laboratory activities in mineral chemistry, solid-state physics and computerized vector analysis, Shinn (1982) observes that 'the internal structure of the cognitive and social arrangements match', and that 'epistemic factors and scientific instrumentation do not constitute a complete explanatory schema', which would also need to include 'social elements'.

It would seem, then, that the attitudes, activities and cognitive styles of groups of academics representing a particular discipline are closely bound up with the characteristics and structures of the knowledge domains with which such groups are professionally concerned. One could venture further to suggest that in the concept of a discipline the two are so inextricably connected that it is unproductive to try to forge any sharp division between them. Even so, if one is to examine the nature of their interconnections, a distinction must be made – at least in theoretical terms – between forms of knowledge and knowledge communities. That contrast will be explored in detail in Chapter 8, though it will crop up on a number of occasions in the intervening discussion.

Unity and diversity

While it is convenient in some contexts to represent disciplines as clearly distinguishable and reasonably stable entities, it has to be acknowledged that they are subject to both historical and geographical variation. The changing nature of knowledge domains over time has already been remarked upon, and such change has its impact on the identities and cultural characteristics of disciplines. Apart from the traumas of the birth of new disciplinary groupings, the death of old ones, or the occasionally dramatic metamorphosis of those in middle life, the process of steady evolution has its own recognizable consequences. Not only are relatively fast-moving fields such as biochemistry noticeably more sophisticated and more specialized than they were a decade or two ago, even the apparently more reflective and conservative subjects (e.g. history or modern languages) have undergone significant long-term changes. But, as Toulmin (1972) remarks, 'each discipline, though mutable, normally displays a recognisable continuity', its differentiation over time is seldom such as to obliterate all significant resemblance.

The same is true of changes in spatial location. Here, Toulmin draws attention to the 'differences of emphasis in the characteristic judgements of different research centres'. On a localized scale, Ruscio (1987) has sensitively explored the 'subtle, intricate interaction' between 'the various disciplines and . . . the many institutions, each with its own culture'. He uses the biological analogy of a genotype and a phenotype: 'The genotype represents the fundamental instructions to the organism and its potential for survival and growth; the phenotype represents the actual manifestation of that potential in a particular physical setting.' His study shows the phenotypical variations to be substantial, but he is confident that one can none the less identify genotypical 'cultures endemic to each discipline'.

Ruscio's study was confined to universities and colleges in the USA. But even if one takes a more global perspective, namely that of the cross-national manifestations of disciplinary cultures, there are noticeable similarities as well as discernible differences. Some of the variations stem from identifiable features of a particular society, such as the structure of its education system or its level of economic development. Others, however, would seem more broadly to reflect national traits and traditions. Among relevant sources in the published literature, Galtung (1981) has explored 'teutonic, gallic and nipponic approaches' to 'structure, culture and intellectual style'. His conclusions are broadly similar to those of Jamison (1982): 'for most of its recent history, natural science has been affected by particular national styles' in terms of the direction of scientific research, the form that scientific conceptualization has taken and the intensity of scientific development.

Within my sample of academic disciplines, the respondents in physics felt able to talk about 'typical French papers', or to contend that 'run-of-the-mill physics in Russia is very different from its counterpart in Britain'. National stereotypes of a conventional (and relatively crude) kind were evoked. For example, one academic engineer remarked that:

the French use what might be called an asbolute approach, beginning with a highly mathematical exploration of the feasibility of each problem; US engineers adopt a comparative approach, starting straight in on solutions and looking at the relative merits and demerits of different ones.

Another referred to the 'heavy-handed' nature of German mechanical engineering. Among the historians who in their turn identified 'different national habits of mind', one remarked that:

> History is not and cannot be culture free. There is a national way of looking at things. Even if you take a strong and clearly defined ideology such as Marxism, the English Marxist historian differs from the German Marxist historian, and both in their turn differ from the Russian.

Significantly, however, the same respondent added that 'even if it contains different ideologies and cultures, there is nevertheless a definable world of historians'. Similarly, 'there are different national profiles, but economics is an international discipline in the sense that economists in one country can understand what economists in another country are talking about'.

No one who writes or speaks of national differences seems to want to deny that strong resemblances persist between different branches of the same family.[3] To vary the metaphor, we might say that disciplines provide a carrier wave on which the signals of distinctive national groups are modulated.

Tribalism and tradition

Despite their temporal shifts of character and their institutional and national diversity, we may appropriately conceive of disciplines as having recognizable identities and particular cultural attributes. We shall need next to consider the forms which such identities and attributes may take.

In a characteristic piece of reminiscence, Evelyn Waugh (1956) wrote of pre-war English aristocratic society as:

> divided into spheres of influence among hereditary magnates . . . the grandees avoided one another unless they were closely related. They met on state occasions and on the racecourse. They did not frequent one another's houses. You might find almost anyone in a ducal castle – convalescent, penurious cousins, advisory experts, sycophants, gigolos and plain blackmailers. The one thing you could be sure of not finding was a concourse of other dukes. English society, it seemed to me, was a complex of tribes, each with its chief and elders and witch-doctors and braves, each with its own dialect and deity, each strongly xenophobic.

The tribal aspects of academia are not too far removed from this, as a crowd of witnesses attests. Among them, Clark (1963) writes:

It is around the disciplines that faculty subcultures increasingly form. As the work and the points of view grow more specialised, men in different disciplines have fewer things in common, in their background and in their daily problems. They have less impulse to interact with one another and less ability to do so. . . . Men of the sociological tribe rarely visit the land of the physicists and have little idea what they do over there. If the sociologists were to step into the building occupied by the English department, they would encounter the cold stares if not the slingshots of the hostile natives . . . the disciplines exist as separate estates, with distinctive subcultures.

An individual's sense of belonging to his or her academic tribe is manifested in a variety of ways:

The culture of the discipline includes idols: the pictures on the walls and dustjackets of books kept in view are of Albert Einstein and Max Planck and Robert Oppenheimer in the office of the physicist and of Max Weber and Karl Marx and Emile Durkheim in the office of the sociologist (Clark 1980).

It also involves artefacts – a chemist's desk is prone to display three-dimensional models of complex molecular structures, an anthropologist's walls are commonly adorned with colourful tapestries and enlarged photographic prints of beautiful black people, while a mathematician may boast no more than a chalkboard scribbled over with algebraic symbols.[4]

It is, however, through the medium of language that some of the more fundamental distinctions emerge. A detailed analysis of disciplinary discourse (such as those attempted by Bazerman 1981, or Becher 1987b) can help not only to bring out characteristic cultural features of disciplines but also to highlight various aspects of the knowledge domains to which they relate. It is possible by this means to discern differences in the modes in which arguments are generated, developed, expressed and reported, and to tease out the epistemological implications of the ways in which others' work is evaluated.

On the latter point, Geertz (1983) remarks that 'the terms through which the devotees of a scholarly pursuit represent their aims, judgements, justifications, and so on, seem to me to take one a long way, when properly understood, toward grasping what that pursuit is all about'. My own research data bring out some of the connections between the terms of appraisal which are widely used in a particular discipline and the nature of the relevant knowledge field. That historians will commend a piece of work as 'masterly', and will be ready to single out the quality of 'good craftsmanship' (features that are rarely identified in other disciplines), suggests a particular emphasis on gaining command of, and shaping into an aesthetically pleasing, purposeful and well-articulated product, a body of miscellaneous and formless raw material. The high premium placed on 'elegant', 'economical', 'productive' and 'powerful' solutions to mathematical and physical problems points towards a knowledge field in which it is possible to identify structural simplicity, reducing explanation to essentials, and where, in a close network of interconnected phenomena, certain discoveries hold within them the means of generating many others. The epithets 'persuasive', 'thought provoking' and 'stimulating', seemingly more common in sociology than elsewhere, suggest a particular concern with the quality of the analysis itself and with its effects on the audience, as against its substantive content. In similar vein, one might note that among physicists, 'accurate' and 'rigorous' are double-edged tributes, since no physics worthy of the name should lack either property; while in both history and sociology to use the word 'biased' is 'to betray one's naiveté', in that every interpretation must have this feature to some degree.[5]

More generally, the professional language and literature of a disciplinary group play a key role in establishing its cultural identity. This is clearly so when they embody a particular symbolism of their own (as in mathematics and theoretical physics), or a significant number of specialized terms (as in many of the biological and social sciences), placing them to a greater or lesser degree beyond the reach of an uninitiated audience. But in more subtle ways the exclusion also operates in those disciplines (such as history and, perhaps, to a decreasing extent, literary studies) which pride themselves on not being 'jargon-ridden', since the communication here none the less creates what linguists would call its own register – a particular set of favoured terms, sentence structures and logical syntax – which it is not easy for an outsider to imitate.

The tribes of academe, one might argue, define their own identities and defend their own patches of intellectual ground by employing a variety of devices geared to the exclusion of illegal immigrants. Some, as we have noted, are manifest in physical form ('the building occupied by the English department', in Clark's words); others emerge in the particularities of membership and constitution (Waugh's 'complex of tribes, each with its chief and elders and witch-doctors and braves'). Alongside these structural features of disciplinary communities, exercising an even more powerful integrating force, are their more explicitly cultural elements: their traditions, customs and practices, transmitted knowledge, beliefs, morals and rules of conduct, as well as their linguistic and symbolic forms of communication and the meanings they share. To be admitted to membership of a particular sector of the academic profession involves not only a sufficient level of technical proficiency in one's intellectual trade but also a proper measure of loyalty to one's collegial group and of adherence to its norms. An appreciation of how an individual is inducted into the disciplinary culture is important to the understanding of that culture.

Getting to know the ropes

In its very nature, being a member of a disciplinary community involves a sense of identity and personal commitment, a 'way of being in the world', a matter of taking on 'a cultural frame that defines a great part of one's life' (Geertz 1983). For a would-be academic, the process of developing that identity and commitment may well begin as an undergraduate, but is likely to be at its most intense at the postgraduate stage, culminating in the award of a doctorate and, for the chosen few, the first offer of employment as a faculty member.

Socialization into a particular form of academic life involves a number of different elements. Among them, Taylor (1976) singles out the power of the discipline's own ideology, built up of 'heroic myths'. Illustrating this with particular reference to geography, he remarks that:

> other disciplines are portrayed as involving specialist 'blinkers' or not fully appreciating the importance of the spatial dimension. In contrast there is the myth of the geographer as 'the great synthesiser', the 'foreman' who combines the individually futile ideas of the blind labouring specialists.

Representations of this kind, Taylor adds, need little empirical evidence; they are 'vast generalisations which have the basic role of creating an overall purpose and cohesion' out of what appears in practice as a highly disparate activity.

Other common components in a disciplinary ideology would include 'specially reconstructed histories', involving a judicious selection from past events, and a careful choice of folk heroes (as Taylor wryly remarks, 'Most other disciplines would be surprised at geographical claims concerning Immanuel Kant and Sir Francis Galton for instance'). These legendary aspects of a disciplinary culture have, incidentally, a wider role: they serve not only as part of the machinery of socialization, but also as weapons to be deployed in the course of internal disputes and controversies – a point to which we shall return in Chapter 5.

Myths and legends are, however, only part of what Bourdieu (1979) has termed the 'cultural capital' which one inherits in acquiring the member-ship of a disciplinary community. At a more mundane level, initiates are steeped in a folklore and a code of accepted or required practice which conditions the way they see the world. A telling example of how this 'hidden curriculum' operates, even at the undergraduate level, is provided by Snyder's (1971) analysis of intellectual and social life among engineering students at MIT. Becker *et al.* (1961) offer another in the context of a medical school, showing in fascinating detail how professional attitudes and values are gradually shaped through the interaction of students with one another, with their instructors, and with their work.

A rich source of observations on how socialization takes place among doctoral students is provided by Gerholm (1985), who takes as his unifying theme the notion of 'tacit knowledge'. His contribution will form the basis of my concluding paragraphs on this theme. Introducing his analysis, Gerholm observes:

Any person entering a new group with the ambition of becoming a full-fledged, competent member has to learn to comply with its fundamental cultural rules. This applies also to academic departments. To function smoothly within the group of teachers, fellow students and secretaries, the student needs a considerable amount of know-how. Most of it will be acquired slowly through the interaction with others and without anyone ever making a deliberate effort to teach the newcomer the rules of the game. Nonetheless, failure to comply with these implicit rules will undoubtedly affect the student's standing within the group.

He goes on to distinguish the technical aspects of such knowledge from its personal elements:

a graduate student, as part of his or her socialisation into an academic discipline, will come into contact with two main categories of tacit knowledge. One of them is the knowledge that has grown out of long experience in the discipline. It is a practical, almost subconscious, knowledge or competence that the department elite fully masters. The most important ingredient is the knowledge and command of the repertoire of scientific discourses. The other category of tacit knowledge is generated by the students themselves as they try to make sense of what they are experiencing in the graduate studies program. Like the former type, it is likely to be used as a guide for action. And for an understanding of what goes on in Academia they are both of great importance.

The first category, as Rorty (1979) has pointed out, calls among other things for an ability to recognize 'what counts as a relevant contribution, what counts as answering a question, what counts as having a good argument for that answer or a good criticism of it'. Within the language domain of a given discipline, Gerholm suggests that there are more subtle nuances: the official, 'front stage' style of research reports and other formal communications; the more domestic genre adopted in 'internal settings, such as local seminars'; and the type of 'back stage' discourse in which research students engage among themselves. Membership of a disciplinary community in its fullest sense involves 'the ability to define the situation correctly and to use the type of discourse required by that very situation'.

Complementing this external, communally defined component of tacit knowledge, the graduate student also has to acquire his or her own sense of what the disciplinary values comprise. It is not enought to recognize, and be seen to subscribe to, the official norms, such as those enumerated by Merton (1973) in relation to academic scientists:[6]

for every [such] institutional norm . . . one can find at least one counternorm prescribing a diametrically opposed line of action. Scientific findings, for example, should be part of the public domain and thus rapidly communicated to whomever might be interested. But we all know that many findings are being kept secret for some time in order not to give other scientists a clue which they might use to get ahead.

In addition to the *de jure* rules of conduct (which Gerholm likens to 'a scientific version of the Ten Commandments'), a career-minded academic must 'familiarise himself with the more Machiavellian rules of conduct' that exist *de facto* within any academic community. And much as one must learn which linguistic repertoire it is fitting to adopt in a particular situation, one also has to acquire 'the *savoir faire* which consists in knowing how to handle these conflicting rules, when to invoke one and perhaps practise the other'.

Gerholm provides two entertaining instances of this dualism. In the first he contrasts the high-minded sentiments voiced by Evans-Pritchard (1951) about the makings of an anthropologist – 'intuitive powers which not all possess'; love of scholarship; imaginative insight; and 'the literary skill necessary to translate a foreign culture into the language of one's own' – with the more earthy advice proffered by the same authority to a student departing on fieldwork: 'Take quinine, play it by ear, and stay away from the women.' As his second example, he quotes a study by Kleinman (1983) of graduate students in sociology, sharply contrasting the public emphasis on 'collective identification' with a covert pressure towards individuation. At the inaugural wine and cheese party for the department's new recruits, the standard conversation-starter is 'What's your field of interest?' Even at this early stage, it is implied, each novitiate ought to have developed a distinctive research concern. Collaboration, or even talking shop with other students, is subtly discouraged. As one student reported, 'it is pretty much assumed that at this level you work by yourself'. In so far as students talk to one another about sociology, their conversation is based on departmental gossip rather than on substantive intellectual issues; their time together is spent more in social than in academic activity.[7]

My empirical enquiries have been directed at a broader, more general level than the studies quoted here. In an indirect way, they do however confirm the efficiency of the initiation process into academic life. My interviews with research students yielded few distinctive issues when compared with those put forward by their seniors: the pattern of responses from the two groups was along broadly the same lines. Given that nearly all the postgraduates were in their final year, one might infer that they had already 'got to know the ropes', having been successfully imbued with the cultures of their chosen academic communities.

Some cultural characteristics

So far, we have been concerned with the general characteristics of disciplinary cultures – their unifying features, cultural correlates and initiation processes. Little has yet been offered in the way of concrete exemplification of what a disciplinary community is like. There are, however, difficulties in attempting to characterize the nature of any particular academic tribe to any satisfactory degree of depth. A likeness, to be at least recognizable if not revealing, must involve not only painstaking observation but the detailed refinement of what is seen and its communication in accessible form. Not many of those seeking to depict one or other aspect of academic life have attempted to offer such portrayals: and among the occasionally rich delineations that do exist, few, if any, lend themselves to easy reproduction. To scale down and simplify is to change the art form from portraiture to caricature.

A treatment of this theme, then, must depend upon a number of distinct strategies, each more or less unsatisfactory. The most ambitious among them would be (continuing the pictorial analogy) to assemble an exhibition of full-length canvases of notable subjects – the drawback here being the demands it must make of its audience in both time and attention. A watered-down option would be to present a gallery of much simplified stereotypes in the effort, while forgoing any pretence to accuracy of detail, to put across some impression of individual variety. A third possibility would be to abandon the attempt to assemble first-hand material, but instead to compile a catalogue directing those interested to the separate locations of some of the relevant published works. None of these strategies is of course exclusive of the others.

The first entails the presentation of contrasting cases in enough detail to gain a sense of what their respective cultures comprise. Such a presentation would be possible from my data: indeed, appropriate syntheses of the interview material, which I plan to publish separately, already exist for biology, history and physics. Evans (1988) offers, for the general reader as much as for the connoisseur, a superb example of how a particular disciplinary culture, that of modern languages, can be displayed in all its aspects.

The gallery-of-stereotypes approach enables me to draw directly on part of my research data. One of the questions I raised with a number of respondents related to the impressions they had formed of colleagues in certain other disciplinary fields. I found most of the answers to be surprisingly hazy: the stereotypes which emerged of both subjects and practitioners – most of them shared among people from quite diverse backgrounds – seemed to me neither particularly perceptive nor particularly illuminating.[8] None the less, at a rather rudimentary level, they pinpointed a number of contrasts. I shall here concentrate on four sets of such caricatures (those for engineers, sociologists, biologists and academic lawyers), adding some comments on the (often equally simplistic) attempts at self-portraiture among the same four groups.[9]

Engineers give rise to a fairly clear, if unsurprising external image. Their practicality and pragmatic values are frequently emphasized; they are respected as being 'in touch with reality'. But at the same time they come across to their more hostile observers as dull, conservative, conformist and

mercenary; as unintellectual, unacademic and 'not very clever'; as politically naïve and uncultured – 'technocrats with no refinement'. Those who
take a more favourable view see them as hearty, likeable and enthusiastic;
as creative, lateral thinkers; and as having a broad outlook.

Among the engineering respondents themselves, one with a psychological bent identified himself and his fellows as 'stable introverts'. Another
made a similar point in less technical language: he found his students 'not
very outgoing – any sense of fun they might have is squashed by the weight
of their course material'. The need to be hardworking was emphasized in
relation both to gaining an academic reputation and to making extra
money through consultancies. If engineers are conservative, argued one of
those I interviewed, that is because 'when you have to make something
useful and safe, you tend to become conformist'. One's failures are
frequently matters of public concern: since failures do occur, 'engineers,
unlike physicists, have not got much to be arrogant about'. Agonizing over
status, to which academic engineers in Britain seem especially prone, is (the
same respondent went on to remark) of little help: 'You don't gain much
sympathy by going round saying you are undervalued.' A commonly
acknowledged limitation is that 'engineers cope badly with people', and
lack much bent for politics or philosophy – 'they like hard and fast rules';
'they have a need for things to be clear-cut'. Another recognized cause for
apology is a lack of 'communication skills'; engineers (it was said, as was
much else, with contradictory cogency) are 'not good speakers'; 'traditionally bad at self-expression'. On the positive side, 'you have to be able to
think clearly, to know what you're doing, how and what for'; 'the good
engineer knows how to cut out the dross and get to the heart of things'.

Sociology always seems to have a bad press. It is widely condemned by
those in other disciplines as fragmented and pseudoscientific, dubious in its
methodology and 'open to ideological exploitation'. By the same token,
sociologists are seen by some as highly politicized, guilty of indoctrinating
students, and 'very left'. They are held to be woolly in their thinking,
dubious in their ability, prone to overgeneralize and, perhaps predictably,
jargon-ridden and inarticulate. By way of small recompense, one fellow-
academic described them as 'friendly – a bit like Methodists' and another as
'interesting – they can be quite nice people'. They were thought by some to
be engaged, ineffectively, in some form of social engineering; and one
interviewee was unsure whether or not they taught social workers.

The awareness that their discipline has 'a dirty name' is not easy for
sociologists to escape. While they understandably regard this as the
consequence of ignorance and prejudice, they confess to a feeling that as a
community they are 'embattled' and 'beleaguered'. The frequent accusations about jargon may at times be justified, in that it can be used as a 'kind
of protection', a means of mystifying, and so defending oneself from,
critical outsiders; but its proper function, in sociology as elsewhere, is to
provide a form of professional shorthand, encapsulating a complex of
ideas in a single word. The most notable feature of the discipline itself is its

fissiparous, sectarian – even divisive – nature. It is 'a series of enclaves'; 'marked by factionalism'; it has a 'longstanding convention of internal dissent'.[10] Nevertheless, in the view of its proponents, it offers a powerful insight into collective human behaviour, making it possible to penetrate below superficial appearances and to reveal the mechanisms which underlie them. It has 'a great deal to contribute to social understanding.'

Perhaps because of the highly diverse nature of their subject matter, biologists do not seem to project as clear an image as do engineers and sociologists. They are described in contradictory terms, as interesting, serious, committed and hardworking people, and as having time to sit about and talk; as patient experimenters, and as 'ethereal folk who spend time cutting up flowers and being very delicate'. The discipline is seen by some fellow academics as 'highly descriptive', as a 'sort of watered-down physics, less difficult and less interesting', and by others as 'fast-moving – in its hey-day'. Its practitioners are variously rated as not much different from physicists, and as less dull and more expansive. Alongside this tendency to describe biologists in analogical terms, a number of respondents said they had no clear idea of what the subject or those who profess it were like.

The sense of disciplinary diversity is reinforced by the comments of the biologists themselves, who seem more prone than other academic groups to mutual stereotyping. Thus, 'microbiologists are narrow, but geneticists are lively'. 'Zoologists are more adventurous and less conventional than botanists', but tend to be 'arrogant and overconfident'. 'Botanists are more cautious'; 'not necessarily the brightest'; 'people who hide behind herbarium cases and hate one another'. These disparate groups do however share certain common features. A stronger emphasis is given than in the other sciences to clarity of communication: you are expected to 'read and write well', to 'talk coherently and intelligibly' and to develop 'a sense of style'. There is 'a tolerance of divergent values'. A biological training also offers 'a grounding in manipulative skill, a capacity for reasoning, and an ability to cope with complexity'.

The predominant notion of academic lawyers is that they are not really academic – one critical respondent described them as 'arcane, distant and alien: an appendage to the university world'. Their personal qualities are dubious: they are variously represented as vociferous, untrustworthy, immoral, narrow, arrogant and conservative, though kinder eyes see them as impressive and intelligent. Their scholarly activities are thought to be unexciting and uncreative, comprising a series of intellectual puzzles scattered among 'large areas of description'.

This generally negative view seems to be shared by its victims, a number of whom diagnosed a common 'tendency towards self-denigration' and 'a sense of doubt about one's intellectual quality'. An American law professor spoke of English legal scholars as 'narrow and uninteresting'; another thought them 'atheoretical, *ad hoc*, case oriented and not much interested in categories and concepts'. This was not a matter for much disagreement: one English respondent acknowledged that 'you don't have to be particularly scholarly', and another suggested that English law schools shared 'the anti-intellectual ethos of practising lawyers', in contrast with the 'higher tradition of worthwhile academic thought' in the USA (though the Americans also confessed themselves worried that their 'techniques and methodologies are not sufficiently probing or fundamental'). The English academic legal community was acknowledged to be 'insular', 'separate from other disciplines', and 'based on a narrow and isolated education'. If the American academic lawyers were part of a larger conurbation, the village-like, parochial qualities of their English counterparts were displayed in a heavy reliance on gossip and 'reputations based on very little knowledge' – 'the word *potential* is used a lot'.

These brief vignettes say as much, perhaps, about the people making the judgements as they do about the disciplines on which they pronounce. But what they do establish, clearly enough, is that the profiles – or at least the silhouettes – of the four subjects in question are discernibly different.

The third and final strategy for tackling the ethnography of academic tribal groups – the compilation of a catalogue of works relevant to the topic – is likely to prove less satisfactory in some respects than the previous two, in that it places squarely on the reader the burden of seeking out and scanning through an inevitably heterogeneous mass of material. However, it does offer the advantage of pointing anyone who is sufficiently motivated to a series of original expositions, as against mediating them at second hand. In the bibliographical exercise that follows, I have done no more than set out, with the occasional comment or annotation, a list of some of the publications that happen to have caught my eye during the course of my enquiry. As will be seen, the majority of the references are confined to disciplines in the interview sample.

Physics, and in particular the glamorous subfield of high-energy physics, has undoubtedly been the most popular area for study. The more substantial treatments include those by Gaston (1973), Pickering (1984) and Traweek (1982), though there are many other studies using physicists as a basis of comparison with other disciplines, or as a vehicle for advancing some particular thesis. The other scientific disciplines are poorly attended to in comparison: in chemistry, for example, the substantial study by Strauss and Rainwater (1962) relates to the wider profession of industrial and government-employed chemists and has little to say about the discipline as such. Among writings on the theme of mathematics, Startup (1980) has contributed a useful but somewhat pedestrian review article. Fisher (1973), though ostensibly concerned with mathematicians in general, bases his argument for the most part on a detailed study of 15 mathematicians working on one particular, and highly specialized, topic. Wilder (1981) approaches the subject matter of mathematics as a cultural system, tracing its evolution and the cultural forces which have dominated it, but has little to say about its practitioners. Hardy's (1941) apologia, though a classic of its kind, offers an unashamedly personal interpretation. Among the social sciences and humanities, economists appear to have a strongly hagiographical bent. While there are, subject to the exception to be considered shortly, few if any analyses of economics as a disciplinary community, there are numerous writings on the lives and works of eminent individuals. Blaug (1985, 1986) provides the prime example in his potted biographies of the 100 best economists before Keynes, and the 100 best economists after. On a more modest scale, Klamer (1984) deferentially records his conversations with the nobility among the new classical macroeconomists. An attractive intellectual history of anthropology is to be found in Kuper (1975). Sociological writers on sociology, whom one might expect to have taken a reflexive interest in the workings of their own collective enterprise, seem in practice to have been surprisingly reticent on the subject, daunted, perhaps, by the prospect of a destructively critical audience. Platt (1976) offers an admirable, and highly readable, study of the process of social research, which illuminates a number of aspects of the working lives of professional sociologists. For the most part, however, writings in this category take the form of descriptive accounts of research practice, prescriptive discussions of methods of enquiry and historical treatments of the way the discipline has developed. Historians, in their turn, offer a fairly prolific choice of historiographical works, and of quasi-philosophical or methodological disquisitions on the nature of 'the historian's craft', but have little to say about themselves as an academic community, or about the social and cultural aspects of the discipline itself.[11] And although, as Evans (1983) points out, academics in the modern language field 'constitute a fairly well-defined professional group', in sociological and political terms 'Modern languages is uncharted territory' – or at least was so, until the publication of his masterly account, referred to above (Evans 1988).

Among my sample of 12 disciplines, academic law represents the social, and engineering and pharmacy the science-based, professions. The almost total neglect of these areas, in terms of any documentation of their cultures, may be connected with the fact that they are far from easy to demarcate from their surrounding domains of professional practice. Thus, for example, the (now somewhat dated) account of engineers offered by Gerstl and Hutton (1966) deals almost exclusively with the professional socialization of practitioners, allowing academic engineers no more than a few lines of text. The same is true of the briefer but more up-to-date discussion of pharmacy by Holloway *et al.* (1986). In the case of law, with the exception of an interesting discussion by Campbell and Wiles (1976), my attempt at a literature search drew a complete blank.

As a postscript, it is perhaps worth remarking on a small category of writings by insiders on the habits and customs of their own tribal groups. Typically, such writings take an allegorical form and adopt a self-consciously jocular tone: they convey an impression of archness and of occasionally rather laboured humour. None the less, as with other examples of conscious self-parody, they offer a number of revealing insights. Works in this *genre* include Leijonhufvud (1973) on economists,

Jones (1980) on sociologists and Ziman (1973) on high-energy physicists. The first of these is both the wittiest and the most meaty. A flavour of it is conveyed by the author's comments on the initiation process:

> The young Econ, or 'grad', is not admitted to adulthood until he has made a 'modl' exhibiting a degree of workmanship acceptable to the elders of the 'dept' in which he serves his apprenticeship. Adulthood is conferred in an intricate ceremony the particulars of which vary from village to village. In the more important villages, furthermore (the practice in some outlying villages is obscure), the young adult must continue to demonstrate his ability at manufacturing these artefacts. If he fails to do so, he is turned out of the 'dept' to perish in the wilderness.

Jones' (1980) study of 'The Nacirema Tsigoloicos' includes a reference to the same topic:

> This process [initiation] begins when the neophyte enters a Tsigoloicos temple, whereby he more or less withdraws from the profane world; the subsequent trials, which sometimes take many years, involve a series of severe ritual abstinences, including the eating of impure foods, fasting, loss of sleep, infrequent bathing etc. – all under the eyes of the old men of the clan, who serve him as godfathers.

A note of qualification

In the intricate, Byzantine world of academia, nothing is as simple as it seems. If, as the argument so far has suggested, knowledge communities are defined and reinforced by 'the nurturance of myth, the identification of unifying symbols, the canonisation of examplars, and the formation of guilds' (Dill 1982), their territorial borders are simultaneously blurred and weakened by a rival set of pressures. This does not of course invalidate the exercise of identifying the distinctive cultural characteristics of individual disciplines: it merely underlines the fact that such an exercise depends on the adoption of a particular frame of reference, more specific than that relating to knowledge fields, but still sufficiently broad and general to obscure several important qualifications. We shall go on to consider some of these as they emerge in the examination of internal and external subject boundaries. As a fitting comment to close this chapter, and to introduce the next, one could do worse than to quote an observation from Gaff and Wilson's (1971) sample survey of faculty values and attitudes in American colleges:

> There are significant differences between faculty members in different fields of study on such aspects of culture as educational values, teaching orientation, and life style. These differences seem sufficiently great to [constitute] distinct faculty cultures. . . . This is not to say that

these cultures are discrete; indeed, there are areas of overlap on every item and every scale. [Moreover] the analysis . . . suggests that there are significant subcultural differences as well.

Notes

1 To be fair, Toulmin elsewhere presents a more balanced view, emphasizing that the nature of a discipline is dependent not only on concepts but on those who conceive them (Toulmin 1972).
2 He adds an important rider (which will be taken up in Chapter 7) that both knowledge and social organization are also 'to a large degree determined by macro-sociological' considerations.
3 One of the geographers I interviewed brought out clearly why this was so. He took off his shelves a list of faculty members, and demonstrated that in most departments their higher degrees were gained in leading institutions in a variety of countries – the mixture of academic backgrounds was highly cosmopolitan. And as he pointed out, the international composition of many disciplinary communities is further reinforced by mutual visits and by specialist conferences which bring together people from a diversity of national backgrounds. (Indirect evidence suggests that this characteristic is less prominent in non-élite departments: however, I have already argued in Chapter 1 that it is the élite who set the defining disciplinary values.)
4 I am indebted to Tomas Gerholm for this ethnographic observation (personal communication).
5 It is clear, in the context of such remarks, that no sanction is given to bias in the sense of distortion or lack of attention to contrary evidence (see also p. 133).
6 The four principal norms of scientific conduct, according to Merton (1973), are universalism (the need for truth claims to be subject to 'pre-established impersonal criteria'), communism (the common ownership of scientific findings – to which 'secrecy is the antithesis'), disinterestedness (as exemplified less in individual conduct than in institutional procedures), and organized scepticism ('the temporary suspension of judgement and the detached scrutiny of beliefs'). His account has been much quoted, but also much criticized. A well-argued disputation of his thesis is provided by Mulkay (1969); other critiques include those of Barnes and Dolby (1970) and Rothman (1972).
7 The same tendency towards gossip rather than shop talk is reflected in the practice of historians, and is in marked contrast with that of physicists. Here is one of many instances in which the social and cognitive aspects of a discipline reflect one another (see Chapter 5 for a more detailed discussion of individualistic and collaborative enquiry).
8 Why, it may be wondered, should that be so? Is it that all stereotypes are, by definition, deficient in these respects? Or is it the case that academics, in common with many other people, seem stubbornly to preserve their simplistic, and often pejorative, views of alien groups in the face of conflicting evidence from individual members they know well? The reasons remain open for exploration.
9 I have chosen this cross-section to include one natural science, one science-based profession, one discipline drawn from the humanities and social sciences, and one social profession. The four subject areas are among those I studied in some depth (see Appendix), and are, for comparison, also represented in the discussion of knowledge fields in Chapter 1.

10 An elaboration of the point is offered by Porter (1984), quoting an interview with Ray Pahl, a well-regarded British sociologist. According to this source, Pahl identifies 'a combination of paranoia, indiscipline and anti-hierarchical egalitarianism' as grounds for the low esteem in which the subject appears currently to be held:

> Sociologists are . . . a difficult lot to defend – their own worst enemies – with an alarming propensity to score 'own goals' . . . the well known spiral of self-labelling, stigmatization and amplification has caused sociologists to project a kind of self-fulfilling lack of confidence . . . there is no agreement as to whom we acknowledge as 'leaders'. . . . and certainly no deference of the kind that would give them the prestige and general recognition to speak out in defence of sociology, and be listened to.

One might remark on the apparently unconscious irony with which those who make such observations contribute to the 'spiral of self-labelling, stigmatization and amplification'.

11 Exceptions to this generalization include Church (1973, 1976, 1978) and, in the context of nineteenth-century academic life, Rothblatt (1968).

3

Overlaps, Boundaries and Specialisms

Adjoining territories

It was noticeable, though not unexpected, that the respondents in my study had no difficulty in enumerating the disciplines which were more or less closely related to their own, and that there was very little disagreement between their views on the matter. It seems natural enough to think of knowledge and its properties and relationships in terms of landscapes, and to saturate epistemological discussion with spatial metaphors: fields and frontiers; pioneering, exploration, false trails; charts and landmarks.[1] So my enquiries about neighbouring areas of knowledge almost invariably produced clear and detailed conceptual maps (and even, in the case of one geographer I interviewed, a neat pencil-and-paper sketch of his discipline and its adjoining territories). Thus, for example, economics was said to have one common frontier with mathematics and another with political science; some trade relations with history and sociology; and a lesser measure of shared ground with psychology, philosophy and law. Biology was portrayed as being bounded on the one side by mathematics and the physical sciences (especially physics, chemistry and physical geography) and on the other by the human sciences (in particular by psychology, anthropology and human geography). And in this vein the catalogue continued across all 12 of the disciplines concerned.

Within the published literature, too, one may come across instances of similar mapping exercises. Thus Buchanan (1966) confirms the areas of 'spillout' and 'spillin' identified by my respondents in economics, but adds some further if less direct connections with engineering and physical sciences; and Mikesell (1969), confining his attention to human as against physical geography, notes its varying degrees of contiguity with anthropology, sociology, political science, economics, demography, psychology, history and area studies, again closely reaffirming the testimony of the geographers I interviewed.

However, the process of locating a discipline in relation to its neighbours is in itself of limited interest, and should be seen as no more than a preliminary to other more fundamental issues. Boundaries, after all, do not exist merely as lines on a map: they denote territorial possessions that can be encroached upon, colonized and reallocated. Some are so strongly defended as to be virtually impenetrable; others are weakly guarded and open to incoming and outgoing traffic.

The nature of the divisions between disciplines, one might contend, varies with the nature of the disciplines concerned: some borders allow a greater latitude than others. Disciplinary communities which are convergent and tightly knit in terms of their fundamental ideologies, their common values, their shared judgements of quality, their awareness of belonging to a unique tradition – in short, their fraternal sense of nationhood – are likely to occupy intellectual territories with well-defined external boundaries. What is more, when the patriotic feelings within a discipline run high, deviations from the common cultural norms will be penalized and attempts to modify them from the outside will be rejected. Any systematic questioning of the accepted disciplinary ideology will be seen as heresy and may be punished by expulsion; any infiltration of alien values and practices will be appropriately dealt with, either by direct resistance or by incorporation into the prevailing framework of thinking. Thus, within economics, those who question the basic axioms of the subject are regarded as deranged if not positively dangerous, and are liable to find themselves cast into a wilderness of their own; deviants in other marginal fields, such as the statistical areas of mathematics, may be cut off and left to form an independent and self-sufficient community.

The inverse is true of disciplinary groups which are divergent and loosely knit, i.e. where the constituent members lack a clear sense of mutual cohesion and identity. In their case the cognitive border zones with other subject fields are liable to be ragged and ill-defined, and hence not so easy to defend. It may indeed at times begin to seem as if there is, in Whitley's (1984) terms, no 'central core which firmly controls intellectual boundaries and reputations'.[2] Geography appears to be a case in point. Its practitioners readily absorb ideas and techniques from neighbouring intellectual territories, and even identify themselves with other academic professions than their own (through publications in their journals, attendance at their conferences and membership of their communication networks). Pharmacists share some of the same centrifugal tendencies, often preferring to see themselves primarily as members of more clearly identified and more prestigious knowledge fields such as pharmacology, biochemistry, or one of the relevant branches of chemistry. Scholars in modern languages are less inclined to form allegiances outside their own broad subject area, but many of those who specialize in literary criticism are hospitable to itinerant theories from psychology, sociology or structural anthropology.

Once again, one can observe connections here between the social and cognitive aspects of knowledge. Impermeable boundaries are in general a concomitant of tightly knit, convergent disciplinary communities and an indicator of the stability and coherence of the intellectual fields they inhabit. Permeable boundaries are associated with loosely knit, divergent academic groups and signal a more fragmented, less stable and comparatively open-ended epistemological structure. But it should be noted that the correlation is not a perfect one (we shall return in Chapter 8 to consider some significant exceptions to it).

Areas of common ground

It often happens that adjoining disciplinary groups lay claim to the same pieces of intellectual territory. This does not necessarily entail a conflict between them. In some cases, depending on the nature of the claimants and the disposition of the no-man's land, it may involve a straightforward division of interest; in others it may mark a growing unification of ideas and approaches.

As Toulmin (1972) has pointed out, 'any particular type of object can fall within the domains of several different sciences', depending on what questions are asked about it. He instances the behaviour of a muscle fibre, which can fall within the spheres of interest of biochemistry, electrophysiology, pathology and thermodynamics, and may also be made a topic for, say, quantum mechanical or psychological investigation.

What demarcates one disciplinary perspective from another in a theme or topic which they share may vary between a distinction in style or emphasis, a division of labour or a difference in conceptual framework. Examples of the first are provided by Megill (1987) and Barry (1981). Focusing on 'the philosophy/history frontier', Megill contends that:

> philosophers, in their writing, are inclined to consider at great length matters that historians will pass over quickly, and *vice versa*. Judged as philosophy, works of history are likely to seem weak. Judged as history, works of philosophy are likely to seem irrelevant.

In similar but more detailed terms, Barry contemplates 'the relation between the kind of theoretical works on politics that gets done by people in political science departments and the kind of thing that people in philosophy departments do when they turn their attention to politics'. Here, he suggests:

> the most noticeable difference is that philsophers tend to be short on background and political scientists long on padding. . . . 'Background' and 'padding' both refer to contextual information: the difference lies in the use made of it. To have a good background in a theoretical subject is, I take it, to have a firm grasp on the relevant empirical phenomena associated with it, and also to be on top of the theoretical literature concerned with it. . . . Padding, by contrast, is the presentation of factual material or the rehearsal of previous opinions or old

controversies to make up for the fact that the author personally has relatively little originality to contribute to the subject.

Other cases clearly display a separation of intellectual spoils, the task of exploration being divided by common agreement between the interested parties. In an entertainingly graphic passage, Horton (1967) describes:

The curiously menial role in which the modern British anthropologist has cast the psychologist – the role of the well-disciplined scavenger. On the one hand, the psychologist is expected to keep well away from any intellectual morsel currently considered digestible by the anthropologist. On the other hand, he is tossed all indigestible morsels, and is expected to relieve the anthropologist of the embarrassing smell they would create if left in the house uneaten.

My interview data contain a number of examples of the same phenomenon. To take a case in point, one of my informants, a physical chemist, began by observing that the scientific background of physicists is based on deductive solutions, whereas that of chemists is based on induction. This distinction, he suggested, pervades the practice and marks the common boundary of the two disciplines. Physics is limited in range: when a problem turns out to be too hard, the physicist marks it down as 'dirty' and abandons it to the chemist. If the chemist also finds it too hard, he passes it on to the biologist, who adopts a phenomenological, rather than an inductive or deductive approach. However, this tidy division of effort is disappearing as more physicists begin to tackle problems previously left for the chemists, while the chemists are now encroaching on the biologists' share of the pickings.

The third way in which territorial rights are divided up among rival interest groups – by distinctions in conceptual framework – is not entirely separable from the other two (i.e. contrasts in style or emphasis, and the division of intellectual labour), but goes beyond them to encompass more fundamental and far-reaching disciplinary variations. A cogently argued analysis by Yates (1985) highlights a dichotomy between anthropologists and sociologists. Even when they are studying essentially the same phenomena, crucial differences emerge. Sociologists 'seem obsessed with methodology and scientific status while anthropologists seem more relaxed on those issues'. To the anthropologist, 'fieldwork is not meant to be about data, it is about experience'; the method of inquiry is 'an internal process, itself inseparable from the experience in which it is realised'. In sociology, to the contrary, 'unpredictable subjective qualities are detrimental to the [researcher's] role as an instrument of science, especially as a recorder of what is actually there'. One might say that 'in social anthropology relationships *are* data, whereas in [sociology] relationships *produce* data'. Summing up, Yates concludes that for sociologists, 'methodology is external and technical and related to the possibility of objective knowledge', whereas for anthropologists 'methodology is the internal apprehension of relationships and their transformation through sets of cultural meanings . . . what is of significance is competence of introspection'.

But the sharing of ground, as already remarked, can lead to convergence rather than a separation of interests. In his comparison of 'historical sociology' and 'theoretical history', Jones (1976) begins, as Yates does, by marking the epistemological contrasts between the two fields. He berates, with equal vigour, history for its failure to theorize and sociology for 'the vague and shifting character of much of its knowledge, its proneness to passing theoretical fashions and the triteness of some of its "laws" '. None the less, the two are, he maintains, more intimately related than superficial appearances suggest. At base, 'they are only different aspects of a single concern: the construction of a historical science'.[3]

On a grander and more sweeping scale, Geertz (1980) identifies a 'culture shift', a 'refiguration of social thought' bringing the humanities and social sciences closer together in their intellectual kinship:

> What we are seeing is not just another redrawing of the cultural map – the moving of a few disputed borders, the marking of some more picturesque mountain lakes – but an alteration of the principles of mapping. Something is happening to the way we think about the way we think.

Geertz characterizes this as 'a turn . . . by an important section of social scientists, from physical process analogies to symbolic form ones', and illustrates his argument be referring to the growing use of comparisons between society and 'a serious game, a sidewalk drama, or a behavioural text'. This change in 'the instruments of reasoning' has 'disequilibriating implications' for social scientists and humanists alike. The 'social techno-logist notion of what a social scientist is . . . the specialist without spirit dispensing policy nostrums' is now brought into question; but 'the cultural watchdog notion of what a humanist is . . . the lectern sage dispensing approved judgements' is by the same process being systematically under-mined.

The cause of unification

Geertz and Jones, together with those who argue along similar lines, appear content to uncover intellectual similarities which already exist or to discern disciplinary mergers which lie in store over the horizon. There are, however, others who adopt a more activist stance, seeking positively to promote unification rather than passively to identify it: to break down boundaries, not only to diminish their significance. Their calls to arms are of some interest, in that they lead on to a consideration of whether there are systematic connections between disciplines, and if so what form they take – from the espousal of one kind of cause to the investigation of another.

The contrast drawn by Barry (1981) between philosophers' and political scientists' approaches to the same question has already been mentioned. He goes on to suggest that the differences are counterproductive, demanding a change in 'organizationally induced incentives . . . ways in which the political philosophers and the political theorists can move toward one another without jeopardising their positions in their own departments'. The structural reforms he outlines are thus directed towards 'a great increase in the amount of organizational boundary crossing'.

Campbell (1969) is more ambitious, espousing as his goal the achievement of 'a comprehensive, integrated multiscience'. The major obstacle in the way of achieving this goal is 'the ethnocentrism of disciplines', the internal dynamics which favour the growth of what is regarded as the disciplinary core and allow the relative atrophy of its peripheral or marginal elements.

What is of particular interest in the present context about Campbell's argument is that, as in Barry's case, his diagnosis of what he sees as our present intellectual malaise, as well as his suggested remedies, are organizational rather than epistemological. The blame can, he contends, be laid firmly at the door of disciplinarily- and departmentally-based structures: the 'tribalism or nationalism or ingroup partisanship' which acts as a powerful centrifuge, promoting an artificial alienation and distance between even closely-related specialities on either side of a boundary. Thus, 'centrality becomes reinterpreted as common root, trunk and fountain head when initially it meant only remoteness from the boundaries of other departments'.

Campbell's analysis leads him to assert that the 'present organization of content into departments is highly arbitrary, a product in large part of historical accident'. (One might, incidentally, wish to make the same charge against nationhood.) Writing in the same volume – devoted to the theme of interdisciplinarity in the social sciences – Wax (1969) adopts a closely similar stance. The attempt, he suggests:

> to structure the social-scientific disciplines into a set of mutually exclusive and exhaustive enterprises . . . is not so much impossible as it is destructive. For, from the viewpoint of a systematic and logical division of scientific labor, the very existence of the disciplines or sciences that are taken to constitute the social or behavioural sciences makes but little sense. Sociology, anthropology and their siblings are not the outgrowths of a systematic division of social-scientific labor, but are instead the arbitrary consequences of particular social processes . . . social scientists must become far more conscious of the arbitrariness, deliberate bias and ethnocentricity of their critical assumptions.[4]

Elaborating on his theme, Wax argues that the problem is not so much that 'the social sciences are chaotically organized and that the various disciplines are professional rivals for the same subject areas . . . each studying the same subject matter, while giving different labels to their activities', but rather that 'the gaps among our disciplines are much too large'. The prime need, then, must be to bridge or fill in these gaps, a goal which Campbell endorses and one whose realization, he believes, has to be based on promoting 'collective comprehensiveness through overlapping patterns of unique narrowness' – on creating 'a continuous texture of narrow specialties which overlap with other narrow specialties', as against 'trying to fill these gaps by training scholars who have mastered two or more disciplines'.

Disciplines under the microscope

With this move, Campbell deftly shifts the focus of attention and the locus of analysis from disciplines to specialisms. It may be worth pausing briefly to review the steps which have led from the macroscopic view of knowledge to the microscopic one which now presents itself.

Chapter 1, it may be recalled, concerned itself in part with the delineation of broad epistemological categories. In Chapter 2, the framework was narrowed to allow for the evident disciplinary variations within such categories. Once it is conceded, however, that disciplines comprise an untidy level of analysis in certain respects, in that the boundaries between them are constantly shifting and sometimes poorly demarcated, and that there are numerous apparent gaps and overlaps in their pattern of coverage of knowledge domains, it becomes necessary to introduce a yet more finely meshed set of explanatory concepts. Much as disciplines have to be invoked to accommodate the anomalies within broadly defined fields of knowledge, specialist areas or segments seem to offer the most appropriate analytic currency to account for the complex internal and external relationships which are made manifest in any close scrutiny of disciplines themselves.

In their replacement of discipline-based categories by those of specialisms, Campbell and Wax manage to convey a sense of movement from the superficial to the fundamental. The heart of the academic enterprise, the true basic unit of intellectual organization, is the specialist field; it is, they believe, within its narrow but profound matrix that the closest contact is achieved between human understanding and the realm of epistemological reality it seeks to explore.

Two further points need to be considered before we move on to a more detailed discussion of the specialisms which fragment the internal structure of disciplines as well as those which straddle their boundaries. First, there has been noticeably little mention in all this of the views of natural scientists, humanists or those in professionally oriented fields: nearly all those who have been quoted in the discussion so far are social scientists. That may be because of a greater tendency for the latter to concern themselves with the social aspects of knowledge; or perhaps because academics in other knowledge domains take it more for granted that they have interests in common and areas of overlapping coverage with their disciplinary neighbours. But that such a blurring of boundaries also occurs in fields outside the social sciences cannot be in dispute. For every statement, such as the one by Buchanan (1966) that 'it is easier for an economist working with non-market decisions to communicate with a positive political scientist, game theorist or organizational theory psychologist than it is for him to communicate with a growth-model macro-economist with whom he scarcely finds any common ground', it is possible to point to comparable assertions in my interview data from informants in other knowledge domains. Thus, one respondent, a chemist, spoke of the 'strong connections with physics' which characterized the elementary chemical reactions which he was studying at the molecular level; another, a mechanical engineer, remarked: 'I have more in common with the mathematicians who study fluid mechanics that I have with other engineers who study combustion – though combustion is my main research topic'.

Secondly, in marking the transition from a concern with disciplines to an emphasis on specialisms, one can note an accompanying elaboration of the metaphors it seems natural and appropriate to use. To be sure, it is still possible to talk of boundaries and border disputes; but there is also a strong tendency to invoke another and rather different family of concepts. Campbell's (1969) ideal of 'a comprehensive social science, or other multiscience' calls for what he calls a 'fish-scale model' in which specialist research areas overlap like the scales on a fish, so bringing about 'a collective communication, a collective competence and breadth'. Polanyi (1962) envisages 'a chain of mutual appreciation . . . the whole of science [as] covered by chains and networks of overlapping neighbourhoods . . . the consensual chains which link [each individual] to all the others'. And Crane (1972) in her turn observes that each specialist field 'appears to be related to a few others, but in such a way that all fields are interlocked in a kind of honeycomb structure'. And so in this convergence of scales, chains and honeycombs, it becomes possible to contemplate the vision of a return from the incohate to the coherent, from fragmentation to wholeness: *e pluribus unum*.

The notion of a specialism

It is not only at their borders that disciplines can prove a troublesome unit of analysis. When one begins to look closely into their epistemological structures, it becomes apparent that most of them embrace a wide range of subspecialisms, some with one set of features and others with others. There is no single method of enquiry, no standard verification procedure, no definitive set of concepts which uniquely characterizes each particular discipline. It is in some contexts more meaningful to speak about the identifiable and coherent properties of subsidiary areas within one disciplinary domain or another. And once this change of emphasis is adopted it becomes possible (as we shall see in later chapters) to recognise between subspecialisms certain patterns of similarity and difference which cut right across disciplinary boundaries.

The move from the arena of disciplines to that of specialisms calls for a corresponding shift in perception. One aspect of the change is brought out by Crane (1972), generalizing from her close study of communication among academics to society at large:

> Instead of seeing society as a collection of clearly defined interest groups, [it] must be reconceptualised as a complex network of groups of interacting individuals whose membership and communication patterns are seldom confined to one such group alone.[5]

There are two features particularly worth noting in this view of collective life under the microscope. The first is that the complexity, like that of an active biological culture, is inevitable and inexorable: the individual cells subdivide and recombine, seek to defend their integrity while changing their shape and disposition, as if this constant process were a necessary part of survival. Ruscio (1985) writes of specialization as 'an iron law [that] controls the progress of science and similarly the academic profession'. He adds some useful reminders of why this is so:

> There are epistemological reasons: the sheer volume of knowledge and its rapid expansion compel a scientist to carve out his own niche of expertise. There are also sociological reasons: Academics achieve status within the profession by advancing knowledge, a dynamic that requires precise contributions. Institutions of higher education them-selves compete for status, reinforcing the individual's motivation.

The second feature is a consequence of the first: it is that there is little to be found here of the relative constancy and stability of the disciplines themselves. Once inside the framework of academic specialties, one can only clutch at the metaphysics of Heraclitus: all is in a state of constant flux.

A specific illustration of this shifting, kaleidoscopic process was given by one respondent, a mathematician, in his remark that the *Mathematical Reviews Index* – an important bibliographical tool within the discipline – has found it necessary to change its classification system in more or less drastic ways at least once a decade. The notion of specialisms as elements whose only constant feature is their lack of constancy is reinforced and extended by Bucher and Strauss (1961) in their study of medical specialization. Stressing the heterogeneity of professional groupings, and the divergence of interests between them, they develop a 'process model' which entails 'the ideal of . . . loose amalgamations of segments pursuing different objectives in different manners and more or less delicately held together under a common name at a particular period in history'.

This last comment suggests a nominalism which the incohateness of pattern makes it tempting to adopt: specialisms, it might seem, can only be defined in terms of the labels with which groups of people choose to identify themselves at any given time.[6] To make matters worse, specialist fields may, like disciplines, themselves be represented as subject to internal fragmentation. Thus Gaston (1972) observes of high-energy physics that 'differentiation is not only within the same discipline but within the same speciality'. And Bucher and Strauss (1961), in developing their process model, elect to refer to the 'groupings which emerge within a profession' as 'segments', adding in parentheses that:

> Specialties might be thought of as major segments, except that a close look at a specialty betrays its claim to unity, revealing that specialties, too, usually contain segments, and, if they ever did have common definitions along all lines of professional identity, it was probably at a very special, and early, period in their development.

Later in the same paper they refer to 'the different organizations of work activities that can be found within single specialties', and comment that 'while specialties organize around unique missions, as time goes on segmental missions may develop within the fold'.

One is reminded of the physicists' unending quest for the ultimate particle of matter, in which it seems that every new candidate turns out itself to be a composite; or of the more commonplace conception that 'big fleas have little fleas upon their backs to bite 'em; little fleas have lesser fleas, and so *ad infinitum*'. It is perhaps scarcely surprising in the circumstances that Whitley (1984) argues that, especially in weakly co-ordinated disciplines with a high degree of 'task uncertainty', it is 'difficult to establish . . . the division of the field into separate yet interdependent specialisms'.

The looseness and untidiness of the terminology reflects that of the situation to which it applies. As a rough approximation, it might be said that disciplines take institutional shape in departments, and that specialisms are less formally recognizable in terms of organized professional groupings, dedicated journals and bibliographical categories. However, some specialisms cover such a broad span of knowledge that it becomes useful or necessary to subdivide them (Mulkay 1977, notes a possible classification of solid-state physics into 'twenty-seven relatively distinct fields of investigation'). Such subspecialisms are harder to identify, being variously associated with 'social circles', 'networks', 'invisible colleges' and other comparable notions, and may vary considerably in character and scope, being attributed to active research populations of anything from half a dozen (Roberts 1970) to around 200 (Price and Beaver 1966).

Some social considerations

It is not easy to disentangle the social from the cognitive aspects of the specialization process, although some writers tend to emphasize the former at the expense of the latter. Thus, Griffith and Mullins (1972) write about 'some members of a scientific speciality' as 'small, coherent, activist groups

. . . that subsequently had major impacts on their "home" disciplines'. To quote Bucher and Strauss (1961) again, in amplification of this:

> Professional identity may be thought of as analogous to the ideology of a political movement; in this sense, segments have ideology. We have seen that they have missions. They also tend to develop a brotherhood of colleagues, leadership, organisational forms and vehicles, and tactics for implementing their position. . . . [But] it must be pointed out that not all segments display the character of a social movement. Some lack organised activities, while others are so incohate that they appear more as a kind of backwash of the profession than as true segments.

The contrast noted by Griffith and Mullins (1972) between 'a loose communication network' and one with 'high levels of communication and organization' is one of many which can be drawn in the attempt to analyse the process of specialization. The first, in which group members have many contacts outside – 'suggesting that scientists work in and influence more than one speciality' – is, they contend, characteristic of what Kuhn (1962) designated as 'normal science'. The second, highly organized type of group typifies 'revolutionary science' ('groups that are in the process of formulating a radical conceptual reorganization within their field . . . convinced that they [are] achieving the overthrow of a major position within their discipline or making a major revision in methodology'). However, in modification of this claim, Griffith in an earlier paper with Miller (1970) pointed out that 'the use of special methodology might spread through or even define a speciality within the literature without creating a highly coherent group or any sense of being at a major research front'; and, more generally, 'a research literature may be the product of a coherent group in continual contact or of individuals operating almost completely independently of one another'.

As an aside at this point, it could be argued that knowledge is likely to be rendered, in Campbell's terms, more cohesive and less fragmented by the activity of loosely knit specialist groups, since it is they who promote communication across the boundaries of specialisms. In contrast, closely knit groups might be claimed to contribute more to the overall advancement of knowledge, particularly if they are associated with major intellectual revolutions that succeed.

Conceptual revolutions cannot, however, be legislated for – like accidents, they just happen (though a combination of circumstances can serve to prevent them). There is a risk, too, that they may go wrong and in doing so create a pathology of their own – that of in-breeding within the group concerned. Griffith and Miller (1970) observe that 'the focusing of the group's attention on a single series of phenomena and the development of a distinctive scientific style results in a considerable restriction of the range of information regarded as relevant', and a 'virtual indifference to the work of others'. Ruscio (1985) refers to specialized groups which become separated from other subfields within their own discipline, and quotes a political scientist he interviewed as saying that close identity in research 'should not be seen as something that's putting everybody in communication with one another; it's not that kind of thing at all. Instead, what's happening is that very distinct groups of communicators are growing up.' Crane (1972) writes of circumstances in which the operational definitions given by techniques cannot be reconciled, so that narrow fields cannot merge into broader ones. There is in consequence little intercommunication: 'little concern for theory or for the implication of ideas for other groups. . . . Gimmicks develop, often in the form of a procedure, equipment or task which is then mechanically repeated.'

Some cognitive considerations

Specialization does not however have to be regarded as a predominantly social process. It is easy to sympathize with Chubin's (1976) complaint that sociologists of science – who have contributed a major part of the writings on the topic – have underemphasized the extent to which 'intellectual, cognitive or problem content can generate different kinds of structure'.[7] By taking 'social structure as an antecedent of specialties – that is, as impelling a convergence of interest on a research problem or set of problems', they seemingly deny 'the possibility that intellectual events and the relations they engender give rise to a social structure that we treat as a specialty'.

It would be wrong to play down the importance of social factors in determining the characteristics of a specialized knowledge field. Indeed, it will be necessary to develop further the analysis of networks, along with the role of intellectual fashion, in the exploration of some of the main mechanisms of academic life in Chapter 4, and the question of career motivation in Chapter 6. However, it is also as well to recall, with Elzinga (1987a), that 'differentiation is certainly more than just the result of a social and micropolitical process in the world of higher education'.

To restore the balance, we ought to begin by noting that it is in the domain of hard pure knowledge, as it was defined in Chapter 1, that specialization is apparently at its most intense. Hard pure areas seem to exert an almost hypnotic effect, allowing many attempts at analysis to ignore the fact that specialization also occurs in hard applied fields (as the study by Bucher and Strauss 1961, makes plain) and in soft pure and soft applied contexts as well. It is perhaps the linear, cumulative and atomistic character of hard pure knowledge which creates a natural arena for specialization and a natural target for the study of intellectual networks of communication. But while closely focused areas of shared interest and their associated interest groups are a less predominant feature of other epistemological categories, they are none the less readily to be found, and they have a good many of the same characteristics as specialisms in the hard sciences.

One may indeed discern a similar spectrum within the social science disciplines, the humanities, and the technical and social professions, from loosely knit confederations to closely cohesive segments. Close-knit groups are often clustered around 'a distinctively different theory or a new or modified research methodology in opposition to a clearly established position' (Griffith and Mullins 1972); looser ones are commonly based on a shared area of content or a shared field of professional practice. The most noticeable disciplinary difference lies in the response to radically new ideas. In closely articulated, hard pure, knowledge areas, revolutionary theories may have the effect of overthrowing and replacing the current orthodoxy (Kuhn 1962); in other domains (because, one might say, there is no clear orthodoxy to replace), they tend rather to be absorbed into the more organic, amorphous conceptual structures which are in their very nature not readily amenable to being superseded.

Types of specialization

It is important for some purposes to recognize that specialisms fall into distinct logical categories. Law (1976) marks them in straightforward and readily understandable terms as theory-based, technique- or methods-based and subject matter specialities. The last of the three is perhaps the most familiar, in that it designates a particular area of knowledge (tax law, say, within legal studies) or set of problems (algebraic geometry, say, within mathematics) on which research activity is focused. The definition of a specialism of this kind can of course be more or less precise: an academic may in some contexts identify himself or herself as concerned with classical drama and in others as being a student of the late Elizabethan theatre, or as interested in a particular playwright or even as working on a particular play. But the reference here is to the object of study rather than to the mode of investigation employed or the perspective which is adopted.

Methods-based specialisms (Law gives crystallography as an example) introduce another dimension, in that 'methodological differences can cut across specialty – and even professional – lines with specialists sharing techniques with members of other specialties which they do not share with their fellows' (Bucher and Strauss 1961). Moreover, someone armed with a suitable technique may invade a number of subject specialisms in turn and use it to produce novel results; a process which, with an illuminating difference of metaphor, physicists tend to describe as 'skimming the cream' and chemists as 'turning the handle'.

Theory-based specialities may be broader still, in that they derive from sometimes quite general ways of looking at the world. The richest of them are capable of being carried across disciplinary boundaries to attract followers in a diversity of fields. For example, catastrophe theory, stemming from topology, has helped to clarify a variety of problems in the biological and social sciences; structuralism, with its origins in linguistics, has made inroads into anthropology, sociology and literary criticism. Espousing a theory – as against choosing a subject field or learning to apply a technique – can have ideological as well as straightforwardly cognitive implications, with the result that those with conflicting theoretical stances may show much the same mutual antagonism as the adherents of rival political creeds.

The three types of specialism are not necessarily separated in practice, in that a given subject area may be closely associated with a particular method, some methods are a natural accompaniment to particular theories, and certain theories are in their turn confined to specific bodies of subject matter. None the less, the category in which a specialism is located can make a considerable difference to the types of things one can say about it.

To put some flesh on these bare logical bones, it may be useful to draw upon a few examples from outside the overworked domain of the natural sciences. For historians, the *Annales* school has represented not merely a methodological break, but a new theoretical conception of what should count as acceptable evidence and where the boundaries of historical subject matter should be drawn. The oral history movement, in contrast, has to be seen as a predominantly methodological specialism, even if – in its nature – it is currently confined to the subject field of modern history. Within economics, monetarism is a theory-based specialism, econometrics is defined in terms of technique, and labour economics is a subject field. Modern languages also encompasses all three types of specialism: deconstruction among the theoretical approaches, practical criticism as a methodology, and language, period and genre as dimensions of subject matter. Among the professions, Bucher and Strauss (1961) remind us that, 'Within a core specialty like internal medicine there are many different kinds of practice ranging from that of a "family doctor" to highly specialized consultation'; but more 'profound divisions . . . frequently arise around the exploitation of a method or technique, like radiology'.

Frames of reference

In the discussion so far, disciplines and specialisms have appeared as competing forms of analysis. The disadvantages of attempting to chart knowledge fields in terms of disciplines were emphasized by Geertz and others, who noted their overlapping boundaries and their conceptual congruences, and by advocates of interdisciplinary enquiry, such as Campbell, who charged them with a failure to tackle important interstitial areas of enquiry. But an alternative account in terms of specialisms was seen not to be entirely satisfactory either; at least in part because of imprecisions in their definition and instabilities in their inherent characteristics. Whitley (1984) further reinforces the causes for complaint:

Taking the immediate specialism to be the basic unit of intellectual and social organization . . . creates substantial problems. . . . First, it is not always very clear how these are to be identified across the sciences. . . . Second, the present high degree of intellectual specialization is historically specific and thus temporal comparisons would be difficult to carry out. Third, they are often highly fluid and changeable so that comparisons of their structure and operations as relatively stable work organizations is [*sic*] fraught with obstacles. Finally, because the degree of specialization and intensification of the division of labour varies across the sciences . . .

Even so, it is difficult not to agree with Chubin (1976) that ' "specialty" is a viable concept whose various representations capture better than conventional units of analysis, especially "discipline", the process and structure of research'.

But perhaps, in the end, there is no need to postulate an irreconcilable rivalry between the macro and the micro – between broad knowledge fields at the one extreme, narrow specialisms at the other, and disciplines poised uneasily between the two. Particle physics does not have a monopoly of scientific truth which renders the study of astronomy invalid. Alternative frames of reference only serve to emphasize different aspects of the same reality, allowing a trade-off between comprehensiveness and specificity. To see the whole is to see it in breadth, but without access to the particular vision: to see the part is to see it in depth, but in the absence of the general overview.

Notes

1 'That our epistemological metaphors are (at least partially) culturally specific, and that our knowledge of knowledge is therefore (at least partially) culturally constrained' is argued by Salmond (1982) in an interesting comparison of contemporary Western with traditional Maori conceptions of knowledge. The latter represent knowledge not in spatial terms, but as a shared and valued possession, a source of power and wealth, analogous in some ways with Bourdieu's notion of 'cultural capital'.

2 In another context, he distinguishes fields in which 'how the core is separated from peripheral, or "deviant" areas is of critical concern' from those where the matter is given lesser importance. Thus, the physicists' 'policing of intellectual boundaries and fears of "pollution" from "applied" issues are as marked as those of economists, especially in European countries, and are a strong contrast to the more relaxed attitudes of chemists' (Whitley 1984).

3 The intellectual links between historians and sociologists have been the subject of discussion by both disciplinary groups over the last couple of decades. The *British Journal of Sociology* **17**(3) (1976) has other relevant articles besides that by Jones (see also Erikson 1970, Smith 1982, and, for a more extensive and thorough-going analysis, Burke 1980).

4 In the course of passionate argument the occasional rhetorical flourish can be

forgiven. The accusation of arbitrariness however goes too far for comfort. While the institutionalization of disciplines into departments might be said to distort the way in which they develop, the cognitive distinctions between disciplines are in many cases too fundamental to attribute to mere historical accident. Some territories may be demarcated by political artifice (as the 49th parallel sets apart Canada from the USA); but other divisions follow the lie of the land (as the Himalayan range disjoins India from Tibet).

5 The analogy with nationhood remains as close here as elsewhere. Drawing upon a quite different intellectual tradition, the historian Eugene Weber (1977) writes in strikingly similar terms about the emergence of France as a distinct national entity:

> Perhaps . . . the nation is a complex of collective bodies, all in process of perpetual change and in a constantly varying relationship with one another. The static view of the nation as a precise entity that having once been forged is thereafter stable . . . is thus replaced by a Bergsonian model of continual interaction much closer to what actually went on.

6 A nominalist stance neatly rules out a whole range of bothersome epistemological questions. But against this attraction must be offset the misleading nature of the claim that inventing labels is the only issue at stake, i.e. that there is no point in asking what those labels are meant to be tied to. In terms of the metaphor of knowledge production, a claim to a specialism is a claim to a distinct product, and one which is saleable and useful. It can of course be questioned on the (social) grounds that no one else is interested enough to buy it; but it can also be denied on the (epistemological) grounds that the product is not new, does not stand up to critical testing, or does not serve any discernible purpose.

7 A trap into which Chubin, on his own admission, falls in the later part of the same article.

4

Aspects of Community Life

The quest for recognition

The discussion up to this point has focused, in one way or another, on knowledge territories, and in particular on their internal and external boundaries. Sociological phenomena have been seen as connected to, and in some sense reflections of, epistemological characteristics. In the present chapter and the two that follow it, the thrust is in a converse direction. The emphasis is more on academic tribes than on the territories they inhabit. Rather than exploring social issues in terms of cognitive ones, we shall concentrate on key features of intellectual communities and consider how the various forms of knowledge may be related to them.

The two approaches are not in contradiction with one another; nor is either in conflict with the underlying theme of the argument, that forms and communities of knowledge are interdependent in many important respects. The change is one of perspective, not of the object in view. It is necessary to make it because certain features can be more clearly seen through the lens of social observation than through that of cognitive scrutiny. In marking this new departure, an appropriate starting point will be to explore the patterns of work in academia: to try to see what makes the whole thing tick.

It is sometimes argued (as, for example, by Waterman 1966) that research endeavour is sustained by a concern for the disinterested pursuit of truth and spiced with the joy which comes from a new discovery or an enhanced understanding. Whether or not that is seen as a matter of pious but unsubstantiated belief, another more direct motivating force is identified by many who have given careful thought to the issue: namely, the need to earn professional recognition. On this view, the main currency for the academic is not power, as it is for the politician, or wealth, as it is for the businessman, but reputation.

Merton, who has some claim to be the only begetter of the sociology of science, was one of the early proponents of this view (Merton 1957), though his insight was anticipated by someone who was primarily a practitioner rather than a theorist, G. H. Hardy. Reflecting on his life as a mathematician, Hardy (1941) wrote of the 'dominant incentives to research' as 'intellectual curiosity, professional pride, and ambition', a conjunction which he paraphrased later in the same work as 'desire for reputation'. Another such practitioner, this time a physicist (Reif 1961), subsequently developed the theme with particular reference to competition among scientists:

> The scientist . . . is extraordinarily dependent on the good opinion of others, and . . . his reputation becomes translated into many concrete consequences for him. Personal recognition thus assumes even more importance for the scientist than for most other people, and he competes persistently to achieve maximum prestige . . . the very nature of scientific activity implies the need for recognition of the value of one's work by others in the field.

This need, as my own research data underline, is not confined to the sciences alone but manifests itself across the whole range of academic disciplines. Thus, an engineer could speak of 'a major incentive in the feeling that you are recognised in your field', and modern linguists and economists alike would comment on the crucial steps to be taken in establishing 'a scholarly reputation'.

Knorr-Cetina (1982), writing on 'the scientist as an economic reasoner', emphasizes that what is at stake in the academic's 'preoccupation with value . . ., is not the value of some product, but the value of the scientists themselves'. The outcome of one's work, whatever tangible form it may take, is not an end in itself but a means to the end of one's own professional achievement. What counts towards success in an academic career may vary from one field to another. In the technical professions, such as medicine or engineering, a name can be made by discovering or inventing a product (a prime example would be penicillin or the jet engine); in the social professions, such as law, it is possible to become an eminent academic consultant without having had to write a great deal. But for the most part, in leading academic circles, credit is earned through the publication of one's research findings; excellence in teaching counts for little towards recognition by established colleagues in the same field.[1]

A consequence of the emphasis on reputation is the academic's concern to establish and to safeguard his or her rights to intellectual property (Ravetz 1971). As one of my informants explained: 'You get a sense of possessiveness about an idea, and automatically feel you have to defend it.' Powerful taboos exist against plagiarism. Taking and using other people's ideas without acknowledging them is regarded as no better than theft of a more material kind: it can lead to the ruin not only of one's reputation but of one's whole career. Even the inadvertent repetition of previous findings is frowned upon: you need to know what the people who came before you have said, and you only make a fool of yourself by unwittingly saying it again and claiming it as a new insight. The legitimate counterpart is the process of paying a tax on intellectual borrowing, in the form of the citation of relevant sources – though that has a variety of other functions, as we shall see in Chapter 5.

There were some among the junior academics I interviewed who were unclear whether a good reputation was more strongly determined by quantity than by quality of published writing. However, the more senior and established academics generally took the view that it was quality that counted.[2] There has been a fair amount of systematic research into this question, though – as usual – much of it is confined to the natural sciences and, perhaps because it draws heavily on the dubious techniques of factor analysis, its results are to some degree mutually contradictory. Gaston (1970) asserts that quality of research is one of the main determinants of 'visibility' as a physicist, though he defines quality exclusively in terms of the number of citations. Cole (1970, 1978) also shows a reassuring confidence that quality will out in the end: 'Only a small proportion of significant work is overlooked for more than a few years. . . . Good papers have a high probability of being recognised regardless of who their authors are.' A dissenting view is put forward by Lightfield (1971), who suggests that, in terms of recognition, quality is not acknowledged or rewarded 'to the extent that has been supposed', and that the quantity of publications is 'as important, if not more important than the quality'. However, his study is atypical, in that it concentrates on what he terms 'output and recognition' in sociology as against physics. A refinement on the argument is introduced by Cole and Cole (1967), who contend that quality is rewarded in highly prestigious physics departments (some of whose members produce few papers of great significance), whereas quantity is the more significant criterion for advancement in less prestigious ones (where some members produce many papers of little significance). Other findings suggest that quantity and quality are interrelated. According to Price (1963), the more prolific authors tend to make the more significant contributions: there is 'a strong correlation' between merit and volume of output (Cole 1978, even goes so far as to quantify it across a range of subject areas, quoting correlation coefficients of 0.72 for chemistry, 0.71 for biochemistry, 0.59 for physics, 0.54 for sociology and 0.53 for psychology). Perhaps on the strength of this relationship, some writers blur the distinction, referring more globally to research productivity.

The way to get on

While publication constitutes the formal and explicit criterion for recognition, there is (here as elsewhere) an informal and tacit dimension which also has to be taken into account. However important quality may be, it is not only what you write but who you are and where you come from that counts. In her study of 'productivity and recognition', Crane (1965) observes that:

in terms of his chances of obtaining recognition, a scientist gained more from affiliation with a major university than from high productivity or from his sponsor's prestige, probably because the major university provided better opportunities for contacts with eminent scientists in the same discipline.

Reskin (1977) reaches a similar conclusion. Moreover, as Cole (1978) remarks, a scientist who acquires a position in a highly ranked department may experience a rise in the perceived quality of his work. Cole was able to detect no significant differences here in the way in which the reward systems operated across the five disciplines he studied (three in the natural and two in the social sciences; see above). Hargens and Hagstrom (1967), in a study of patronage *vs* open competition among American academic scientists, identify (for fairly obvious reasons) the prestige of an individual's doctoral institution as a more important factor than research productivity in early career advancement. Among economists, Oromaner (1983) suggests that there is a tendency to cite articles by those from prestigious institutions, while Lightfield (1971), in his study of social scientists, contends that recognition is affected by the status rank of both the doctoral department and the present academic location. Without any prompting, one of my informants (an academic lawyer) made a precisely similar point: 'Of two equally bright people, one might have a better reputation than the other. That will almost certainly have something to do with the institutions where they got their degrees and the institutions they teach at now.'

On the question of sponsorship as a source of career advancement, most of those I interviewed, regardless of discipline, took the same line. It could be useful to have a well-regarded patron in applying for one's first appointment or two: but after that, one was expected to be judged by one's own efforts.[3] As one historian remarked, 'the best scholars tend to attract the best students . . . if you are a protégé of one of these leading figures, you may well have some advantage in getting your first job – though seldom beyond that'. The biologists also allowed some scope for patronage, and one observed that 'some research supervisors have an extensive range of contacts, which helps them to place their students – traces of the old boy network still remain, though it is less strong than it once was'. On the whole, the scholarly population has become too large, too diffuse to allow for the survival of a once-powerful patronage system.[4]

The academic study of law in Britain seems to be the one interesting exception (the American scene is very different in this respect), perhaps because its related professional community, and the Bar in particular, still depends to a considerable extent on close informal contacts and personal recommendation. Thus one of my legal informants averred that 'there is preferment and sycophancy in some law schools – if you want to get on you have to have a mentor, work in his areas of interest and follow up the leads he gives you'. Another (from a different institution) spoke of the world of academic law as 'bitchy and sycophantic, with a certain amount of mild corruption in the form of preferment'.

Another aspect of acquiring a reputation is not easily detected in studies (such as those already quoted) which rely largely on bibliographical analysis. It comes out quite strongly in the competitive environment of hard pure knowledge domains, though it seems more muted elsewhere. A number of biologists made the point with characteristic clarity: 'There is a large element of public relations involved'; 'you have to make yourself known, to sell yourself at meetings'; 'you have to put your work across to the right people'; 'few people get there by pure talent, though you do have to be able as well'; 'you get an FRS not only on the basis of what you know, but of who you know'. Reif (1961) writes of the need for physicists:

> to create, either through personal contact or through published work, a favourable impression among as many key scientists as possible. Professional mobility of the scientist depends . . . in an essential way on the reputation he has acquired among prominent people in his field.

And by way of confirmation, one of the US physicists I interviewed, speaking half-admiringly of a colleague who had 'made it', remarked 'he's not that smart, but he's very tough and good at promoting himself'.

This phenomenon seems to be related to one observed by Griffith and Mullins (1972), whose study of a diversity of 'coherent activist groups' led them to identify 'two different leadership roles, intellectual and organizational [which] may or may not be filled by the same individual'. The organizational leader, as the title implies, is responsible for arranging 'times, funds and facilities for research', and in general providing the necessary administrative underpinning for a complex collective enterprise. Although, as Griffith and Mullins emphasize, 'In all cases the organizational leader, if different from the intellectual leader, was a respected researcher in his own right', one cannot but reflect that a reputation gained on these terms, like that acquired for being a well-read scholar or a great teacher, must be more ephemeral than that which, because it rests on a widely respected contribution to the advancement of research, leaves its tangible results in the literature of the subject and the acknowledgements of others.

Pecking orders, élites and the Matthew effect

One of the striking features of academic life is that nearly everything is graded in more or less subtle ways. People are quite open in designating the leading journals in their discipline, about which there is virtual unanimity; they are willing, when pressed, to list institutions and departments in order of intellectual precedence; there is a constant process of implicit and explicit ranking of individuals (the outstanding scholar, the student with the 'first class mind', and, more often by implication or omission, those who are less well regarded).

There is also a prestige which attaches to some subjects in particular,[5] and in some areas even a rough pecking order between the component specialisms. Physicists consider themselves, and are regarded by others, as better than the common crowd; historians are accepted to be a cut above geographers; economists look down on sociologists; and so the catalogue continues. Roughly speaking, hard knowledge domains are regarded more highly than soft ones, and pure than applied. Within what might be called, in sociological parlance, the more stratified disciplines (those with clearly marked internal status distinctions), certain fields of activity are seen as prestigious and others as less so. In general, theoreticians are reckoned to have to deal with the most difficult intellectual tasks. Thus Gaston (1973) remarks that in high-energy physics, 'recognition is, first, a function of scientific productivity and, second, a function of the type of [sub-specialism]. Theorists are recognized more than experimentalists for their research.' Again, among my respondents, mathematical economists were considered the *crème de la crème* within the discipline; 'messy' areas such as labour economics were generally given a low rating. But the orders of priority here are susceptible to conflicting criteria (the more applied fields often attract the largest share of the grants), and subject to intellectual fashion (to keep to economics as an example, one respondent noted that 'area studies used to be a low prestige field, but there is now a boom in research on the Soviet economy').

Any detailed discussion of disciplinary pecking orders can open up a host of intriguing issues. Why, for instance, do historians, sociologists, lawyers and mechanical engineers apparently find it difficult to rank their specialisms while mathematicians and pharmicists are at least able to do so to a limited extent? What is it that makes people by and large accord chemists a higher status than biologists? Such questions, which are ostensibly about knowledge communities, are (as has already been implied) to do with epistemology as well: with the nature and precision of criteria for judging merit; with the degree of elegance of the intellectual field; with the extent to which it lends itself to abstract thinking or responds to mathematical modelling. Such considerations will be taken up again in Chapter 8. For our present purposes, however, it is necessary to return to the question of institutional and personal prestige.

The standing of a particular department is determined in part by the status of its parent institution, and also in part by the reputation of its individual members. But the relationships here are reciprocal, in that an institution's standing is made up in large part of the reputations of its constituent departments, which themselves condition the regard in which their individual members are held. The ascription of status is thus a delicate and complex business; this does not, however, appear to inhibit the pervasive process of evaluating intellectual worth.

One outcome of this constant exercise of discriminative judgement is the creation of élites and the marking down of those who are not among the front runners. Aldous Huxley once wrote of 'A million million spermatozoa,/All of them alive:/Out of their cataclysm but one poor Noah/Dare hope to survive.' A less dramatic version of the same syndrome can be seen across the whole range of academic communities. Selectivity is at its most ruthless in hard pure domains, where the pyramid has a broad base and a sharp pinnacle. Mulkay (1976) argues that a small élite of scientists enjoys a disproportionate share of grant resources and peer recognition; Gaston (1973) observes that there is a relatively small number of scientists at the centre of the information network; and 'most work by average scientists is hardly ever acknowledged, much less rewarded with citations and prizes'. A number of bibliographical studies (e.g. Price 1963) have shown that, taking the science community as a whole, a sizeable proportion of individuals publish no more than one or two papers; of those papers which are published, a significant number (Price 1965, Gustin 1973) are never cited, and some, one might conjecture, will be read by only a handful of people.

The gulf between fame and anonymity is progressively widened by the operation of what Merton (1973), invoking a well-known passage in the first of the Four Gospels, called the Matthew principle: 'To those that have shall be given, and from those that have not shall be taken even that which they have.' Mulkay (1977) refers to 'a self-reinforcing elite structure' – citing as confirmation the studies of the stratification of science by Cole and Cole (1973) and Zuckerman (1970) – and adds that 'The more eminent a scientist becomes the more visible he appears to his colleagues and the greater the credit he receives for his research contributions.' As one of my biologist informants remarked, 'It's a cumulative process. Once you earn a name for yourself, it acts as a magnet: you get invitations to join societies, give papers and take up offices.' Lightfield (1971) notes that those sociologists who are productive in their early careers are likely to remain so, while those who are not are unlikely to become so: the evidence that success breeds success spans the social sciences, the humanities and the professional disciplines.

Great men, gatekeepers and the exercise of power

Even among those who reach élite status during their professional careers, there are few who achieve recognition as great men. Perhaps true eminence is hard to judge except retrospectively: many cases have been known, over time, of pygmies turning into giants. It is also possible to speculate, as Griffith and Small (1983) have done, whether there is some difference between hard and soft knowledge areas in the ease with which ability is recognized and commonly acknowledged. They suggest that

' "softer" clusters are more likely to be dominated by the work of only one or two men' – the 'few ancestral spirits', in Jones' (1980) spoof account of American sociologists, who 'are endowed with extraordinarily creative powers . . . a very few of [whose] inscriptions are sometimes said to embody all the sacredness diffused throughout the whole clan'. It is certainly in the hard pure knowledge areas, where significant discoveries are easy to identify, and where criteria of merit are less open to wide interpretation and dispute, that prizes and other public symbols of recognition abound, and that eponymy is commonplace ('Fermat's last theorem'; 'Maxwell's equations'; 'Halley's comet'; 'Darwin's finches').

It stands to reason that the personal qualities which go to make up greatness are as many and diverse as the disciplines within which it is achieved, and as the people who inhabit them. Attempts to define genius, or even to pinpoint exceptional creativity, have met with only the modest success that attends most speculative psychological investigation. However, there are certain social and cognitive features which appear to distinguish major from minor intellectual contributions. One of these is range of applicability. 'Prestige accrues predominantly to those whose discoveries prove fruitful as a basis for further work by other scientists' (Reif 1961); people who, according to the biologists I interviewed, had changed the shape of the discipline in some significant way. Another is breadth of reference. Crane's (1972) analysis of invisible colleges suggests that it is the most productive scientists who have the highest number of professional ties outside their own specialism; and it became clear from my discussions with historians that those who seek greatness must be 'more than narrow scholars'. In the disciplinary groups in which the same people's names kept cropping up in the course of my interviews (Sauer, for example, among American geographers, or Kahn-Freund among English academic lawyers), they were singled out for their 'broad, philosophical view of the subject', their 'range of knowledge, breadth of education and concern'.[6]

The achievement of a measure of eminence in one's lifetime brings with it a potentiality for the exercise of power. As one informant, a sociologist, remarked, 'Power resides in the membership of salary and promotion committees: people suddenly realise that they are being judged by their seniors'; another added, 'rank counts when it is a question of getting references for jobs – you are subtly confronted by the need for support from your superiors'. Whitley (1969) comments that 'Power in the sciences is seen as an adjunct of prestige' entailing one's appointment to key positions such as journal editors and referees. Mulkay (1977) develops the point:

Because judgements of the highest quality can only be made by men who are already eminent, those at the top of the various informal scientific hierarchies exercise great influence over the standards operative within their fields. And those scientists who wish to advance their careers and to produce results which are accepted as significant contributions to knowledge must comply with the standards set by these leaders.

A certain element of continuity is built into this judgemental process, in that 'as a result of their academic training, editorial readers respond to certain aspects of methodology, theoretical orientation and mode of expression in the writings of those who have received similar training' (Crane 1967).

The role of 'gatekeeper' – the person that determines who is allowed into a particular community and who remains excluded – is a significant one in terms of the development of knowledge fields. 'Generally', Cole (1983) points out, 'the stars of a particular discipline occupy the main gatekeeping roles. By their acts as gatekeepers and evaluators, they determine what work is considered good and what is unimportant.' A prime example emerged from my interviews with mathematicians, when it became apparent that one distinguished member of the discipline in Britain had played a key part in all the significant appointments to his field over several years, and had also had considerable influence on the promotion pattern in neighbouring specialisms. Whitley (1984) remarks that the significance of gatekeeping may vary between subject fields:

> Anglo-Saxon sociology and economics, for instance, differ greatly in the influence a relatively small number of intellectual leaders are able to exert over research strategies and significance criteria. . . . Generally, the more concentrated is control over the major communication media, the easier it is for a small elite to set standards and direct strategies.

This qualification seems plausible in the light of the differences which have already been noted (see especially Chapters 1 and 3) between different knowledge forms and communities. The more closely defined and better-defended the boundaries are between hard specialisms, and the more tightly knit the groups associated with them, the easier it is to maintain the integrity of received doctrines by the ostracism or expulsion of internal dissidents and the refusal to provide entry permits to outsiders with dubious credentials. Yet traces of the gatekeeping function may be found even in epistemologically soft areas whose associated specialist groups are loosely knit. In history, one of my informants spoke of the need to 'defer to the elders of the tribe', and another remarked that it was at least a matter of courtesy, if not of expediency, when one wanted to enter a new specialism, to write to one or more of the leading experts for initial advice and guidance.

Peer review and the process of validation

Although particular weight is given to the pronouncements of the more eminent academics in any community, they are not alone in shaping its values and standards. The responsibility for quality control is a collective one, distributed across the whole membership of a given group; except in the strongly hierarchical subject areas, leadership is only granted on sufferance, and those who are accorded it have to continue to justify themselves as especially competent and active exponents of their discipline or specialism. The right of any member of a particular field to criticize the work of any other member, regardless of their relative status, is strongly defended in principle even where it is only weakly exercised in practice. This right rests on a procedure which is commonly termed peer group judgement or peer review.

The notion of an academic peer group is not clearly defined. It has some affinities with a specialist network, some with an 'invisible college' and some with a wider disciplinary community, though the contexts in which the term 'peer group' is used differ from those in which the other labels are commonly found. It is related to the exercise of a number of key evaluative functions (Zuckerman and Merton 1971) performed by suitably selected members of a body of reasonably close colleagues. It forms the basis of the grant-awarding process in the case of many research funding bodies (proposals are typically sent out to two or more independent referees with appropriate expertise), and is also used in assessing articles submitted for journal publication and in determining eligibility for the membership of learned societies. Senior members of the peer group may be invited to act as external examiners for degree awards, to participate in the process of appointment to senior posts, and to offer comments on candidates for promotion within an institution.

The principle of mutual judgement by informed specialists seems well-founded, in that only those with a mastery of a particular field are capable of making an authoritative appraisal within it.[7] In terms of research activity, as Mulkay (1977) argues:

> trustworthy assessments of the quality of a given piece of work can only be made by those who are working on the same or similar problems and who are known to be capable of producing results of at least the same level of quality. There can be no separate formal hierarchy of control in scientific research. All participants, as they use, modify or disregard the results communicated to them, are continually engaged in judging the adequacy and value of their colleagues' work. As a result of those judgements, recognition is allocated and reputations are created; not only for individual researchers, but also for research groups, university departments and research journals.

Peer review, it may be said, serves to maintain overall standards as well as to recognize individual excellence.

Like many useful social mechanisms, however, the peer group has its drawbacks. The indictments are as numerous as they are varied. One fairly obvious one was noted earlier: that those who have already earned reputations tend to be consistently favoured at the expense of those who have not.[8] Another is that in the more highly specialized areas, the scope for informed and impartial judgement is limited – the selection of referees may have to be made from those whose professional acquaintance with the field is only indirect (and whose judgements will in that sense be amateur), or from the few people with shared expertise who may wish to protect their own standing against rival claims.

A third common and predictable set of complaints arises from the fallibility of human judgement. The failure of experts to agree is commonplace, in this as in other spheres, and especially so at 'the research frontier' where 'getting a research grant depends to a significant extent on chance'; though, perhaps reassuringly, 'the great bulk of disagreement . . . is probably a result of real and legitimate differences of opinion among experts' (Cole *et al.* 1981). It should be noted that Cole's later research identifies less difference in this respect between the natural sciences and the social sciences than has usually been assumed: they have 'similar [that is, comparatively low] levels of consensus at the research frontier' (Cole 1983).

Cole, who has made a particular study of peer review procedures, argues that leaving aside questions of reliability – i.e. consistency of judgement – their validity must also be suspect, in that they often fail to predict the winners:

> In one subject we studied, algebra, . . . people whose proposals [for grants to the National Science Foundation] were declined actually turned out to be on average slightly more productive than those whose proposals were accepted. Although there may be some discoveries which are immediately judged to be significant and do indeed turn out to be highly significant, for most science it is not clear to participants, when work is produced, whether it will turn out to be important. Although we have always assumed that this is true for the social sciences, [a number of studies] suggest that it is also true for the natural sciences (Cole 1983).

Apart from these congenital weaknesses, peer review tends to operate unevenly between different knowledge fields: 'Disciplines vary in the extent to which articles by authors from diverse intellectual backgrounds are selected for publication in their principal journals' (Crane 1967). Soft areas with relatively permeable boundaries are in their nature more tolerant of divergence than those whose subject matter is hard and whose boundaries are closely defined. It was commonplace among my respondents[9] that different speciality groups within the same disciplines adopted different standards of academic rigour: the variations between disciplines in this respect were acknowledged to be endemic (and often held to be related to their ranking in the intellectual pecking order).

Where the system shows signs of breaking down, it too does so in different ways according to the knowledge domain in question. The venial sin of 'sloppy refereeing' seems most prevalent in mathematics, where it can be particularly difficult and time-consuming to enter into someone else's frame of reference and follow the train of reasoning within it (in contrast, respondents in some more loosely organized disciplines re-marked on the importance accorded to meticulous evaluation procedures). One of my mathematical informants condoned the fact that 'people don't take enough care to check papers for accuracy', remarking that 'there is no reward system built in for that kind of work'. Another observed that 'people used to be more conscientious in the old days, when they weren't so pressed for time', but commented that the comparatively slipshod current practice was not damaging to the subject in the long run, since any important errors would eventually get known – it merely demanded 'more vigilance from the general mathematical public: and in any case it is the author who cares most passionately about not making mistakes'.

The last comment, incidentally, underlines an interesting disjunction between supposition and actuality. Perhaps because of the insistence of positivist philosophers of science that the validity (or falsity) of an empirical proposition ought, at least in principle, to be tested by replication of the supporting experimental procedures, it seems to be widely supposed outside the natural science community that this is indeed the normal practice. However, my own data are unequivocal in confirming Thagaard's (1987) contention that:

> Replication of previous findings is seldom performed because rep-lications are difficult to publish. Publication of papers requires presentation of new aspects. One way to meet both the demands for new findings and for verification of new results is to work on similar projects, which usually implies the same design.

In effect, validation by the peer group, even in the universalistic world of hard pure knowledge, is less a matter of the careful, repetitious checking of one another's results than of a seemingly more haphazard process: assuming that people's findings are correct and building upon them until something is clearly seen to have gone wrong, at which point some credit may be given for tracking down the original error. 'There is almost always', one of my respondents remarked, 'a deeper reason to replicate – it isn't something people do in the normal run.'

The very notion of validation has (as the discussion in Chapter 1 attempted to make plain) to be translated into different terms in the particularistic, interpretive domain of soft pure knowledge – which demands some form of 'authenticity' – and in the contrasting domains of hard applied and soft applied knowledge, where the respective re-quirements might be identified as functional efficiency and procedural utility. The peer groups concerned with establishing standards in these diverse knowledge areas are thus faced with dissimilar tasks. It is not surprising that they have to tackle them in distinctive ways, and that breakdowns in procedure may be traced to different sources of weakness in the system.

When the hard scientists – pure as well as applied – in my sample referred on occasion to unethical refereeing, they frequently had in view cases of sharp practice or plagiarism. Their stories, mythical or personally experienced, related to eminent referees who had caused others' submissions to be rejected or long delayed, and who had then proceeded themselves to publish suspiciously similar findings. In soft knowledge domains, this form of corruption is uncommon, because few people are working on the same issues, and even if they are, their interpretations of them are very rarely identical. On the other hand, there is more room in such fields for the venting of personal preferences or antipathies. Any member of the peer group may be open to the accusation of 'log rolling' for friends and protégés (by treating their efforts more kindly than they deserve) or of 'doing down' enemies and rivals (by unduly harsh criticisms of their work). The deliberate freezing-out of contributions which are seen as in some way threatening (usually because they purport to undermine an established ideology or school of thought) is not confined to any one knowledge area, manifesting itself from time to time with comparable partiality in every kind of discipline.

The limitations of the exercise of peer judgement are easier to discern in the more or less publicly accessible arena of book reviewing or the refereeing of journal articles – where opinions are at least open to being challenged or appealed against – than in the closed world of making appointments and promotions, approving grant proposals, according honours or awarding prizes. Here the only recourse against the suspicion of unfairness is to try one's luck at another time or in another place, with the attendant risk that one or more of the same unfavourable referees will be employed. Where the achievement of a coveted goal is open to strong competition from people in a diversity of fields, the problem of making a just choice is all the worse. Faced with an array of well-supported, highly qualified candidates from disciplines whose standards are not easily comparable with one another, the temptation to lapse from the niceties of intellectual judgement to the coarser pursuit of political bargaining can become intense, as many of those who have been involved in such situations may be prepared in their unguarded moments to acknowledge.

Taking the long view, however, such complaints about the peer review process may be of no great import. They serve a useful purpose in signalling familiar pitfalls to be guarded against or in suggesting modest reforms in current practice,[10] but they cannot be allowed to constitute a major indictment against the system as a whole. Most of those who advocate parliamentary democracy as a method of government are prepared to acknowledge its manifold weaknesses: their defence of it rests on the claim that there is no preferable substitute. So too, it can be argued, the exercise of peer group judgement must be tolerated, for all its admitted faults, because no one has yet come up with an approach to academic evaluation that would not be discernibly worse.

Networks and social circles

The concept of a peer group has affinities with that of a network, as may be seen from the following comment by Crane (1972):

> Behind the seemingly impersonal structure of scientific knowledge, there is a vast interpersonal network that screens new ideas in terms of a central theme or paradigm, permitting some a wide audience and consigning many to oblivion.

That a network also has a close relationship with the notion of a specialist area or segment may be seen by relating some of the observations in Chapter 3 to this statement by Mulkay (1977):

> Research networks are amorphous social groupings which, partly due to migration . . . and partly due to overlapping membership . . . are in a state of constant flux. At any one time the research community as a whole, as well as particular disciplines and specialties within it, is composed of numerous networks at various stages of formation, growth and decline.

An attempt to locate a tidy pattern in both sets of relationships might go something like this. A general distinction can be made (Becher and Kogan 1980) between what individuals or groups of individuals do – which may be termed their operational mode – and what their values, aspirations and loyalties are – which may be labelled their normative mode. The two modes are interdependent, in that significant changes in one will tend to be reflected in changes in the other. The peer group represents the academic community in its normative mode, where its predominant concern is with establishing standards, assessing merit and evaluating reputations. The network represents its operational mode, in which the focus is on the development and communication of knowledge as such. The interconnections may be seen in the way in which knowledge development is tested against professional norms (screened, in Crane's words, 'in terms of a central theme or paradigm') and the comparable way in which reputation may affect the collective identification and communication of 'new ideas'.

The distinction between norms and operations has a different frame of reference from that between the social and the cognitive aspects of academic life, though a shadowy connection may be discerned between them. It is in terms of this second dichotomy that networks and segments are related. It was suggested in Chapter 3 that the term segment might be seen in cognitive terms to signify divisions in knowledge at the microscopic level, whether or not such divisions fell within disciplinary domains or straddled the boundaries between them. The term network may be reserved to designate the corresponding social divisions: 'amorphous social groupings', as Mulkay describes them, of which 'the research community . . . is composed'.

A useful analogy, in attempting to characterize networks in more detailed terms, is that of a 'social circle' (developed by Crane 1969a, 1972). The parallel is a neat one, in that social circles are 'amorphous', 'overlapping' and 'in a state of constant flux'. They are centred upon, and drawn around, both individuals and groups. That is, they can be defined in both personal and interpersonal terms – one may speak for some purposes of 'X's social circle', and for others of 'the social circle to which X belongs'. They also allow for pluralism, in that an individual may be said to belong to more than one such group. The attributes of social circles may vary. They may be large or small, active or moribund, important, colourful and exciting or insignificant, drab and mundane. They may be cliquey or open, and the relationships between members may be close or relatively distant, somewhere on the spectrum from best friends to nodding acquaintances. And they may be seen to be 'at various stages of formation, growth and decline'.[11]

The abundant research literature on the theme has three noticeable features. The first will by now seem familiar: it focuses largely (though not exclusively, as we shall see later) on the hard pure domain of the natural sciences. The second is its tendency to concentrate on the high life, on those active, glamorous situations in which interesting things are always happening, at the expense of those which follow the everyday routines of what Kuhn (1962) calls 'normal science'. The third characteristic of network studies is that they more or less consistently adopt the group as against the individual perspective, which sometimes has the effect of reifying the concept into an independent, substantive entity, divorced from the consideration of membership and, as Chubin (1976) complains, careless of the question of intellectual content. In contrast, my data, being drawn more widely from a scatter of disciplines, tend to emphasize everyday circumstances as against contexts of high intellectual excitement, and to reflect the individual's standpoint rather than that of the group as a whole. The two approaches turn out in the event to be complementary to, rather than contradictory of, one another. The ensuing discussion will deal briefly with both.

To start with the material from my interviews, one phenomenon is clearly evident in the testimony from members of virtually every discipline; namely, the existence of an inner and an outer circle of professional acquaintance. The outer circle is in many cases quite large in compass, numbering somewhere between 100 and 400 people, with a norm of about 200. Its members comprise those colleagues with whose names and work one is more or less familiar – the distant intellectual relatives and passing professional friends one might occasionally meet and greet at conferences, those who might appear on one's mailing lists for offprints or publisher's notices. The inner circle is usually surprisingly small, ranging from half a dozen to a score, with a dozen as a fairly common average. The bonds here are tighter and more resilient, singling out those colleagues with whom one has a direct affinity and a closely shared interest; those critical friends to whom one would send draft papers for comment and whose own drafts one would take some trouble to read; the kind of people one would go to for assistance over a knotty problem, advice on research tactics, or support at times of intellectual adversity, and whom one would expect to help in one's turn.[12]

The size of the outer circle shows some variation from one type of specialism to another, with practitioners in socially well-organized, cognitively hard knowledge fields (physics in particular) often claiming large numbers, and those in loosely organized soft areas (social geography, say, or minority languages) usually quoting smaller ones.[13] The inner circle, however, seems to reflect no such cognitive contrasts. Variations in size here seem more a function of individual gregariousness than of subject field, leading to the speculation that this phenomenon is more a social than an epistemological one. Rather than reflecting a curiously uniform property of knowledge in all its different manifestations – the ability to be neatly parcelled up into small units capable of accommodating some 20 active researchers at most – the incidence of such small groupings seems more likely to arise from the difficulty academics have in sustaining more than a limited number of close affinities. Links of the intense kind in question are demanding as well as rewarding: they take time to develop and sustain. Moreover, there is usually a limit to the extent to which one is prepared to confide in others about one's own half-formed ideas, or to be receptive to theirs.

Previous researches into academic networks give some indirect support to this contrast between inner and outer circles, though they do not address it directly. Thus Crane (1972) quotes Roberts' contention that groups could be as small as half a dozen (Roberts 1970), but attributes this to low paradigm development in the humanities; and Mullins (1973a) ascribes the size of 'clusters' – a 'minimum core of 13 to 15 active students, teachers and researchers' – to a particular phase in the cycle of growth of coherent intellectual groups.

A more commonly noted contrast in network research is that between open and closed groups. Mullins (1968) and Knorr-Cetina (1982) are among those who focus on the incidence of informal contacts across group boundaries. The first author, however, in a joint paper with Griffith (Griffith and Mullins 1972) also discerns certain highly coherent groups which develop their own enclosed and private worlds: 'these groups generate "tribal folklore" and customs, including distinctive lifestyles, mock ceremonies and awards, special ingroup roles, and even, on occasion, a group sport'. Close cohesion is generally seen to be more common in 'revolutionary' than in 'normal' contexts. Those who are united in an attempt to contest the prevailing orthodoxies, or to strike out in a novel direction, tend to show a higher level of interaction and a more intense pattern of communication than those who are engaged on central problems demanding accepted modes of practice in areas in which the appropriateness of the subject matter, methods and theories are not in dispute (we shall return to a more detailed consideration of this point in Chapter 5).

Case histories of particular networks, understandably enough, tend to focus on the interesting exceptions to everyday routine. They are not confined to groups in the hard sciences, though these remain the dominant focus. Thus, alongside Gaston's (1973) detailed scrutiny of high-energy physicists, and the briefer ones by Nadel (1980) on specialists in superconductivity and Mullins (1972) on the phage group in molecular biology, there are comparable explorations by Mullins (1973b) on the school of ethnomethodologists in sociology, by Murray (1983) on anthropological linguists, and even a short foray by van den Braembussche (1979) into the *Annales* school in history.

Studies along these lines commonly represent the evolution of their chosen problem area as falling into three or four phases. Mullins, one of the front runners in such research, labels them as 'normal', 'network', 'cluster' and 'specialty', giving them somewhat surprisingly precise definitions, sizes of membership (Mullins 1973a, 1973b) and collective lifespans ('10 to 15 years is typical'; Griffith and Mullins 1972). Leaving aside the first of these, which can be taken simply as the characteristic form of loose network underpinning most academic activity, the remaining stages are usually identified in terms of (1) a disorganized, spontaneous growth of interest in a new development, as a result of which a network begins to coalesce and its defining doctrines to crystallize; (2) a more systematic structure of communication, recruitment and training, during which small internal interest groups appear and external boundaries become more firmly staked out; and (3) a stage at which the area becomes institutionalized, the excitement dies down and routine sets in. In the end, 'the penalty of success . . . is the death of the group as a distinct social and intellectual entity' (Griffith and Mullins 1972); 'growth turns imperceptibly into decline as recruitment falls away and as established members of the network move elsewhere into problem areas in the process of formation' (Mulkay 1977). The process can be aborted at any stage. Where a particular area of intellectual development proves to be less promising than it initially seemed, support ebbs away and the network dies a premature death – though here, as elsewhere, a rump of the highly committed converts may remain to pursue their unfashionable concerns in what will by that point have become an intellectual backwater.

The influence of fashion

Every one of the 12 disciplines covered by my study appeared to be subject to fashion (or, as one sociologist preferred to call it, 'paradigm choice or shift'). Some informants considered this a healthy feature of their academic community, allowing scope for individuals to move in new directions and ensuring that ideas did not stagnate. Others took a less positive view, deploring the tendency of some colleagues to 'behave like a flock of lemmings' in pursuit of novelty, noting the adverse effects on the systematic development of the field, and commenting on the consequent overpopulation in some areas at the expense of underpopulation in others. One of the chemists interviewed summed up a common worry: that susceptibility to fashion served to create 'a cyclical pattern of glut and scarcity'. Another remarked on the 'tendency to flock into new areas while other fields become comparatively neglected'.

The term itself, as some respondents noted, is value-laden, in that the same research activity might be represented as 'a mere fad' by those who disapproved of it, where those in favour would describe it as 'a hot area', and hence as rightly attracting new recruits.[14] Crane (1969b) attempts a neutral account in her observation that:

> The key factor in fashion is that similar perceptions of an area come to be shared by large numbers of scientists due to a process of social validation occurring in a rapidly expanding communication network.

Recruitment to meet the need for expansion 'depends upon the number of scientists in related areas who are capable in terms of training of moving into [a new field]'. It tends to stem from three main groups of academics. The first consists of those who are highly mobile by temperament and profession: people who eschew fixed loyalties to a single line of research and are eager to seek out novel ideas as they begin to appear over the horizon. The second is the group of individuals who, at any given time, have become disenchanted with their current line of research – usually because it is, or they themselves are, apparently going stale – and who are therefore looking out for promising fresh departures. The third group comprises the novitiates to the discipline, the research students who arrive with no fixed loyalties, keen to make their mark in areas which have not yet been heavily worked over, and susceptible to recruitment and proselytization by seniors wanting to attract a following into a new area of development.

Fashion takes a particularly intense form in those hard pure areas in which it appears relatively easy to identify promising new issues (see Chapter 1). Ruscio (1985) reports one of the biologists he interviewed as saying:

> a lot of people who have been trained in molecular biology . . . jump around from one biological system to another. Some of these people are more technologists than biologists who operate with a question in mind and then take their systems and techniques to answer that question. I call it the bandwagon effect: they work on one problem and then something else turns up and a whole bunch will switch over to that and then over to the next one that comes up.

Mulkay (1972) documents the comparable practice, in hot areas of physics, of 'skimming the cream' and 'moving on', a theme which was also frequently touched on in my interviews with physicists (one of whom likened the associated groups of intellectual predators to 'shoals of piranha fish').

In most instances of fashion, the race is to the swift. Those who lag behind the trendsetters and opinion leaders often end up with the skimmed milk:

> in many cases a major proportion of the innovative work is completed before the field has begun to acquire a significant proportion of its eventual membership . . . opportunities for making a notable scientific contribution and the chances of receiving an unusual amount of professional recognition decline very quickly (Mulkay 1977).

It is not only in the natural sciences that fashion holds sway, though it takes distinctive forms in other knowledge fields. Soft pure areas, where new issues are not sharply defined in terms of the existing state of enquiry, allow the exercise of a more eclectic choice, perhaps 'promoted by foundations' or by 'the activities of elites or special interest groups', in contrast with those domains in which the selection of problems is made 'on the basis of strong theoretical imperatives' (Crane 1969b). Applied disciplines are different again. Here fashions tend to follow the demonstration (or at least the plausible claim) of success with novel techniques or procedures, sometimes with the backing of an associated theory but at other times on a straightforwardly heuristic basis.

Some types of development are more amenable to fashion than others. This may well be because as Crane (1969a) argues, the acceptability of a new idea is affected by 'the amount of cognitive reorganization required to integrate the new information with previous knowledge'. As the Ruscio quotation above suggests, the extension of existing ideas and methods into a new subject field offers an attractive hostage to fashion. Methodological innovations, provided they are reasonably straightforward and do not demand a substantial amount of special training, are also relatively easy to take up. Significant changes in theoretical orientation and requirements to adopt complex new techniques (the use of computers in engineering design, say, or the earlier introduction of electron microscopy into biological research) are another matter, in that they demand a major reinvestment of time and effort, a theme which we shall explore further in considering the reactions of academics in general to innovative ideas.

Fashion, then, is a pervasive aspect of academic life, taking a variety of shapes and sizes. It may appear, as an eminent cell biologist once observed, in the guise of a mink coat, expensive and difficult to carry off, or in the form of a chainstore outfit, so cheap and simple as to be accessible to anyone who wants to go for it (Fell 1960). However, it owes its prevalence in the context of higher education less to frivolity than to a concern on the part of many academics to find a rapid and effective way of enhancing their own reputations. And it needs to be remembered that there is a cognitive price to pay for most such social self-improvement; namely, the need to show that one has succeeded in some discernible way in advancing the cause of learning.

Reactions to innovative ideas

Among the paradoxes which abound in academia, one of the most curious is the apparent coexistence of radical chic with entrenched conservatism. Many of my respondents who complained about their discipline's susceptibility to fashion were equally ready to assert – within the compass of the same interview, if not in the same breath – that the jealous guardianship of the *status quo*, especially among the more senior of their colleagues, acted as a barrier against promising innovations. This conflict between tradition and change is enshrined in the title of Kuhn's (1977) essay on the subject (which is also the title of the book in which it appears): *The Essential Tension*.

Resistance to new ideas is inborn among academic communities, as can be clearly shown by the length of time it often takes for a major insight or discovery to gain general acceptance. Merton (1973) canonizes the phenomenon as 'organised scepticism', one of his four basic norms of scientific behaviour, and Mulkay (1969), although critical of the norms themselves, does not dispute the contention that such a tendency exists. One among many instances is provided by Duncan (1974), in his account of how the seminal ideas of one geographer, Hägerstrand, after years of being written down or ignored, eventually succeeded in promoting a new approach to the discipline. Barber's (1961) general treatment of the subject offers other examples, in the process of suggesting why it is that new findings are only reluctantly conceded.

On this point, the explanations are various. Kuhn (1962) puts it down to a concern to maintain an existing paradigm, even in the face of conflicting evidence. Cole (1983) claims to have found 'many examples' of the contention that:

> If the experimental results do not fit the predictions made from the theory, the theory is not assumed to be incorrect. Rather, the scientist will assume that there was something wrong in the experimental techniques and that a proper experiment will bring about results which do indeed fit the theoretical expectations.

Boissevain (1974) adds two further considerations: besides 'the logical momentum of a scientific theory', he identifies 'the social climate . . . and the considerable power differentials inherent in all scientific communities' as factors 'which contribute to the persistence of all paradigms once they become dominant'.

Mulkay (1977) contests Kuhn's suggestion that major scientific advances typically demand a conceptual revolution, maintaining that 'although uncompromising intellectual resistance does occur . . . it is by no means as pervasive as Kuhn suggests'. He concedes, however, that 'a closed orthodoxy may be more probable' in highly socialized, socially isolated and intellectually distinct areas, and that 'intellectual control may be more likely in networks with a stable elite', a view echoed by Whitley (1984):

> Radical intellectual change – such as is implied by the term 'revolution' – is improbable where work goals and procedures are relatively uniform and stable and the hierarchy of problems and areas is reproduced and controlled by a strong authority structure.

In contrasting fields 'lacking strong paradigms', Collins (1975) offers a markedly different interpretation of resistance to change, seeing it as a wish 'to keep the organization decentralised and thus relatively egalitarian. The development of any theory that would change this situation . . . involves a power struggle of a particular sort.'

Such accounts appear to ignore one straightforward motive – which emerged consistently during my interviews – for standing out against new ideas. In many fields it takes time and trouble to acquire the necessary expertise to make a significant research contribution. People who have spent some years – to take only two of several examples given by my respondents – building up the vocabulary and conceptual structure demanded of a specialism in mathematics such as homotopy theory, or undergoing training in Freudian psychoanalysis in order to use it as an approach to literary criticism, understandably see themselves as being committed to a sizeable intellectual investment. And as with investments of a more familiar kind, there is a consequent wish to capitalize on them, recouping in collegial credit the efforts spent in laborious endeavour. A new development which threatens seriously to undermine the value of one's existing intellectual shareholding is unlikely to be welcomed with much enthusiasm.

It was noted in the discussion of intellectual fashion that some forms of innovation are more readily acceptable than others; particularly so, perhaps, where they do not entail the costly process of abandoning existing assets and reinvesting in new ones. In soft pure areas where the internal boundaries are weak and movement across them relatively uninhibited, new theories are liable to succeed one another with disconcerting rapidity. Opposition to change is relatively low, too, 'when ideas from one area are being applied to another area that has not been active previously' (Crane 1972). Analogously, 'because new areas have, by definition, not been conceptualized before, their discovery will not normally generate intellectual resistance' (Mulkay 1977).

The familiar contest of the Young Turks against the Old Guard can also readily be explained in such terms. Those who have as yet made no major intellectual commitments have little to lose by investing in potentially high-risk, high-profit commodities; those who already have a substantial blue chip portfolio tend to see the emergence of rival markets as a threat rather than a promise.[15] The market metaphor has a certain appropriateness here, in that a persuasive analysis along these general lines was first put forward by a distinguished economist, Harry Johnson.

Johnson's (1971) thesis involves the identification of 'the social and intellectual conditions that make a revolution or counter-revolution possible'. The precondition is 'the existence of an established orthodoxy which is clearly inconsistent with the most salient facts . . . yet is sufficiently confident of its intellectual power to attempt to explain those facts, and in its efforts to do so exposes its incompetence in a ludicrous fashion'. Against this background, Johnson argues, a revolutionary theory must depend for its success on five main characteristics. First, it has to 'attack the central proposition of conservative orthodoxy . . . with a new but academically acceptable analysis that reverse[s] the proposition'. Next, it has 'to appear to be new, yet absorb as much as possible of the valid . . . components of existing orthodox theory'. Thirdly, it must be 'so difficult to understand that senior academic colleagues would find it neither easy nor worthwhile to study', hard enough to 'challenge the intellectual interest of younger colleagues and students but actually easy enough for them to master adequately with a sufficient investment of intellectual endeavour', thus allowing youthful iconoclasm 'quickly [to] earn its just reward . . . by the demolition of the intellectual pretensions of its academic seniors and predecessors'. The fourth and fifth requirements are, respectively, that it should offer 'a new methodology more appealing than those currently available', with 'a high degree of apparent empirical relevance', and that it should provide 'a new and important empirical relationship'.

These are stringent demands, which not all accredited revolutions, even within hard pure fields, let alone those outside, would be able to meet. None the less, Johnson's analysis presents a sharply delineated picture of the type of struggle that characterizes a major generation gap within a particular academic community, relating social to cognitive considerations in an appropriately subtle way. Taylor (1976) shows it to be broadly applicable to the controversy over quantitative geography in the 1960s and early 1970s,[16] adding some useful observations about how such controversies may eventually be resolved.

Taylor argues that 'the traditionalist must overcome the disrespect of the young by using one of two strategies – he must either banish the heretics or else integrate everybody into a new unity'. Proponents of 'the hardline view' opt for confrontation, seeking to show that the new proposals fall outside the proper scope of the discipline and should be regarded as intellectually invalid, or at best as forming the basis of a separate enterprise. This claim may well be supported by a judicious re-presentation of the history and traditional values of the disciplinary community in question. The alternative course is one of conciliation: 'a very common general strategy in all types of social communities outside the academic world . . . the incorporation of the "avant-garde" into the establishment'. That, however, may not be the end of the story. Both Johnson and Taylor remind us that revolution may breed counter-revolution. The Keynesian revolution, attacking the prevailing economic orthodoxy, was succeeded by the monetarist attack on Keynesianism; and in geography, 'as the establishment, or at least part of it, quantifiers have to take their turn in coming under attack from new young geographers'.

The revolutionary and the normal

It is easy to be carried away into imagining that all academic life shares this quality of high intellectual theatre. But major revolutions, it needs to be recalled, represent the grand opera of the scholarly community, much of whose everyday entertainment falls within the more humble genre of improvised street theatre. 'In mature fields with accumulated resources', Bourdieu (1981) contends, 'great periodic revolutions' give way to 'countless small permanent revolutions'. Change is for the most part small-scale, steady and persistent.

None the less, among the relatively élite groups in which most research (including my own) into academic cultures has been conducted, professional life is never entirely static. If one wishes to acquire and maintain a reputation, it is essential to keep up with, and indeed to contribute to, new developments in one's field. Such new developments are a feature not only of highly active academic areas but also of those in which a less hectic pattern of life prevails. Academia offers an environment in which progress and development, not stability, is the normal expectation.

The basic mechanisms explored in this chapter can be seen as ways of living with intellectual change: its promotion through the reputational system, its concentration through differential recognition and the gatekeeping process, its evaluation through peer review, its promulgation through networking, its amplification through fashion, its containment through resistance, and its apotheosis through revolution. But the final and perhaps the most important point to be made about these various aspects of collective academic life is that they are projections into a particular environment of understandable, everyday social phenomena. To paraphrase the conclusion of Taylor's (1976) study, they are not the product of cool, rational analysis by objective intellectuals living in a social vacuum, but fairly predictable arrangements adopted by a set of people who happen to operate in a certain kind of community.

Notes

1 Among some notable exceptions are people whose ideas are developed largely in seminars and lectures, but given public recognition by their disciples. An example would be H. P. Grice, an Oxford philosopher who published little, but who was widely respected by those he taught and others who knew him professionally for the originality and clarity of his views.

2 To adapt the often-quoted words of Mandy Rice-Davis, 'Well they would, wouldn't they?' It is unlikely that those who had made the grade would want to suggest that they did so by the sheer width of the library shelving their works took up.

3 Cole's (1978) quantitatively based study reached the same conclusion in respect of the natural and social sciences: that sponsorship is primarily important in initial employment, but that it has little effect on later job acquisition.

4 Sheldon Rothblatt (personal communication) has a characteristically pertinent comment to make on this point:

> At one time it was possible to see this [the replacement of personal connections by reputational systems in determining academic worth] as a gain, since the academic circles were relatively closed and club-like and it was difficult for outsiders to break in. The elite institutions dominated the hiring network, and recommendations for positions were discussed by closed circuit. But given the number of ways in which reputational systems are created and manipulated, it hardly appears that we have advanced at all.

5 By way of illustration, one of my respondents, a chemist, referred to 'a hierarchy of arrogance. . . . Physics represents the hardest, most abstract reasoning – people know they're smart. Chemists feel defensive in relation to physicists, but superior in relation to biologists.' Another, an economist, remarked wryly, 'it's part of the status hierarchy that we don't talk to people who have to deal with reality'.

6 Compare Ruscio's (1986) findings, on independent evidence, that 'A highly regarded peer is "broad and well-read and able to bring knowledge from other disciplines to broaden the perspective within his own" ', and that ' "Landmark contributions" come from people who "are not drowned by a particular orthodoxy but having chosen a problem look at it from a number of points of view" '.

7 My colleague Trevor Pateman has pointed out that the notion of a peer group has its origins in the eighteenth century, when encyclopaedism and the amateur tradition were giving way to specialized professional knowledge. The idea of authority as derived from expertise is raised by Condorcet in the 1780s in his arguments against Mesmer's doctrine of animal magnetism (Darnton 1968), and the theme is developed at greater length in Lewis (1849). Bazerman (1987) confirms that 'in the middle of the eighteenth century, referees were introduced to maintain professional interests and quality' in the Royal Society's *Transactions*.

8 Cole *et al.* (1977) state:

> Scientists with an established track record, many scientific publications, a high frequency of citations, a record of having received grants from the NSF [US National Science Foundation] and ties to prestigious academic departments have a higher probability of receiving NSF grants than other applicants do. Nevertheless, the granting process is actually quite open . . . the scientific enterprise is an exceedingly equitable, although highly stratified social institution.

9 The research literature appears somewhat confused on this point (see the comments on differential rejection rates of journal articles across disciplines in

Zuckerman and Merton 1971, and Hargens 1975). But Ruscio's (1986) study supports my findings: 'In a discipline where there is disagreement about the legitimacy of one approach or another "and where it is hard to know who is doing path breaking work across the fields", the solution is to allow each subfield to set its own standards.'

10 For example, 'blind refereeing', in which the author's identity is not made known to the referee, even though it may sometimes be inferred.

11 An analogy along a different dimension is prompted by recent work in the field of applied linguistics. The notion of a 'discourse community', as elaborated by Swales (1988), has six defining features: common, public goals; a recognized set of mechanisms for intercommunication between members (in Swales' terms, a 'forum'); an existing process of information exchange; particular *genres* that 'articulate the operations' of the community; a shared and specialized terminology; and 'a critical mass of members' with relevant expertise in both content and discourse. Although the concept embraces a wide range of activities – Swales cites philatelists specializing in the postal history of Hong Kong and a local society of birdwatchers as two examples – it is clearly applicable also to specialized academic networks.

12 Members of the inner circle are not necessarily to be found within one's own department: when they are, they rarely exceed one or two in number. The geographical scatter of membership is often very wide.

13 It also, not surprisingly, seems to vary with the stage of academic career. Doctoral students have not usually managed to build up as wide a circle of professional acquaintances as have established, active researchers, though they will usually have identified those working on closely similar topics, both through the literature and through the contact networks of senior colleagues.

14 An essentially similar point is made by Barber (1968) and Crane (1969b).

15 The point is developed in greater detail in Boissevain (1974):

> the 'young Turks' . . . advance new theories not only because they have not been fully socialized into the rules of the dominant paradigm, and are hence particularly likely to see that those rules no longer define a playable game . . . [but also] because they seek recognition. They are trying to gain status in a competitive community, to advance higher from their position at the bottom of the scientific totem-pole. In terms of the culture prevailing in all scientific communities, one way of doing this is to demonstrate the inadequacy of an existing theory and, if possible, to advance a new, more adequate, theory.

He goes on to argue that:

> The outsiders attack with one of the few power resources not monopolized by their rivals: ideas. Hence the seeds of change are always present in the structural asymmetry between those with more power and those with less power. Those with more power try to maintain the asymmetry, and hence their superordinate position, sometimes even innovating to accomplish this end. They defend the status quo. Those with less power try to reduce the gap by pointing out anomalies.

16 See also Goodson (1983) for a discussion of the emergence of 'the new geography'.

5

Patterns of Communication

The life-blood of academia

Communication is central to the academic enterprise. The validity of that claim is readily established, in that both the promotion of knowledge (the main cognitive concern) and the establishment of reputation (the key social consideration) are necessarily dependent on it. A fresh insight, a new discovery, a novel invention, unless made available to others in the public domain, will remain no more than a piece of private intellectual property, fated to accompany its owner to the grave. That owner in turn, unless he or she is able both to establish first ownership and to relinquish possession to others, will be given no credit for its origination.

The claim can be yet more strongly advanced. Communication is the force that binds together the sociological and the epistemological, giving shape and substance to the links between knowledge forms and knowledge communities. As Gaston (1972) contends, the reward system and the communication system are closely interconnected; as Griffith and Small (1983) suggest, certain key epistemological distinctions may only emerge through a study of the structure of communication; and as Griffith and Miller (1970) demonstrate, communication patterns reflect the characteristics of the field of enquiry as well as those of the relevant research community.

A study of patterns of communication is accordingly important enough to deserve consideration in its own right. A beginning might best be made with an issue which has emerged from my enquiry as a key to the explanation of a number of otherwise unconnected and apparently random phenomena: namely, the density of population in a given specialism and the related scope and tractability of its component problems.

Population density

It was in my interviews with physicists that my attention was first drawn to the notion of 'the people-to-problem ratio'. In some specialist fields, it became clear that the number of issues currently being pursued was relatively small, though the number of people in pursuit of them might be quite substantial. At the other end of the scale, knowledge areas could be identified in which the questions that could be asked at any given time, with some reasonable expectation that they might be answered, were virtually unlimited, while the number of those engaged in answering them was negligible in comparison. In order to elucidate the idea of the people-to-problem ratio, it will be tactically useful to focus on the extremes of the spectrum, while acknowledging the existence of many intermediate instances where the ratio is neither spectacularly high nor strikingly low.

There are certain areas in almost any knowledge domain, whether it be pure or applied, hard or soft, which from time to time enjoy a high level of active interest. Sometimes, the attraction may stem from what appears to be a strikingly novel perspective with powerful implications – in Kuhn's (1962) terms, a revolution based around a newly emergent paradigm. But in the case of a thoroughgoing conceptual reassessment, though the initial problem base may be small, it must soon widen out to encompass all or most of the intellectual territory whose existing paradigm is in dispute (an attempted coup which is eventually confined only to part of the hinterland is accorded no more than the status of a minor insurrection). In such a case, the people-to-problem ratio remains abnormally high only for a short while, until the process of 'normal science' is set on its realigned course. The same is true of other, more transient population movements, focused on the fashionable topics referred to in Chapter 4, to which academics who are not committed to substantial investments in rival concerns may be attracted for one of a variety of reasons, whether personal or professional or both. Where the occasion is recognizable in hindsight as no more than a passing fad, the residual population – regardless of how large or small the problem scope might be – is likely to dwindle to a point at which the people-to-problem ratio is not much changed from its original level (yesterday's fashion is as marginal as tomorrow's, lacking even its anticipated glamour).

There remains, however, a significant group of specialisms which continue to attract a level of interest high enough to exonerate them from the charge of mere faddishness, while they remain concentrated within a sufficiently narrow cognitive framework and stable enough in terms of their associated social structure to be disqualified from revolutionary status. A further distinction, subtle but important, needs to be made here between a school or sect (terms which imply a relatively rigid and static set of intellectual beliefs)[1] and a close specialist community which is at a constantly high pitch of intellectual activity. A sectarian approach, in the academic as much as in the religious context, combines a narrowness of outlook with a breadth of application. It is a matter of seeing the world which one inhabits only from one particular angle: but it is the whole of that world, and not simply a limited part of it, which falls within the scope of the sect's defining dogma. Along another dimension, one might say that a sect is a revolution which has become established without achieving orthodoxy, permeating the whole of its relevant domain but winning the hearts and minds of only a minority of the population. In any event, however many adherents a particular school of thought may have, since the interests of those adherents are cast across a broad field, the people-to-problem ratio is liable to remain small. It is only in the second category – the tightly knit but dynamic specialist group in a closely defined knowledge field – that the population can become for more than a short time (the passing of a fashion or the establishment of a successful revolution) heavily concentrated on a limited number of problems.

Framing an analogy between urban and rural ways of life, I want to liken specialisms which have a high people-to-problem ratio to urban areas, and those with a low one to rural areas. In the first, there is alongside a densely concentrated population a generally busy – occasionally frenetic – pace of life, a high level of collective activity, close competition for space and resources, and a rapid and heavily used information network. By and large, the rural scene, though it may offer frenetic and competitive moments, occasions for communal involvement and a potential for spreading rumour and gossip like wildfire, displays the opposite characteristics.

Urban and rural scenarios

Urban and rural specialisms differ in a number of ways, not only in their communication patterns, but in the nature and scale of the problems on which their inhabitants are engaged, in the relationships between those inhabitants, and in the opportunities they have for attracting resources. Urban researchers characteristically select a narrow area of study, containing discrete and separable problems, where their rural counterparts typically cover a broader stretch of intellectual territory in which the problems are not sharply demarcated or delineated. The urban population is clustered around comparatively few salient topics, as against being spread out thinly across a wide range of themes. The urban mode is to tackle questions with relatively quick, short-range solutions, whereas rural researchers are liable to become engaged on long-range issues which may take years to puzzle out.[2]

Competition in urban life can become intense, even cut-throat, taking the form of a classic *Double Helix* pattern:[3] an all-out race to find the solution to what is seen as a seminal problem. In rural life, it makes better sense to adopt the principle of a division of labour – there are plenty of topics, so there is no point in tackling one on which someone else is already engaged. Teamwork is another feature more common in urban than in rural settings. Where several people are engaged on the same issue, it may pay to work collaboratively with a group of colleagues: joint activity has less occasion, and a less obvious justification, when there is ample opportunity to avoid close overlap with others. A competitive urban environment carries other implications – fears of plagiarism, a temptation to be secretive, and a concern with rapid publication to ensure priority – which we shall shortly consider in more detail.

There were frequent illustrations of these contrasts in my research data (from which they were in fact derived). Independent corroboration of them may be found in a number of places in the literature. To take one example, the investigation by Gilbert (1977a) of radar meteor research in the 1940s and 1950s (a rural branch of radio astronomy) offers a striking juxtaposition with the study by Gaston (1973) of high-energy physics in the 1960s. Gilbert's analysis shows that 'the ratio of the number of authors to the number of topics' in the group of researchers he studied was typically as low as 1.5, i.e. 'there were about three participants for every two topics under investigation'. Taking into account the fact that 'over the years 1945–1960 the average number of authors per paper varied about a mean of 1.6', this implies that 'there were on average approximately the same number of collaborating groups of researchers as there were topics. It is therefore unlikely that competition on a significant scale would have occurred.' Gilbert contrasts this situation with the one described by Gaston, remarking that 'competition will be prevalent when there is general agreement among the participants of a research area on the overriding importance of finding solutions to one or a small number of clearly defined problems'. Gaston (1971) himself argues that 'in fields of science in which there is not such a concentration on so few problems . . . there is less risk of anticipation' and competition is less likely. In another clear instance of a rural pattern of activity, Griffith and Miller (1970) observe of one specialism in psychology that:

> there are so few active researchers in this area that there is little perceived danger of overlap among research efforts. This may . . . reduce the need for rapid informal communication, since there appears to be little need to determine whether anyone else is doing research on similar problems.

The urban and rural research environments are as noticeably different as the activities which take place within them. The urban world has touches of modishness and occasional moments of intense excitement which are lacking in the measured pace of rural life. It can where necessary command sizeable resources and a high level of technology, where rural research is more modestly equipped and provided for. Research Councils and Foundations tend to concentrate their energies and funds on urban groups, both because they have a higher profile than rural ones and because they more commonly make large claims for supporting grants. For the most part, the urban context favours what Price (1963) designates as 'big science'. The rural setting embraces a number of 'little science' specialisms, but also takes in most soft pure, hard applied and soft applied areas as well.

Informal communication channels

Some of the most striking urban/rural differences emerge in the character-istic forms of communication within and between the various kinds of specialisms and networks discussed in Chapters 3 and 4. In the exploration of this theme a distinction needs to be made between the procedures involved in published work of a conventional kind (books, monographs, journal articles, reviews and the like) and the less formal mechanisms which do not fall so evidently and unrestrictedly within the public domain. To begin with the latter, a good deal of interchange takes place by word of mouth or in private or semi-private writings. Besides the everyday mechanisms of shop talk, gossip, and other familiar modes of personal correspondence, there is a clear incidence in certain fields of what are commonly termed 'preprints'. The phenomenon is one which has arisen mainly in urban research specialisms. It involves a fairly large-scale, semi-private circulation of photocopies of papers in typescript before they appear in orthodox journal form (as a sizeable number subsequently do). This practice has the advantage of helping to establish the priority of the authors' findings without the delay often attendant on formal publication. At the same time, however, it serves to create a privileged network of those who are on the mailing list, at the expense of equal access by those who do not enjoy insider status.

The contrast between insiders and outsiders is heightened by the tendency in urban circles to hold invited lectures by leaders in the field, engage in small, invitational conferences and symposia, undertake fairly frequent visits to laboratories in other centres, and exchange letters and telephone calls on a regular basis. The move towards closure of this kind, with its attendant risk of exclusiveness and inbreeding, can in some contexts become very pronounced: one respondent drew the comparison with an unstable economic system in which there is more traffic in black market currency than in legitimate coinage.

Word-of-mouth communication is a common feature of urban and rural settings alike, though it takes a different form in each. Generally speaking, the more hectic the pace of urban research, the more the reliance on informal sources. Gaston (1972) notes that, within the intensely competi-tive British high-energy physics community, experimentalists go in more for verbal information and theorists more for written information; Traweek (1982) singles out a common preference of American and Japanese practitioners in the same field for 'informed gossip', with little attention given to reading the relevant journals; and Crane (1972) finds a similar distinction across the broader groupings of physicists and chemists: 'Physicists placed a higher ranking than did chemists upon informal sources of locating information such as conversation and correspondence.'

Gossip is rife, too, in the small rural communities characteristic of anthropology (Cohn 1962), sociology (Kleinman 1983) and, as became clear from my interview data, in British academic law. Here, however, it takes the form of rumour and the dissection of personalities rather than the more sternly professional shop talk indulged in by serious-minded scientists – though it may also leave room for folklore of the sort common among less enclosed semi-rural groupings such as those in history. Historians, for example, 'tend to gossip about their sources, about their merits and whereabouts – they talk more about the tools of the trade than the trade itself'. They 'don't talk much shop', perhaps because the nature of the subject lies in details, so that a problem cannot often be adequately defined in conversation.

It is understandable that urban academic groups with a closely shared set of problems should be more occupationally gregarious than rural groups whose work shows little overlap even with that of their few near neighbours. Besides the more private social activities attributed to them above, urban researchers typically attend more national and international conferences than their rural opposite numbers. In my sample, the variation both between and within disciplines in this respect was noticeable. One senior and cosmopolitan biologist in a hot area claimed to be involved in a dozen gatherings a year, a couple of them overseas (as against most proponents of the same discipline, who regarded conferences, in the words of one respondent, as 'pleasant but inessential', and who normally reckoned to attend only two or three annually). Modern linguists, whose research predominantly follows a rural pattern, might typically go to one national conference in a 12-month period and one international conference once every 3 years.

Formal modes of interchange

The published literature of any field is its most accessible and durable manifestation of the research activity it embraces. The types of informal contact which have so far been considered, while they may assume a particular importance in accelerating the flow of ideas within an active urban community, are both less visible and more ephemeral than the commonly accepted means of recording and transmitting new findings through the medium of the printed word.[4]

The importance accorded to written communication is evident in urban and rural specialisms alike. But the resemblance hardly goes beyond that point, since even the most superficial observation reveals a host of consequent differences between the two. It may be argued, for example, that urban research activity favours the writing of journal articles at the expense of books, whereas in rural research the priorities are reversed. Whitley (1984) puts this contrast in practice down to the greater 'technical task uncertainty' of some specialisms, which means that they:

> have to be able to convey how research is undertaken, its purpose and implications in greater detail than where tasks and outcomes are more

standardized. The high degree of ambiguity of results means that their presentation has to be more elaborate and has to justify the particular interpretation being put forward. Thus typical articles are quite long and often work is communicated through books, whereas a lower degree of task uncertainty enables research to be effectively communicated in a short space through esoteric and standardized symbol systems.

Griffith and Small (1983) make a similar point, more succinctly, in relation to 'the social and behavioural sciences literature':

The journal article is, for many parts of social science, a poor vehicle of communication, ill-suited to discuss extremely complex issues. Books are, in fact, the medium through which change is really affected.

Steig (1986), in her turn, explains the contrast between history, with its multiplicity of monographs, and physics, with its relative paucity, in terms of the 'loosely organised character of Western historical scholarship', adding that:

monographs and therefore book reviews are a major method of disseminating and evaluating historical research[5] . . . since history first emerged as a scholarly discipline, the monograph has been the dominant form of publication, and the article has never successfully challenged its preeminence. . . . Articles have been perceived as a way of getting started.

Book reviews, as Steig indicates, are a significant element in historical scholarship, accounting for over half the text in the leading academic journals (Becher 1987b). They are also prevalent in other disciplines in the humanities and social sciences, though virtually non-existent in hard pure and hard applied subject areas, where they are commonly replaced by thematic surveys of particular topics. *Reviews of Modern Physics* provides a typical example of the genre. Here, each contribution offers a conspectus and synthesis of the main recent contributions to its chosen theme, with a list of references that will normally run to two or three double column pages. Almost invariably, the cited papers are discussed in factual rather than evaluative terms, the only obvious form of criticism being omission.

At the level of individual disciplines, a clear set of distinctions emerged in my sample between history and modern languages, where books were clearly held to earn more prestige for their authors than articles, and the hard pure and hard applied subjects (physics, chemistry, engineering and pharmacy), where book publication (apart from student texts) accounted for only a small minority of the written output. Mathematics and biology allowed for some longer publications in monograph form. In the pure and applied social sciences (economics, sociology, geography and law), respondents indicated no strong preference between book-length and article-length treatment. In economics, articles seem to be the norm for developing the more quantitative topics, and books for the more qualitative ones (such as the history of economic ideas); similarly, in sociology, books are more important in the social thought tradition than they are in the more technical specialisms. Stoddart (1967) suggests that books have tended to become less significant than articles in geography, particularly in quantitatively oriented subject areas. In law, books commonly take the form of student texts on particular topics rather than scholarly analyses of a major field or central theme. Translating this in terms of the spectrum from urban to rural specialisms, it may be held to support the earlier contention that books are a predominantly rural phenomenon and articles a predominantly urban one, a finding which in its turn would seem to reinforce the claim that urban researchers tend to focus on limited and short-term problems whereas their opposite numbers in rural settings show some preference for global issues whose resolution calls for more sustained and longer-term enquiry.

Speed, frequency and length of publication

The publication process is subject to the influence of many variables, including the scope and nature of the message to be conveyed, the form chosen to convey it (article, book or whatever), the number of people involved in generating it, and their age and reputation. It would therefore be surprising if any very clear statistical pattern were to emerge from the attempt to analyse the products of the research enterprise in quantitative terms.[6] None the less, there was a rough-and-ready consistency in the testimony given by my respondents which it may be worth touching upon, even though the material is too flimsy to bear much weight of inference.

Three main sets of considerations were covered in the interviews: a rough estimate of the length of time it would take for a journal article to appear after its initial submission; the approximate length of a typical contribution; and the number of papers an individual author might expect to publish in a reasonably good year. It must again be emphasized that my study was focused on élite academic groups, so the results are confined to the upper end of the scale of prestige and productivity: active researchers concerned with acquiring or maintaining a professional reputation, and accordingly tending to submit their papers to the more prestigious journals in their field.

In terms of publication delays, it may be best to begin by drawing attention to a special feature of the very fast-moving hard pure specialisms, especially those within physics, chemistry and biochemistry. Here, the need for the rapid public announcement of findings has resulted in specialist publications which minimize delay by restricting length. A typical example is *Physical Review Letters*, in which highly topical results may be published within 3 months or so of their submission, provided that they are kept within the compass of three or four pages.[7] That such public mechanisms exist alongside a flourishing private preprint network gives a clear indication of the anxiety of authors to win first place in a sprint to the finishing-post.

The waiting period, as one might expect, tends to be longer in specialisms where the population density is lower (so that there is less overlap of topics and little consequent concern with priority). Delay times may vary considerably from specialism to specialism, especially in heterogeneous subjects such as biology, and between the more rural areas of chemistry, such as analytical chemistry, and the dense urban groupings at the biochemical end of the discipline. But the rough averages are indicative. Full-scale journal articles in physics may be held up for 9–12 months, and those in economics for 9–18 months. The comparable figures in engineering would appear to be between 1 and 2 years; in mathematics and in mainstream biology the lower limit is similar but the upper one rather higher. At the other end of the spectrum, modern linguists may have to try their patience for as much as 2 or 3 years before their papers appear in the established journals (though there are less prestigious outlets where the time lag may be as low as 6 months). History and sociology fall somewhere in between, with typical waiting times of around 18 months or a couple of years.

Where time-lags give an appropriate indication of competitive pressures, the length and frequency of an individual author's output say something about the nature and scale of research topics. Again, there is considerable variation in those disciplines with a diversity of types of specialism. A reasonably productive biologist in a setting which might be described as suburban would perhaps reckon to publish one or two journal articles a year of moderate length (say 4000–6000 words), though there is also some pressure to produce the occasional monograph of 20 000 words or more (the figures for mechanical engineers are similar – 'between, say, thirty and sixty papers in a lifetime' – though in their case alternative modes of output commonly take the form of consultancy reports and conference papers). However, in the more descriptive areas of biology (e.g. taxonomy), the annual production rate might be as high as 10–15 short papers. An output of ten or more, often of less than 2000 words and with multiple authorship, would also be characteristic of the hotter specialisms such as biochemistry.

Chemistry is a discipline in which many of the topics are capable of being broken down into small components: this is manifest in the relative brevity of chemists' writings (4000 words tends to be on the high side), in their tendency to put such components together into papers with several authors (see also the section later in this chapter on collaborative research), and in the volume of their output. Ten or a dozen contributions a year is not uncommon, though the rate may decline somewhat with increasing age: the most prolific researchers can notch up totals of 4 or 5 hundred titles over a successful working life. In mathematics, there are fewer coauthors. The average length of article is about double (some 6000–8000 words) and the average output about half that in chemistry. Active economists can be counted on to produce two to four articles a year (at least those who are not simultaneously engaged in writing books), though in their case the upper word limit of about 8000 may be imposed by leading journals in the interests of accepting more articles and reducing publication delays. Where research topics are free-standing rather than cumulative (so that there is not an already established starting point for the work) the rate of output is understandably lower and the length of contribution greater. Reputable historians and modern linguists in particular may thus do well to produce an annual average of one 8000–12 000 word article a year, particularly as they may also be working on a book at the same time.

Citation practices and their implications

Citation – the inclusion in academic writing of formal and explicit references to the work of other authors – is a feature of every discipline. The study of it as a phenomenon can be revealing in a number of different ways.[8] Those with an interest in information science often adopt a quantitative approach, using citation counts and patterns of citations to identify research networks (see, e.g. Griffith and Miller 1970), underline the disparities between more and less prestigious authors (as in Price 1963, 1965), or characterize the rate at which knowledge becomes obsolete in different fields (one instance is given by Burton and Kebler 1960). Those who are interested in research practices tend to favour a more qualitative approach, concerning themselves with questions about purpose and function.

The evidence from my study, which I will use as a starting point for a brief discussion of the topic, was of the latter kind. There was some indication, as one might expect, of disciplinary differences in the incidence of citation. Perhaps, as one informant, a biologist, speculated, 'the softer your subject-matter, the more citations you need to give'. Certainly, a number of mathematicians confessed themselves to be somewhat slapdash in referring to previous work, partly at least because of a preference for approaching certain problems with a freshness or vision unclouded by the knowledge of how others had tried to tackle them before. People in less hard disciplines thought it important to be punctilious in their referencing, for a variety of reasons.

In biology, you are expected in social terms to 'prove that you have read everything relevant' and in cognitive terms to 'acknowledge the foundations on which you build'. In sociology, there are temptations not only 'to use other people's writing to reinforce the statements you put forward – citing other people suggests a greater measure of support for your case', but also 'to cite famous people so as to suggest that you are keeping good intellectual company'.[9] Citation, one historian suggested 'serves a social and institutional as much as an epistemological function'. It enables you to engage in debate with other writers; it protects you from reviewers' criticisms of your failure to acknowledge X's arguments or Y's findings;

and more generally it serves as a mechanism for preserving solidarity among historians. After all, 'if we don't read them, perhaps they won't read us'. But more fundamentally, footnote references to primary and secondary sources 'give the reader a sense of interplay between data and argument – an almost literal sense of tension as the reader's eye moves constantly between the one and the other'. Admittedly, the citation of secondary sources can 'get out of hand, and become over-elaborate'. A number of US respondents considered themselves less extravagant in this regard than their British counterparts.

Among those who have made a close study of the phenomenon, Weinstock (1971) lists 15 discrete 'reasons for using citations', including 'paying homage to pioneers; giving credit for related work; identifying methodology, equipment, etc; . . . criticising previous work, substantiating claims; . . . disclaiming work or ideas of others; disputing priority claims of others'. More parsimoniously, Chubin and Moitra (1975) categorize references as, broadly, affirmative and negational. They subdivide the affirmative group into basic and subsidiary, additional and perfunctory, and the negational group into partial and total. Within physics, which they take as the basis for their analysis, they find very few partially negational references and no totally negational ones – a point to be taken up in the subsequent discussion of academic controversy. Gilbert (1977b) argues that the main function of referencing is to act as a covert form of persuasion; and, in staunch ethnomethodological tradition, Small (1978) contends that cited documents serve as 'concept symbols' – 'in citing a document the author is creating its meaning': besides 'its functional, social and political implications', citation may be used 'to curry favour, to publicise, to favour one approach over another', and so on.

The quantifiers display a very different set of concerns. One of the issues which attracts their attention might be described as the mortality statistics of publication. For example, defining the 'half-life' of a discipline as the period during which half the currently available literature has been published, Burton and Kebler (1960) quote figures of 4.6 years for physics and 5.2 years for mechanical engineering, as against 10 years for botany, 10.5 years for mathematics and 11.8 years for geology. The evidence that hard pure knowledge dates more rapidly than soft pure is to be found in several studies. As long as a generation ago, Stevens (1953) was able to claim that science and technology:

> exhibit a high concentration of papers in a select nucleus of special journals, and also in a brief span of time covering a few current years. In contrast, the literatures of the social sciences and humanities exhibit a great dispersion of publications in different forms, on different subjects, and over a comparatively long span of time.

He illustrates this general claim by remarking that in chemistry more than 75% of the research literature could be located in some 20–25 journals over the previous 15 years, while in US history 75% of the literature was dispersed between 150 journals over the preceding 100 years, together with 'numerous books, manuscripts, files of newspapers and government documents'.

My interviews with economists indicated that 'people rarely quote articles written more than 20 years ago', and indeed that 'normally the time span doesn't go more than 10 to 15 years back'. In contrast, Cole (1983), reporting a 'small pilot study' of citations in the field of literature, observed that:

> although approximately 29% of the [material] was published in the last five years covered by the study, only 13% of the influence citations in *Studies in English Literature* . . . referred to work covered in that period. . . . Clearly, the citation practices of scholars in English literature differ from those of scientists.

The degree of dispersion of references, mentioned briefly in the quotation from Stevens above, is another interesting aspect of differences within and between disciplines. Chubin (1976) quotes an earlier study distinguishing between those articles appearing in 'core journals' and the residue, which tend to be widely scattered:

> If there was no 'scatter', scientists would be divided into small groups sharing the same interests, speaking only to each other, and reading and citing only each other's work. . . . Both [core and scatter] are necessary, the former to permit scientific knowledge to cumulate and grow, the latter to prevent it from becoming a . . . sect-like pheno-menon.

Crane (1972) makes a closely related point:

> Some degree of closure [of scientific knowledge in 'core' journals] is necessary in order to permit scientific knowledge to become cumula-tive and grow, while their ability to assimilate knowledge from other research areas prevents the activities of scientific communities from becoming completely subjective and dogmatic.

The catholicity of interest among scientists may vary, as Nadel (1980) points out, with different stages in the growth of a specialism. Thus, research on superconductivity was characterized at first by a dispersion of articles in a variety of journals, but later became institutionalized by the concentration of published material in a relatively limited number of specialist sources. None the less, in normal science, as Mullins (1968) remarks, formal contacts as much as informal ones may lie outside the discipline or department; and Anthony *et al.* (1969) report that chemists and physicists claim to devote something between a quarter and a third of their reading time to journals outside their own specialism, with 65% of the chemists and 40% of the physicists giving 'undirected browsing' as one of their reasons for reading scientific journals.

In less highly structured and strongly specialized disciplines there is a general expectation that people will read widely outside their own current areas of concern. In history and modern languages, for example, interesting and potentially relevant ideas may be gleaned from a variety of sources, as both the widely dispersed citation patterns and the comments from informants in my sample on the virtues of a broad knowledge of the field made plain. This is likely to be related to the issue of mutual intelligibility between specialisms. For example, in some fast moving areas of biology it was held to be very difficult to keep up with developments outside one's specialism, not only because of time pressures but also because of the incomprehensibility of language and logical structure, even in neighbouring territories. A characteristic view in slower-moving areas within the discipline, however, held that it was 'important to keep in touch with developments in other fields . . . what you learn about other specialisms helps you to change your attitude towards your own – and you can sometimes pick up useful concepts and techniques which other groups have developed'. How easy or difficult it is to understand colleagues in different parts of one's discipline is an important aspect of the style and accessibility of scholarly writing, which is the topic to which we shall now turn.

Questions of style and accessibility

A distinction may be drawn between hard and soft knowledge areas in terms of the extent to which they use mathematical symbols as against common parlance. On the one hand, most writings in mathematics and physics and many in academic engineering are unintelligible to the lay reader, not merely because their content is unfamiliar but because they convey meaning in a special, highly compressed, quantitative code. On the other hand, articles and books in most humanities subjects, though they may use the occasional technical term, are couched in familiar, everyday language and are – on the surface at least – readily accessible to those outside the field. Between the two extremes, disciplines such as chemistry and pharmacy employ a symbolism of their own; researchers in biology, geography, sociology and academic law make varying use of specialist words carrying a particular meaning with which outsiders are likely to be unfamiliar.

There seem to be two main factors at work behind such evident and widely recognized distinctions. The first is cognitively derived, concerning the extent to which research is subject to a contextual imperative, as against a weaker contextual association; the second is social, and is related to the degree of legitimacy allowed within the discipline to public communication with external audiences.

To decompress these statements, it has been remarked on a number of previous occasions that hard pure knowledge in particular develops in a restricted and relatively clearly defined sequence. Its cumulative character depends on the degree to which the central topics of current concern are determined by those in the recent past, and the extent to which they serve in their turn to identify those needing to be tackled in the near future. Most hard pure problems are thus formulated in an established knowledge context. In contrast, the topics in soft areas, though they may in some cases be subject to fashion, and hence grouped together in a more or less close association, do not convey the same sense of obeying an imperative demand. The consequence is that in many hard areas research takes place, and can be reported, within a known framework of assumptions; in soft areas, the context has often to be separately elaborated.[10]

This affects both the length of typical contributions, as has already been noted, and their general style. Both Bazerman (1981) and Whitley (1984) remind us that where relevance to current developments in research is an important criterion, the succinctness and precision of communication is prized above its stylistic qualities. In specialized scientific fields, there is 'an elaborate communication system which uses a highly formalized symbol structure to co-ordinate research across geographical and social boundaries. Ambiguity is reduced by standardizing and formalizing reporting procedures.' In contrast, because of the 'limited degree of standardization of cognitive objects and work processes', and because 'the meaning and significance of results are ambiguous', writers in the human sciences have to tailor their style 'to the particular message being communicated' (Whitley 1984). Developing the point:

> The sociological literature . . . is . . . diverse, unsettled and open to interpretation: therefore, the essay must reconstruct the literature to establish a framework for discussion; in the humanities, the literatures . . . tend to be particularistic and used in particularistic ways. . . . Codification, if it can be called that, is entirely personal (Bazerman 1981).

And here, as Whitley adds, 'an individual's style of writing is an important component of his or her reputation'.

Such considerations do not fully explain why, for example, biologists, and to a lesser extent geographers, place such a high premium on literary and stylistic qualities (see Chapter 2). From the pointers given by informants in a number of disciplines, I am inclined to ascribe this to the existence of a tradition of lay participation, or at least of lay interest. History offers a good case in point. Historians, along with most other academics, are scornful of 'professional popularizers', people who are seen as making money out of other people's ideas; though many of them would like their own ideas 'to reach a wide – though preferably a discerning – public'. Amateur practitioners in history are not subject to the same degree of obloquy, and may even, in areas such as archivy and local history, be acknowledged to serve a useful purpose. The amateur tradition is strong in biology as well: active amateurs can play a significant supporting role in ecological research and in studies of animal and plant populations; passive amateurs help to create a ready market for books in the style of *The Naked Ape* and *The Selfish Gene*. Geography has its tales of polar exploration, not to mention the *National Geographic*; astronomy its active gazers at the stars through the telescope and its passive watchers of their interpreters – stars from a different mould – on their television screens. Because of their openness to public view, such disciplines would seem more conscious of the need for, and benefits of, skills in lucid communication.

The more strongly specialized, professionally closed and linguistically impenetrable disciplines leave no such scope for outside involvement. Nor are they tolerant of attempts to go over the heads of the research community to enlist a wide public interest in new developments. It is firmly understood that even the more newsworthy discoveries must be announced within the family before they are made known outside it. In physics in particular, as Reif (1961) and Geertz (1976) imply, and Traweek (1982) makes plain, there is a strong resistance to premature communication in the popular media, which is seen as a transgression of community boundaries.

This discussion has already taken us some way from the central business of communication – the kinds of messages that are conveyed, the means of conveying them, the time pressures to which they are subject – and into a consideration of its social milieu. The rest of the chapter will concentrate on the latter aspect, picking out three main features of the environment in which the interchange of ideas takes place. We shall begin by considering the various forms of competitiveness in the exploration and transmission of new insights, and some of their side-effects. This will lead on to a brief review of collaboration and teamwork and its manifestation in joint or multiple authorship. In a subsequent section, we shall look at the situations in which the exchange of ideas degenerates into the exchange of hostilities as communication breaks down into controversy.

Competition

The competitive nature of academic life is a function of the emphasis placed on gaining a professional reputation. In rural areas, such competition takes a more subtle form than that of a contest to publish one's findings before they are 'scooped' by somebody else. It may rather be manifested, in the words of a biology respondent, by 'an emphasis on publication, aggressiveness at meetings and a high degree of single-mindedness'. Rivals seek to surpass each other in the quality and significance of their work, in the esteem in which they are held by professional colleagues, and in the honours which are bestowed upon them; they may even vie for the same jobs, but they seldom engage in battle over the very same area of intellectual territory. It is in the most heavily populated urban pockets that the fiercest tussles take place over the division of the spoils of research. As Gaston (1971) writes:

In their attempts to gain recognition for their accomplishments scientists work in a competitive situation which is quite different from that of other professions. . . . Competition in science is more like a race between runners in the same track and over the same distance at the same time.

However, not all hard knowledge is associated with a highly competitive urban research community. Hagstrom (1965) instances mathematics as a discipline in which 'competition tends to be less prevalent because of the absence of agreement on the relative importance of mathematical problems'. Griffith and Miller (1970) suggest that 'positions, resources and facilities for which there [is] much competition' are likely to be a special feature of highly coherent groups. Among the chemists I interviewed, one developed the point in an unexpected direction:

Some people are quite competitive and secretive, but there are others who don't feel that they are in a rat race. They see themselves as being in competition with nature, not with other scientists. The race is only of secondary importance, because the job needs to be done. On the whole, if there is a race for the solution, that solution is probably rather obvious, and not really on the frontier of the subject. The more important parts of science don't necessarily end up as a fight for the finish.

Where strong competition does exist, it has its positive aspects in generating intellectual excitement, personal involvement and a heightening of research productivity; but it does also tend to give rise to a number of problems and pathologies. One is a tendency to produce hasty, careless work in the interests of rapid publication. Both Gaston (1971) and Reif (1961) single out this feature for discussion. The latter quotes a revealing editorial in *Physical Review Letters* in which it is noted that:

when a 'hot' subject breaks and many groups initiate related work . . . [b]ecause of the rapid development and the intense competition we have found it necessary to relax our standards and accept some papers that present new ideas without full analysis, relatively crude experiments that indicate how one can obtain valuable results by more careful and complete work. . . . Such incomplete papers have been accepted reluctantly since we realize that thereby we penalise some physicists who, working along the same lines, want to do a more complete job before publishing.

Another consequence of working in a hot climate is the fact that one's ideas may be stolen – if not directly in the form of plagiarism (which, if proven, carries a heavy sanction), then in the more cunning guise of picking up someone else's idea and running with it fast enough to win the race:

What is stolen in such cases are ideas, general information about the goal sought and the means to be used. Usually the thief must do considerable research himself.... A chemist will learn about an experiment which is planned, but he is obliged to do the experiment himself if he is to publish first (Hagstrom 1965).

And there are of course cases where the borrowing is unconscious, where someone remembers an idea as his or her own, even though it may in fact have been suggested by someone else.

The fear of theft, if not the first-hand experience of it, is one of the motivating sources of secrecy. Another is the direct obverse of the concern for over-hasty publication – the urge fully to exploit the consequences of a promising idea before bringing it out into the open and allowing others to do so. One interviewee, a physicist in an urban network, spoke of a tendency to 'play your cards close to your chest ... to be open about publishing last year's findings, but not this year's'. It is not unknown for 'laboratories to be kept locked, and progress reports to be given in a very guarded way'. The dilemma, as Hagstrom (1965) points out, is between withholding publication with the 'danger of being anticipated in presenting the central idea' and being 'forced to share recognition for its elaboration with others'.

As an aside at this point, it is interesting to note how many writers see the incidence of secrecy as an important distinguishing mark between pure science and technology. Marquis and Allen (1966), for example, note that technologists' communication patterns favour oral transmission and un-published reports, and that secrecy is more prevalent than it is among scientists. Price (1970) contrasts the technologist's opportunity to make capital from discovery with 'the open publication that determines intellectual private property for the sciences'. Dasgupta and David (1985) make a similar point, arguing that scientists regard knowledge as a public consumption good, whereas technologists treat it as a private capital good, with related strategies of disclosure and secrecy. And Baruch (1984) sees the cultures of scientists and technologists as 'almost opposites', in that the former 'leave as their legacy public scientific knowledge', whereas among the latter knowledge 'is developed in secret. Publication is anathema, and the final test of validity is public use.'

It must be said that I found very little evidence of this distinction in my interviews with physicists, chemists and biologists on the one hand, and mechanical engineers and pharmacists on the other. The reason may possibly have lain in the nature of my sample: the technologists interviewed were in relatively prestigious departments, where there was clearly a stronger emphasis on contributing to theoretical development than on generating patentable products. It may be that departments with a strongly applied emphasis would have shown a closer concern with keeping promising inventions under wraps, with a view to circumventing the academic equivalent of industrial espionage. Or it might have been that people preferred not to talk about such issues, because they were not thought to be entirely respectable, though I found no such inhibitions among the physicists. However, another possible explanation derives from the fact that many technological specialisms lie towards the rural end of the spectrum, where the number of people working on the same or closely similar topics is relatively small, the competitive pressures are less evident and the consequent urge to establish priority less pronounced than in the densely urban areas within pure science. In this spirit, one mechanical engineer claimed, 'It's often wise to wait for your work to mature – to be sure you've got it right before you send the final typescript off'; another listed the priorities as 'wanting first to be right, second to be useful and only third to be ahead of the field'; and a third claimed that 'priority in reaching a result isn't all that important, particularly if someone comes along shortly afterwards with a better technique and more accurate measurements . . . progress is a matter of making incremental changes, refining measurements and looking at new variations on existing techniques'.

Some people clearly enjoy the challenge of direct competition; others prefer to avoid it. In most rural areas, there is little choice in the matter, since there is no one else hell-bent on getting there first. But in those disciplines where there is some option, quite a few people – according to Whitley (1984) – prefer 'differentiation and security to coordination and challenge'. Gilbert (1977a) is at pains to emphasize that 'recognition and career success for scientists working in most research areas depend on their being in a position to find and follow up research problems which differ substantially from those being pursued by other participants'. And in their study of radio astronomy in Britain and the USA, Mulkay and Edge (1973) note that

> Research groups tend to avoid competition by concentrating, wherever possible, on techniques and problems which are not the main focus of interest elsewhere. Once one group has achieved a clear lead in a particular field, other groups will tend to choose different areas rather than face duplication and open competition.

As one of my respondents, a botanist, put it: 'There are some competitive areas, but you need to be careful with them – you may want to be near enough to share the warmth, but not so close that you get roasted alive.'

Another means of avoiding a direct conflict of interest is through collaboration (whose implications we shall explore in the next section). 'Outside the more competitive areas', observed one of the zoologists I interviewed, 'there aren't so many people working on the same problem, and those that are usually know each other and keep in touch with progress'. A chemist made the similar comment that 'where different groups turn out to be working on the same problem, some people are bastards and start to clam up, but very often you don't have to make a fight of it – you either divide up the field or agree on a joint publication'.

Collaboration

The publications in some fields are likely to bear the names of two or more authors; in others, single authorship is the established norm. Those with a penchant for statistics – even if somewhat outdated ones – may be interested to learn that only 23% of biomedical papers and 32% of chemistry papers in 1963 had single authors (Clarke 1964); that in the specialism of rural sociology between 1941 and mid-1966 the corresponding figure was 61%, and in finite group theory in mathematics between 1906 and 1968 it was 86% (Crane 1972); while in sociology as a whole in the USA between 1956 and 1965 single authors accounted for 68% of articles, two authors for 26%, three for 5% and four or more for 1% (Patel 1973). In 1968, Zuckerman estimated that about 80% of chemistry papers were multi-authored in the previous year, as against some 60% in physics, 40% in the biological sciences and 1% in such subjects as philosophy, language and literature. More broadly still, Hargens (1975) claimed that at the time he was writing less than half the papers were collaboratively, as opposed to individually, produced in mathematics and solid-state physics, but that the proportion was higher in nuclear physics and other experimental areas of physics.[11]

What such figures make plain is both that there is considerable variation in practice between the hard and soft ends of the continuum and that even in some of the harder disciplines the amount of collaborative work is scarcely in keeping with the image of science as a predominantly corporate enterprise. One limitation of studies based on a counting of heads is that they have nothing to say about the causes which their seemingly precise and confident claims conceal: that deficiency has to be remedied by more qualitative, but by the same token more impressionistic, enquiries. Before moving on to a consideration of what lies behind the statistics, however, it may be relevant to ask why the urge for collaboration arises, and what form it commonly takes.

On the face of it, an individual academic's reputation is likely to be most decisively established if the person concerned takes full, unambiguous responsibility for his or her work. As several of my respondents in such fields as geography and economics contended, once you start publishing with other people it becomes difficult to know who has done what. It might therefore be supposed that, other things being equal, the preference would be for publishing solely under one's own name.[12]

Other things are not always equal, of course. There are various good reasons for wanting to work with other people (the avoidance of competitive duplication has already been mentioned as one of them). In some areas of 'big science', there is little choice in the matter. As Ziman (1981) points out, the apparatus is so complex and costly that its use has to be maximized (particle accelerators like those at CERN or Palo Alto work round the clock, have precise and selective user schedules and often substantial waiting lists, and therefore within reason the larger the group the better): in any case, no individual could handle the instrumentation alone. In some comparatively modest 'little science' areas such as organic chemistry, as was remarked earlier in this chapter, it is easy to divide substantial problems into smaller related components; the resulting possibility of a division of labour is a tempting source of collaborative work. In other cases, the resolution of difficult issues may demand an unusual combination of skills; here, there may be a premium placed on working with colleagues who have complementary contributions to make.

These motivations are consistent with the findings of a small-scale study of four social science disciplines (sociology, psychology, economics and political science) by Fox and Faver (1982), concerned with the strategies adopted by research partnerships. One approach they identified was to 'share the parts' with collaborators working together on the same task at the same time; another was to 'separate the parts', where each collaborator again tackles the same tasks, but this time working individually before the results are 'exchanged, mutually reviewed and combined towards a final draft'; a third was to 'divide the parts', so that each collaborator works separately and on different tasks. Fox and Faver suggest that division of labour is the most common strategy for routine research activities, those under time pressure, and those demanding complementary competences, but that 'more complex tasks . . . may benefit from some combination of sharing and separating the parts'.

The processes which underlie apparently similar examples of teamwork are not necessarily homogeneous, as my interviews with chemists and physicists confirmed. The areas of physics which favour large-scale research collaboration and result in papers with as many as one or two score authors are nearly always examples of 'big science', in which the teams may be likened to those in, say, American football, demanding a high degree of mutuality and involving both shared and divided tasks. The membership is typically composed of groups from two or more institutions with a number of senior academics working alongside more junior tenured and untenured staff, postdoctoral fellows, doctoral students and technicians. The teams in certain of the more populous specialisms in chemistry, though sometimes comparable in size, share few other common features. The demands of instrumentation are far less dominant, so the pressures for inter-institutional collaboration are not so severe. There is seldom more than one senior academic – the unquestioned leader – in the team, the other members being untenured academics and other ranks (technicians, research fellows and students). Tasks are systematically divided out between participants, though there may be some sharing on a small scale, with perhaps three or four people working on the more demanding components of the overall project. The pattern is thus quite unlike that of a team sport and more reminiscent of that of an orchestra, with the conductor taking sole responsibility for bringing together into a harmonious whole the disparate contributions of the various sections of the orchestra – strings, brass, woodwind and percussion.

The distinctions between these two cases help to underline the

importance of attending to cognitive as well as social factors in any attempt
to make sense of academic interaction. Large-scale, collaborative research
reporting in physics is commonly a product of substantial and not always
readily divisible problems demanding complex instrumentation; but
superficially comparable cases of multiple authorship in chemistry would
seem to derive instead from the atomistic, easily fragmented and easily
combined nature of the problems in its knowledge field. To quote one of
my informants:

> In particle physics theory drives the whole thing – the different parts
> are inseparable, and the teams tackle a large, unified operational task.
> In chemistry, the problems can be broken up, and each part solved
> separately, before they are put together again.

Mathematics offers another interesting example of the complex reality
behind an apparently simple façade. There is only a modest amount of
joint publication in mathematical research: the statistics quoted earlier,
together with my own observations, suggest that it is roughly comparable
with sociology in this regard. Yet it was quite evident from my interviews
that the sociologists who worked alone seldom went out of their way to
discuss their work with colleagues, whereas many of the solitary-seeming
mathematicians placed considerable stress on the need to talk over their
problems with other people.[13] One way of accounting for this anomaly is to
observe that research in many areas of mathematics, though not as tightly
structured as that in some of the more urban parts of physics and
biochemistry, is none the less subject to quite strong contextual influences.
Ideas and techniques from neighbouring, or even sometimes apparently
distant, specialisms may turn out to help in the resolution of an initially
intractable problem: so if you find yourself getting stuck at a certain point,
it helps to bounce suggestions off other people and get them to bounce
suggestions off you. On the other hand, many mathematical arguments are
organic rather than atomistic in character, they cannot be carved up into
discrete pieces, but demand to be understood as complex wholes: an
endeavour that can call for an intense, essentially individual effort of
concentration. Such formal collaboration as exists is often between no more
than two people, based on the sharing and separation rather than the
division of tasks ('brainstorming' an idea together, or each – as one
informant put it – 'going home trying desperately to sort out an idea before
your collaborator does, spurring one another on towards the solution').

The preference of many sociologists for solitary over collective research
relfects a different set of social and cognitive norms from those of mathematicians. In this discipline, Kleinman (1983) argues, there is an in-built
bias against collaboration and in favour of the 'lonely scholar' image.
Doctoral students 'learn that the "real work" of sociology – research and
writing – involves distinguishing oneself from one's peers. . . . Professional
development . . . is synonymous with increasing individuation.' More than
one of the sociologists I interviewed pointed out that collaboration tends to

occur more often between empiricists, who may be able to share out
fieldwork, than between theorists. To the extent that biological and
sociological specialisms exemplify the predominantly interpretive character of historical or literary research, another factor comes into play.
Interpretation is a characteristically individualistic process, as my respondents made plain: 'In taxonomy it's virtually impossible to work with
other people – like judges, taxonomists can give opinions but they don't
give joint opinions.' As for theoretical sociology, 'how can three people
write with one pen and speak with one mind?' In modern languages, 'one's
research and one's writings are not really separable – and both are very
personal'. In history, it needs 'a single intellect to turn over the material';
'ideas have to be shaped in the mind of the individual scholar'. When one
adds the consideration that, in the soft pure areas of knowledge, there is a
great range of choice in style, taste, and subject matter, and sometimes in
theoretical orientation as well, it is perhaps scarcely surprising that joint
research enterprises are the exception rather than the rule, and that
disagreements are at least as common as the taking of a shared stand.

Controversy

In academic disciplines, as in political parties, a good, blazing row is as
capable of arousing vicarious enjoyment as it is of damaging credibility and
reputation. Both features have been evident, for example, in the much-
publicized squabbles of the English Faculty at the University of Cambridge
(particularly in the early 1980s, when a young, vocal proponent of
structuralism was refused tenure but subsequently obtained a pro-
fessorship elsewhere). When people's ideological identities are at stake,
passions run deep. This may be one reason behind the tendency in areas in
which values are highly charged – sociology is an obvious case in point –
towards a disproportionate incidence of rifts and schisms.[14]

Yet even in the overtly more dispassionate domain of empirical science,
as Kuhn and others have shown, controversies may become too bitter to
remain concealed beneath the public veneer of amity and consensus. Apart
from the tactically dubious recourse for adjudication to parties quite
outside such disputes, other expedients include the attempt to call in aid
the history and traditions of the discipline, often with a generous degree of
retrospective reinterpretation (see, e.g. Taylor 1976, and Graham 1983).

There is a difference to be drawn here between specific, relatively
localized arguments and broad dissensions over basic theoretical stances. A
mildly entertaining, if somewhat voyeuristic, example of the former is
given by Kemp (1977) in his case study of an increasingly acrimonious
wrangle between two eminent biochemists (scientists exposed as nothing
other than ordinary human beings). Such disputes, however, make little or
no difference to the evolution of the discipline in whose name they are

conducted, and have none of the grand, titanic flavour of the battles between the proponents of fundamentally opposing paradigms.

Personal disputes, whether or not they take the form of strong antipathies between individuals, are generally suppressed from public view. Hagstrom (1965) remarks that 'Public expressions of goal conflict . . . occur relatively infrequently . . . and they can probably be legitimised only by presenting them as factual arguments', though he is here writing specifically about the natural sciences. Crane (1972) speculates that 'confrontation was more typical of an earlier period when scientific communities were smaller'. Even in many of the social sciences and humanities, a number of my informants suggested, the days of acerbic criticism and stinging invective in the style of A. E. Housman[15] are dead – 'it's rather a dull period'; 'it's a time of fruitful fusion, but it's sad that the passion seems to have gone'.[16]

There is a fair amount of evidence to suggest a deliberate avoidance or damping-down of critical comment in contemporary academic writing. Hagstrom (1965) refers to 'the tendency of scientists to withdraw from controversial situations' and quotes one of his interviewees, a theoretical physicist, as saying 'Work rarely gets challenged: it is often superseded or passed over, but not challenged.' It is a convention within economics, so the informants in my sample assured me, for a journal editor to invite – though reserving the right not to publish – a riposte from the individual concerned to a specific criticism of his or her work in a submitted paper.[17] A typical comment in the humanities was that of a modern linguist: 'mutual criticism is usually polite – perhaps out of self-protection'. Another respondent, a geographer, noted that disagreements seldom erupt into hostility, but merely take the form of 'a tolerant distaste'. MacRoberts and MacRoberts (1984) go so far as to identify three distinct strategies in 'the art of dissembling' when a negational reference has to be contemplated: the first is to indulge in excessive praise, the second to make only a perfunctory acknowledgement, and the third to avoid direct citation of anyone powerful enough to cause trouble.

In the case of major ideological disagreements, somewhat different considerations arise. Quoting a celebrated controversy between the proponents of operant and non-operant theories in psychology in the nineteenth century, Crane (1972) remarks that for the most part empirical issues were not in question: 'Nor could empirical data resolve the controversy because the disputants did not agree about their relevance . . . [that] relevance was determined by the very issues which were at the root of the controversy.' The argument between the opposing schools of thought 'degenerated into invective and personal attack designed . . . primarily to influence the views of their followers rather than each other. The controversy was never resolved. Eventually, a new paradigm supplanted both.'

Sometimes, the conflict may go underground, or be deflected: 'Scientists may privately scorn the goals . . . of their disciplinary colleagues, but they

are less likely to express such sentiments publicly, or to a stranger'
(Hagstrom 1965); and 'Supporters of different paradigms usually devoted
their attention to different research areas. This did not prevent each group
from expressing considerable contempt for other viewpoints' (Crane
1972). In other instances, it may take the form of an attempted suppression
by the disciplinary establishment of dissident viewpoints.[18] One of the
physicists I interviewed described how a series of papers produced by his
research group were held up, and later rejected, by members of a rival
faction who controlled the most relevant professional journal. The simplest
available recourse was to take over another journal which could then
emphasize the alternative viewpoint. I encountered similar stories in
geography, where the rebellious exponents of the quantitative approach
were 'squeezed out' of the established periodicals and forced to establish
their own rival publications; and in economics where, as one informant
commented, 'The people in charge take care to keep the mavericks out.
They [the mavericks] even had to found their own journals to get a hearing
at all.'

But here too, as in the case of more parochial disputes, there is a
discernible tendency to steer clear of arguments. The respondent who
commented that his discipline 'is organised in a way that minimises quarrels
– it gets people engaged in fiddly problems rather than major issues' was
speaking, on the evidence of my study, for more than a few other subjects as
well. Documenting the ways of political scientists, Ruscio (1985) exemplifies
how the absence of communication on major issues between rival groups
may come about:

> Journals in the subfield [of political philosophy] have become ex-
> tremely focused. Straussian journals circulate submissions among
> Straussians, for example, while Marxist journals send their sub-
> missions to Marxists, so that Marxists and Straussians seldom review
> each other's work. When the articles are submitted to the mainstream
> journals which cover a broader range of articles, the Straussians and
> Marxists frequently 'kill each other off' by critically reviewing sub-
> missions from the opposite perspective. The result is 'well-established
> little cadres of people who don't argue any more about how political
> theory should be done'.

This phenomenon of the systematic avoidance of controversy, both on a
localized and on a more global scale, was captured in summary form by one
of the economists I interviewed:

> Disagreements sometimes become public, but it's more common
> simply not to communicate with people who hold a radically different
> viewpoint. Those who are in opposing camps just talk past each other.
> In the last few years, a polemical argument has been raging over a very
> abstract technical question, but it's been a pointless argument because
> it hasn't changed anyone's views. On the whole, orthodox and

non-orthodox economists have their own journals and keep to their own circle. Inside any particular camp economists don't criticise each other much. When they do, their comments are usually technical ones.

The inclination to play safe – to minimize the risk of making professional enemies by not opposing or being critical of colleagues' views – is also reflected in the preference, noted earlier, of many academics to steer clear of direct competition with others. It is often the consequence of a deliberate career decision of the kind to be discussed in the next chapter. But as far as the present topic is concerned, one might reflect that the reluctance to say what one thinks, the refusal to join in contest or debate, is the direct antithesis of the view with which this discussion began: that free communication is of the essence of intellectual progress.

Some significant distinctions

Detailed attention has been accorded in this chapter to the varying forms in which ideas are transmitted across disciplines and across specialisms within disciplines. The study of communication patterns has served to bring out certain identifiable features of knowledge communities and to underline various aspects of the knowledge forms to which they relate. We can now begin more systematically to enumerate a number of key sociological and epistemological contrasts, and to discern some apparent connections between them.

The urban–rural dimension, which formed the main initial theme, has proved a significant one. Although it is itself based on social considerations, it has helped to mark the way in which hard knowledge, subject to contextual imperatives, gives rise to characteristic modes of communication which differ fairly consistently from those which typify soft knowledge, subject merely to contextual associations.

Where knowledge is both cumulative and amenable to fragmentation, research labour can be parcelled out and progress thus often accelerated. The ready identification of currently significant problems can give rise to a competitive race to solve them, and to a corresponding tendency towards secretiveness. That in its turn encourages a rapid and intense style of interaction which relies as much on the spoken as on the written, on the unpublished as on the published, word. In this context, citation is relatively frugal and time-constrained. At the other end of the hard-soft spectrum, where knowledge is reiterative and where problems are not easily divisible, there is no clear notion of progress and no strong incentive for the sharing of labour. There is rarely any competition in reaching a conclusion, and hence a general inclination towards openness, but little sense of urgency, in communication. Information is conveyed mainly through the printed text; citation tends to be copious and to cover a wide time-span.

Cognitive features reinforce and ramify the distinctions in working practice. They can, for example, be discerned through the varying length of typical publication forms: a preference for book-length exposition signifies a contextual association, where assumptions have to be developed *ab initio*, whereas that for article-length pieces signals a contextual imperative, where much of the background argumentation can be taken for granted. Variations in the scale and complexity of problems are also the occasion for differences in the frequency with which active researchers publish their findings. Again, soft knowledge areas, which depend on the exercise of individual interpretation, are generally less amenable to collaborative publication than hard areas, which rest on commonly defined criteria of validity. The scatter of problems characteristic of a loosely structured knowledge domain is reflected in the dispersion of literature across a wide range and variety of sources, whereas tightly structured knowledge tends towards concentration in relatively few journals.

Other contrasts which have been touched on include the gregarious as against solitary social patterns associated respectively with hard pure and soft pure knowledge areas, along with the differential tendencies towards plain as against specialized language and the related degrees of accessibility to non-specialist audiences. We shall return to a number of these issues in Chapter 8, where a further attempt will be made to clarify the relationships between the various social and cognitive categories to which the analysis has given rise.

Notes

1 Crane (1972) observes that:

> A school is characterised by the uncritical acceptance on the part of disciples of a leader's idea system ... it rejects external influence and validation of its work. By creating a journal of its own, such a group can bypass the criticism of referees from other areas. ... In extreme cases ... such groups forego the attempt to obtain empirical verification of their ideas altogether.

2 Collins (1975) discerns a complex and somewhat obscure connection between density of population and scale of problem tackled:

> the scope of problems studied tends to diminish under the sheer weight of numbers. ... Both large numbers and a large scope of problems under-taken increase the co-ordination problems within a discipline. The number seems to be a more autonomous variable and thus tends to reduce the scope of problems considered.

Whitley (1982) adds that 'if ... the number of practitioners seeking reputations in a particular field, which already has a fairly formalized communication system, increases, the scope of problems tackled is likely to decrease as specialization of tasks and skill becomes higher'.

3 As documented by Watson (1970).

4 Writings in the public domain, because of their ready availability for scrutiny,

are the predominant sources not only for practitioners but for those who study them: the historians, philosophers and sociologists who choose as their topic the nature of academic knowledge and academic communities. Among the latter, the use of oral testimony is relatively rare.

5 In quantitative terms, 'In 1970 in the United States, 1,995 books on history were published; in all the pure sciences . . . eight or nine disciplines . . . accounted for 2,358' (Steig 1986).

6 This contention is borne out by the highly technical and complex discussion in Allison (1980).

7 Announcements of this kind, because they are refereed, enjoy more kudos than preprints, over which little quality control is exercised: they are not invariably followed up by full publication of the details in standard article form.

8 Cronin (1984) provides a thoughtful and reasonably comprehensive review of the relevant literature on the natural and social sciences, but has relatively little to offer on the humanities or the technological or social professions.

9 Even in the apparently dispassionate and value-free area of physics, Gilbert (1977b) suggests, the same tendency may be identified: 'many references are selected because the author hopes they will be regarded as authoritative by the intended audience'.

10 It seems reasonable further to suggest that the degree to which the background to a problem can be taken for granted, as well as the relative incidence of technical and non-technical language, is connected with the universalistic character of hard pure, as against the particularistic nature of soft pure, knowledge (see Chapter 1).

11 He included some additional specialisms in the lower-ranking groups (physical chemistry, inorganic and organic chemistry) and one in the higher-ranking group (theoretical physics) which seem questionable in the light of other findings.

12 It nevertheless came as something of a surprise to me that I encountered so few examples of large-scale teamwork among the natural scientists and technologists I interviewed. The 'teams' often consisted of no more than the occasional postdoctoral researcher, a couple of postgraduates and perhaps a part-time technician, engaged on a 3-year funded project under a single faculty member. In the physical sciences, and even more in biology, mechanical engineering and pharmacy, a sizeable number of my respondents were working in isolation among their departmental colleagues.

13 Crane (1972) reports that in her particular sample of mathematicians, 'isolates were even more likely than members of large groups to report that informal communication was very important to their research', and that 'isolates and members of two-person groups attended . . . conferences as frequently as members of large groups'.

14 'Social scientists operate in a much less predictable and therefore more anxious environment than physical scientists. . . . This continuous struggle to reach consensus in a relatively unpredictable and uncertain environment is likely to generate high levels of conflict' (Lodahl and Gordon 1972). It is also relevant to note the references in Chapter 2 to the testimony of respondents on the divisiveness and factionalism of the sociological community.

15 An anthology of his more memorable critiques is provided in Carter, J. (ed.) (1961) *A. E. Houseman: Selected Prose*. Cambridge, Cambridge University Press.

16 Whitley (1984) hints that this is due to the increasing professionalism within

even the more loosely structured disciplines: 'technical standardization will be encouraged as [academics] become more dependent upon the reputational system than upon their personal connections'. Collins (1975) similarly contends that 'Increased numbers . . . in the social and humanistic disciplines, and the consequent increase in competition within them, results in a . . . trend towards objective and easily inspectable standards of scholarship . . . usually at the expense of concern for humanistic meanings.' Rothblatt (personal communication) offers a somewhat different, and in my view more convincing, interpretation:

> Given the current emphasis on marketability, especially in the United States, about the only way in which a more equitable distribution of rewards is possible is through a continuing subdivision of specialties. If the fields are small enough, then there is always some level of accomplishment that can be recognized somewhere.

The criteria of judgement thus become more localized and the scope for large-scale intellectual controversy more limited.

17 This means of discouraging negative comment is also adopted, according to MacRoberts and MacRoberts (1984), in a number of periodicals in the natural sciences.

18 The pressure to conform may be indirect, particularly in specialisms in which the research community is small and relatively parochial. Thus Boissevain (1974), writing with particular reference to social anthropology, observes that:

> Power, in the form of control over tenure, research funds, recommendations for jobs, research leave, and so on, tends to cluster at the top. Those at the top are if not the architects, then the hard-working builders of the dominant paradigm. An open challenge on strictly scientific (rational or disciplinary) grounds to the theory on which the life work of one's teacher/chairman/patron is based is viewed not only as unscientific. It is also seen as disloyal, reckless, and probably dangerous to career prospects. Hence the challenge is not made, or if made, is quashed before it becomes public. Most persons who monopolize these resources do not use them consciously to protect their vested theoretical interests. Nonetheless, the *fear* that they might do so, or in other ways take offence, inhibits criticism.

6

Academic Careers

Personality and environment

In the preceding chapters, we have explored academic activity mainly in aggregative terms, tracing the common cultures, internal structures and modes of interaction of disciplinary tribes and their constituent networks. But just as there are new insights to be gained by moving from a broad to a narrow epistemological framework, so too there are benefits to be won in the social dimension from supplementing a conspectus of the large picture with a scrutiny of the small detail – the individual academics who might be labelled as the elementary particles of the intellectual world.

As one begins to speculate on the match between academic fields and the people in them, the familiar rivalry of nature against nurture manifests itself. Is it that particular kinds of people choose particular disciplines, or is it rather that disciplines shape and condition their adherents into becoming particular kinds of people? The classical escape route from most dilemmas is to repudiate them, arguing that the choices they pose are as false as they are stark. The claim in the present context must be that academic careers are subject to a range of causal factors, none of which can be shown as predominant in every case. The activities involved in the transmission and creation of knowledge, Ruscio (1987) writes, 'reflect individual preferences, disciplinary backgrounds and institutional imperatives' in a varied mix of ingredients. It is in the nature of the present study that the second of these should enjoy pride of place, since it is around the notion of disciplines that most of the evidence has been collected; something none the less needs briefly to be said about the first and third.

The relationship between personality and learning style is a longstanding topic of psychological enquiry. Some of the more recent research, including that reported by Wolfe and Kolb (1979), has a number of pertinent things to say. For one thing, it acknowledges more clearly than earlier work in the field that apparently homogeneous disciplinary categories may themselves embrace a fair amount of diversity. The

Kolb–Wolfe review (drawing on a number of investigations of student learning styles, including Kolb's study of '800 practising managers and graduate students in management') remains cautious about the tendency, discerned by Bereiter and Freedman (1962), 'of fields to attract people similar to those already in them':

> What these studies show is that undergraduate education is a major factor in the development of learning style. Whether this is because individuals are shaped by the fields they enter or because of selection/ evaluation processes that put people into and out of disciplines is an open question at this point. Most probably both factors are operating – people choose fields that are consistent with their learning styles and are further shaped to fit the learning norms of their field once they are in it. When there is a mismatch between the field's learning norms and the individual's learning style, people will either change or leave the field.

In a more recent work, Kolb (1984) presses the argument further:

> For students, education in an academic field is a continuing process of selection and socialization to the pivotal norms of the field governing criteria for truth and how it is to be achieved, communicated, and used, and secondarily, to peripheral norms governing personal styles, attitudes and social relationships. Over time, these selection and socialization pressures combine to produce an increasingly impermeable and homogeneous disciplinary culture and correspondingly specialised student orientations to learning. . . . Students' developmental pathways are a product of the interaction between their choices and socialization experiences in academic fields such that choice dispositions lead them to choose educational experiences that match these dispositions, and the resulting experiences further reinforce the same choice disposition for later experiences.

Such claims are not inconsistent with, though they go a fair theoretical distance beyond, the observations about matches between personality types and subjects of study which I gleaned in my interviews. Although it was not part of my purpose to enquire into the private, as against the professional, lives of those I met, it was for example apparent from the incidental remarks they made that the physicists were inclined towards an interest in the theatre, art and music, whereas the engineers' typical leisure activities included aviation, deep-sea diving and 'messing about in boats'. The biologists, along with the historians, tended to the view that theirs was 'a discipline for loners'. Much as Evans-Pritchard (1951) had referred to anthropological fieldwork as requiring 'in addition to theoretical knowledge and technical training a certain kind of character and temperament', one of the physicists in my sample spoke of choosing a research area to match one's temperament, and another of picking a problem to suit one's personality; and a geographer observed that graduate students will usually have a good look at the mode of working as well as the content of subdisciplines, and make a selection on the basis of what they see as their own talents.

For undergraduates, the influence of the institution may be as strong as, if not stronger than, that of the discipline. As Parlett (1977), writing in the context of social psychology, reminds us:

> Everyday academic talk is full of statements such as 'he was a typical Balliol man', or 'he absorbed the MIT philosophy', or 'the college made me what I am'. An individual's intellectual style, working habits, personal values, and even ways of speaking and mannerisms, may all be attributed to the lasting influence of his or her former place of education. Both in reminiscence and biography one finds a pre-occupation with drawing out such connections.

Beyond the point of graduation, institutional influences remain, as has already been remarked in Chapter 4, a significant force in determining academic career chances. On the basis of nearly 150 interviews in a wide range of institutions with academics in physics, biology, political science, English, business studies and medicine, Ruscio (1987) concludes that 'the nature of research is determined in part by the organizational setting . . . other major influences . . . are its rationale or purpose and the institutional attitudes towards it'. He shows convincingly how the interpretations of what research is, and the emphasis which is accorded to it, differ from one type of institution to another:

> Each sector seems to worship the god of research, but organized religion reflects the local culture. . . . At a leading research university, the demands for excellence in scholarship are apt to be precise and well understood. On the other hand, scholarship at a liberal arts college may be more broadly defined.

My study, concentrating as it did on élitist institutions, fully supported his contention about the strength of their research norms: virtually none of the people I interviewed – even the most junior postgraduate students – seemed in any doubt about the expectations placed on them. My findings also reinforced and elaborated his recognition (Ruscio 1987) that across the different disciplines there are different patterns, even within the same sector. It is the nature of those systematic differences which we shall now explore, as we follow through the main stages of the academic life-cycle.

Recruitment and the choice of specialisms

Disciplinary differences are evident at the very beginning of an academic career. In most subject areas it is now more or less obligatory to begin by acquiring a doctorate, but this is by no means the case in those applied, vocationally oriented disciplines in which the professional component is significant within academia as well as outside it. In pharmacy, as in the law, a professional qualification can only be acquired after at least a minimal period of practical experience in the field, and a majority of aspiring academics will choose the safety-net of becoming employable as working professionals before beginning to apply for posts within higher education. In engineering, the main motivation is different, though the outcome is the same: starting salaries in industry are so much more attractive than the financial prospects for a doctoral student that very few graduates are tempted to stay on at university. Recruitment to posts in engineering departments is therefore largely confined to those practising engineers who subsequently come to recognize the attractions of an academic life. It is understandable that in all such fields admittance to the relevant profession serves as at least an initial substitute for a doctoral degree – though the more ambitious academics, once appointed, make it their business to acquire a doctorate as well. The consequence is that in applied subjects, those entering the academic community tend to do so later in life than those in other disciplines (sometimes, in the case of mechanical engineering, at quite a senior level, in mid- to late career); that they may, atypically of academics at large, acquire tenured posts in élite institutions without a higher degree (in one leading law faculty in the early 1980s, there were only 5 members out of 32 with doctorates); and that, with some practical experience and professional contacts behind them, they may stand a good chance of augmenting their academic salaries with a reasonable amount of consultancy work.

For the rest, however, as the academic world has itself become more professionalized (Clark 1987a, 1987b), a doctorate has become a standard requirement, at least in the more élite institutions (only a negligible proportion of those I interviewed in hard pure and soft pure disciplines lacked such a handle to their names). It is therefore upon this rite of passage to the scholarly life that we shall for the moment concentrate attention.

In pure, as against applied, disciplines, a further series of broad distinctions emerges between the hard and the soft. In both alike, as has already been indicated in Chapter 4, it is prudent for the novitiate to seek out the most prestigious available department in his or her field (since this will serve to enhance initial research visibility), and to attach himself or herself to the most prestigious available research supervisor (since the benefits of patronage, at least in acquiring one's first paid job, are generally agreed to be more than negligible). There are certain trade-offs even here, since departmental prestige will no more guarantee a good match for a given individual's needs than will an eminent mentor necessarily have time to spare for providing the ideal amount of guidance and support. However, when the initial engagement is being negotiated between a successful applicant (the quality of whose first degree is, at this stage, though not so much later, an important consideration) and a potential supervisor, the extent of available choice of research topic is significantly different from one knowledge area to another.

Generally speaking, the stronger the contextual imperative, the less scope there is for negotiation over the subject matter of the doctoral thesis; the weaker the contextual association, the greater the latitude of decision allowed to the candidate. There are two related reasons for the constraints in hard pure settings. First, it is quite common for a graduate student to be taken on as as junior member of the supervisor's research team, and to be expected to carry out the task or tasks allocated by the team leader; secondly, the student, being relatively unfamiliar with the field, will not usually be in a good position to judge which problems or parts of problems are both relevant to current developments and at least in principle amenable to solution within the time-span of a doctoral programme. One of the requirements of a good supervisor, in subject areas of this kind, is to be able readily to supply newcomers with topics which are neither too easy nor too hard to meet the requirements, while at the same time ensuring a useful contribution to the work of the group as a whole.[1] Few such restrictions obtain in knowledge domains where the choice of theme is virtually unlimited, where a theme, once chosen, may be addressed in a diversity of ways and at a variety of levels of sophistication, and where the norm (at least at the doctoral stage) is for individual rather than group research.

Research groups in laboratory-based and field-based sciences are for the most part closely knit, so that group leaders will tend to have regular weekly (and occasionally even daily) contact with their doctoral students, and will thus be quite strongly involved in guiding and overseeing their work. At the other extreme, a lone doctoral candidate working on, say, a relatively narrow topic in eighteenth-century history or the interpretation of a hitherto-neglected text in Renaissance Italian literature can expect nothing like the same degree of collective, corporate activity or close supervisory attention. Levels of contact between student and supervisor may vary over time, being generally more intense early and late in the evolution of the thesis; but monthly or less frequent sessions, interspersed with lengthy bouts of solitary reading and writing, are the common pattern.

This contrast throws up another, more complex and subtle distinction. There are some fields in which it is not unusual for a doctoral student to produce a paper of publishable standard. When it appears in print, there are certain disciplines or specialisms within disciplines in which it will be routinely expected to bear the name of the research supervisor as joint author. Various grounds for this practice were put forward by respondents, both in those disciplines where the practice is widespread (chemistry notable among them) and in those in which it is more patchy. One justification is that since the supervisor chose the topic and had a close hand in its resolution, he or she is rightly entitled to a share of the credit. ('The top man doesn't own the workers body and soul, but he does own the products of their labour.') One respondent compared it with the levying of a tithe by a landlord from his tenants; others saw it as a kindly way of giving the student a leg up by association with a more prestigious author, or as a way of underwriting the quality of a piece of work whose value it would otherwise be difficult to assess; whereas those who chose not to adopt the practice – or who were at its receiving end – confessed themselves embarrassed by its exploitative overtones and its implication that research students were 'slave labour' or 'cannon fodder'.

Much as standard lengths of articles differ between one knowledge domain and another, what is required in the way of a PhD thesis will vary from an occasionally highly concise proof of a significant theorem in mathematics to a treatise running to 300 or more typewritten pages on a topic in the humanities. Somewhere in the middle, even the more prestigious departments of economics will now allow a doctoral award for three scholarly papers published in a refereed journal or judged to be of comparable standard, one of which may be jointly authored with the research supervisor. This, it is argued, is more in keeping with the current professional research norms in the discipline than is the conventional lengthy and monolithic doctoral dissertation.

These considerations make it plain that even in their initial stages, the lines of academic development may vary substantially from one knowledge area to another; that there is no such thing as a standard career pattern which spans the range of intellectual activity. The claim, as we shall see, is borne out unequivocally in all the subsequent phases of the life-cycle.

The achievement of independence

Because the job market and the disciplinary traditions bear differently upon different subject areas, it will take longer in some than in others to become launched on an autonomous career as a scholar or researcher in an élite institution. In those disciplines in which there is a strong pattern of team activity, along with the availability of substantial grant funding – largely, that is, in the pure sciences, together with some hard applied areas (notably medical and paramedical research) – the intending academic may be expected to occupy 3 years or more in the limbo of a postdoctoral research post before being offered a job leading to tenure. While this is regarded in some fields as useful further experience, it is essentially a period of marking time in career terms. Except in periods of expansion, it does not in any way guarantee a tenure-track post in a prestigious department. Even among those aspirants who survive the postdoctoral stage, many will end up in teaching jobs with few if any research opportunities, or in posts outside academia. Postdocs enjoy more independence and more responsibility than doctoral students, but they are still essentially what one non-scientist, critical of the system, regarded as an army of 'hired hands and dogsbodies',[2] dependent largely on the goodwill of their seniors. Lacking the necessary institutional standing, they cannot in many universities supervise research students or apply for grants in their own names: they are not fully-fledged freemen in the scholarly community.

The academic career proper begins – in disciplines having a postdoctoral tradition, as in those that lack one – with a salaried but usually untenured and probationary appointment on the lower rungs of the promotion ladder (an already mentioned exception being through recruitment to more senior ranks on the basis of outside professional experience). The provenance of the first regular post is important, since it is less usual to move up the scale from a lower-ranking institution than it is to move down it from a higher-ranking one. Let us, however, at this point, focus on the early research career of a successful survivor of the various initial hurdles, typically someone with a good first degree and a doctorate – both preferably acquired from well-regarded departments in leading institutions – together with, where appropriate, a spell of postdoctoral work in a group run by a well-known researcher.

Since my central concern is with the creation and development of knowledge rather than with its transmission, I will do no more than mention here the paradox that the standard route to a research career is through what is formally a teaching appointment, while a research post as such, except at the highest level, carries little status and no long-term prospects of advancement. It is none the less important to recognize that the common pattern in UK and US higher education – though it is not so pronounced in other national systems – is for elite researchers to have teaching obligations as well. These will often be quite substantial in the period before tenure is granted, so rendering it harder than it might otherwise be to make a major research contribution in early academic life.

The requirement to teach places a high premium on the choice of both an initial research specialism and a particular topic within it. To gain the early visibility commonly associated with a strong professional reputation, a budding researcher needs to concentrate the available research time, i.e. the time which remains after the necessary teaching commitments have been met, on an area of activity that is capable of yielding significant results in a reasonably short period. The selection of this activity is arguably the most strategic decision which faces academics in the initial stages of their careers.[3]

We shall need to distinguish more sharply at this point between a specialism and a specific research topic. Although the beginnings of a specialized interest may sometimes be traced back to the late undergraduate phase, intellectual identities necessarily become more pronounced in the course of choosing and pursuing a doctoral topic. Some individuals may stay with, or close to, their initial choice of specialism for the rest of their lives, selecting a series of research problems which continue to fall within it. On the whole, however, as we shall see in the next section, a strong academic reputation may depend on a reasonable degree of mobility between different specialist areas.

One of the most prized assets of an appointment to a tenure track academic post – identified as such by respondents in each of the 12 disciplines covered by my inquiry – is the perceived freedom to choose the subject matter of one's research. In reality, that freedom is hedged about by constraints – including the lack of necessary resources, the scarcity of time, and in some contexts the absence of incentives. None the less, the degree of autonomy, and in particular the liberty to determine the intellectual issues with which one wishes to engage, is held to be significantly greater than it would be in other walks of life.

The scope for matching activities to temperaments has already been noted. That scope is enhanced by the considerable variety of types of research on offer within virtually every discipline. The individual specialisms an apparently homogeneous subject area embraces will often span the continuum from hard to soft modes of investigation. To give only a few examples, the quantitatively inclined historian may be free to register a commitment to economic or demographic history; the modern linguist may choose between the well-hedged confines of philology and the open pastureland of interpretive criticism; the economist may espouse the mathematical rigour of pure theory or the less easily tamed complexity of the labour market; the mechanical engineer may select from a menu which includes the creative uncertainties of design as well as the numerical precision of studies in fluid mechanics; the biologist may opt between the narrow and relatively certain worlds of taxonomy or microbiology and the broad and unpredictable studies of particular species or habitats; the physicist may escape the urban demands of research into particles or solid state by choosing to investigate such comparatively rural areas as meteorology, relativity or gravitation. The option may not of course be an entirely open one. Echoing a point made earlier in this chapter, one of my informants remarked that 'literature and linguistics demand different mind sets – one could view the choice between them as being temperamentally determined'.

Although a commitment to a given discipline does not dedicate one irrevocably to a specific pattern of thought or mode of enquiry, this is not to contradict the claim (argued in Chapters 1 and 2) that particular disciplines and groups of disciplines display certain aggregated characteristics which distinguish them clearly from others. It is merely to emphasize the variety within the uniformity: the fact that even the apparently softest subject may have hard edges, and that at its margins a seemingly hard one may allow for a fair measure of softness. The resulting catholicity within disciplines may be seen as a fortunate epistemological characteristic, in that it allows in the social dimension for a wide range of intellectual opportunity.

Even when the important choice of an initial research specialism has been settled – usually deriving, as we have seen, from the decisions entered into at the doctoral stage – there are still two well-marked escape routes from what may have transpired as a less than entirely successful match between theme and temperament. The first, to which we shall return shortly, lies in the sometimes far-reaching decision to change from one specialism to another; the second, which we shall now consider, rests on the choice of a particular research topic within a specialism to which a firm commitment has already been made.

Inside their necessarily narrower limits, specialisms themselves may offer something akin to the options which most disciplines can be seen to provide. That is to say, certain topics will be seen as central, and others as more peripheral; some as demanding, and others as comparatively tame. The decision that this calls for, whether to gamble with large stakes for high dividends or to play safe for lesser rewards, is a quite serious one in career terms. As one of my respondents, a chemist, put it:

In underpopulated areas within the discipline, there are fewer grants and fewer fringe benefits – less communication, less meetings, less opportunities to share interests, less of the things that motivate people. Because such areas aren't competitive, they promise better results – but the credit is not so great. People drift into such an area if they are loners and isolated individuals who don't like the limelight. Highly competitive people wouldn't be attracted by fields of this kind.

Perhaps in part because the choice of topic is even more crucial in the brightly lit, jostling urban context than it is in the shadowy and less populous byways of rural research, many of those who have written about it have confined themselves to the domain of the hard pure sciences. Schatzman and Strauss (1966) offer an exception, in that their concern is with a soft applied field, the psychiatric profession:

Psychiatrists-to-be . . . are very soon confronted with critical choices, since the psychiatric limb is itself many-branched. . . . By following one branch line rather than another, a psychiatric professional determines the kinds of interprofessional situations he will later select as appropriate to himself. He determines what situations he will be able to work in comfortably, if at all.

The strategic issues were elaborated in one of my interviews with chemists:

Problems take different lengths of time to solve. It isn't necessarily a good strategy to go for the quick solutions. Although these result in a greater number of publications, they don't necessarily count for much. The result may just be 'shotgun science', with very little coherence or quality. In fact, you need to find a good balance between short and long problems as a matter of expediency. You have to do things with rapid results as well as tackling long-term issues. A large problem can be a large gamble too. It can bring a lot of credit – but you may not be able to complete its solution.

The successful selection of research themes in pure mathematics, incidentally, is celebrated by the epithet 'good taste'. Much like the same phrase used by a connoisseur of the arts, it denotes the independent identification of what is consequently recognized as valuable. It is 'a matter of finding significant and soluble problems not amenable to traditional approaches', problems that are 'difficult, deep as opposed to shallow, and worthwhile in terms of the new possibilities they give rise to'.

If the choice is less firmly underscored in soft pure, hard applied and soft applied domains, it is nevertheless there to be made. There are topics which, on most people's reckoning, are minor and perhaps rather trivial, but may none the less lead to a publication of sorts; and there are those on grander themes which promise to become the subject of widespread critical attention. Not everyone is prepared to make the large commitment which may, or may not, even after years of endeavour, be judged to result in a significant intellectual coup; as in the hard sciences, there is the countervailing temptation to stick to a series of minor, more manageable contributions.

Whatever the area of knowledge, however, the dividends are not necessarily confined to hot (mainstream or currently fashionable) topics. Indeed, the potentially greatest pay-offs may come from apparently marginal areas. It is there that many of the successful revolutions are bred: consider, for example, the lonely wilderness years of a Ladurie in history or an Einstein in physics. But to follow in their path is a high-risk strategy indeed, since the chances are that at the end of the day one's efforts will prove inglorious and one's endeavours remain unsung.

The mid-life crisis

We shall need here to make a leap in imagination from the aspiring to the established. That is, we shall need to assume that the individuals with whose fates we have been concerned have duly achieved both the goal of a professional reputation and the status of a tenured appointment. The mid-career stage, though it does not mark an end to the demands and dilemmas of an academic life, will often signal the onset of a new set of challenges.

The main question which is posed at this point concerns whether or not to continue working within the same specialism, whether to switch to another one, or whether to begin the process of moving away altogether from active research. Consideration of the last of these options is conveniently deferred until later in the chapter, when we shall review the general phenomenon of ageing and burn-out; so we shall confine ourselves now to the issue of intellectual mobility.

The most important consideration must be what relative career gains and losses are likely to result from deciding to make a move: but there is of course the prior issue of why, if at all, a change of direction needs to be contemplated. We have already noted, from a collective standpoint, the inertia (though some would prefer the term conservatism) built into the academic enterprise as a result of the often substantial investment needed to attain a special expertise in a particular field (see Chapter 4). Anyone who has spent long, arduous years in the achievement of a close understanding of one particular knowledge area or in the acquisition of a particular type of expertise,[4] is unlikely without hesitation to abandon it and repeat the process in favour of a new one. The sense of reluctance, while apparent among my respondents in a variety of subject areas, seemed particularly acute where the linguistic and conceptual barriers between specialisms were high, or where one complex but well-established technical skill had to be replaced by another.[5]

Corroboration of this claim, at least in respect of the natural sciences, is provided by Reif and Strauss (1965):

> Once the scientist has acquired a certain amount of recognition and a reasonable position, there are many factors which reinforce further pursuits along similar lines. . . . The scientist has a large investment in his extensive training. He has also spent quite a few years viewing himself as a research scientist pursuing certain lines of work, and it is not easy to change his self-concept, role-models, and values.

Gilbert (1977a) makes a series of related points:

> As a result of his previous research experience, a scientist gains particular skills and knowledge and usually acquires specialised equipment suitable chiefly for his current topic. To abandon work on that topic in favour of a new one involves learning new skills, perhaps demands the modification, construction or purchase of different apparatus and requires familiarity with additional sections of the scientific literature. In addition, moving to a new topic implies breaking some of his informal contacts with colleagues and neglecting the reputation which the scientist may have been careful to build up while working on his current topic.

It should be added that he may continue to receive invitations to write and speak on the theme for which he is best known, thus reinforcing his existing reputation at the expense of a new one.

In the face of such disincentives, the motive to change has to be a powerful one. The reasons for making a move tend to be more numerous in cumulative than in reiterative subject areas, being partly dependent on the way in which knowledge has progressed. It was a common theme of the testimony given to me by physicists that, in the words of one respondent, 'Ten years is about the maximum life-span of a fashionable topic' and that, in the words of another 'If you're lucky enough to hit on a new technique, you may be able to exploit it for up to a decade.' In the less rapidly moving areas in biology, 'your techniques can carry you through for about fifteen years after graduation, but you tend to run out of steam when you are around 40'.[6] Knowledge of instrumentation also becomes dated: 'my students do things with apparatus which I don't know how to do'.

Those who work in non-cumulative areas may be spared such problems, but they share others which arise from personal considerations. Even when the field itself is not subject to rapid development, it may be affected by the swings of fashion, leaving the researcher to feel that he or she has been left mouldering in an intellectual backwater. Or, more commonly, individuals may conclude that they have done all the work they want to do within a particular specialist area, or that they have become bored with it, or simply that they are stale and in need of a change.

The difficulties do not, however, end with the decision to migrate to another arena. The barriers to entry are sometimes even more daunting than the disincentives to departure. Hagstrom (1965) quotes a chemist he interviewed as saying, of the adoption of a new specialism, 'It takes at least one or two, sometimes up to five, years to get to the publication stage.' The time needed to become *au fait* with an unfamiliar field depends on several factors: conceptual compatibility between the old and the new, the amount of necessary background knowledge and know-how, the nature of the particular topics selected, and so on. Mention was made earlier of the practice in physics and biochemistry in particular, of applying a specialized technique in a diversity of different areas, 'skimming the cream' of significant but readily solvable problems. But many subject fields are not amenable to such an approach. At the other extreme, Crane (1965) quotes a psychologist as saying of his own specialism: 'There are no substantial contributions of the hit-and-run type. Substantial contributions come from ten to twenty years of working on basically one problem area.' Hagstrom (1965) contends that:

> Mobility seems to be easiest for experimental scientists in disciplines having powerful and general theories. It is hindered when the specialist must command much relatively unsystematic factual material, and it is also low among theorists working with elaborate and ramified theories.

There are social as well as cognitive constraints on intellectual mobility. Reif and Strauss (1965), in acknowledging that 'the scientist must acquire much unfamiliar knowledge before he can be creative in a new field', add that 'He will also have to compete against the young people trained *ab initio* in that discipline.' As several of my respondents in various subject areas pointed out – supporting the contention of Gilbert (1977a) – there is also the crucial difficulty that one is not necessarily able to transfer one's existing reputation to a new specialism; membership of new networks may need to be negotiated, and credibility with funding agencies re-established. Confronted with these challenges, it is perhaps predictable that most people who make a move do not compound their problems by choosing a more intellectually impenetrable area than the one with which they are already familiar. The tendency, discerned by Mulkay (1974), for migration to take place from areas of high precision to those of lower precision is borne out by the available evidence from my sample. To take a couple of cases in point: 'it's fairly common for theoretical economists to move into the history of economic ideas or to become economic historians'; 'it's only very rarely that people move from ecology to cell biology, but there are more examples of moves in the other direction'.

The strategy of hedging one's bets by keeping one foot in the old specialism while dipping the toes of the other in the new, is singled out by Gieryn (1978): 'complete substitution of one problem set for a completely different one is . . . a less common occurrence than simultaneous problem change and problem retention'. My own enquiries suggested that this practice was not confined to the sciences: respondents in other knowledge areas also argued that, to avoid a complete hiatus in one's publications, it was important to continue some writing in the field one was leaving while gearing up to contribute to the literature of the new affiliation.

So far, the discussion has been concerned with the reasons behind migration and the problems which beset it, rather than with its frequency and scope. But something also needs to be said on the latter two issues. Estimates of the incidence of mobility differ to a considerable extent; some commentators write it down as a relatively rare phenomenon, while others claim it to be comparatively common. The divergence may stem from the nature of the population under review. If the whole body of academics is in question, rather than the much smaller group of active researchers, then it could well be the case that 'few scientists change research area during their career' (Thagaard 1987); and that 'the vast majority of researchers stay in a single specialty or work in a related set of specialties' (Chubin 1976). But the evidence from my sample of academics from élite departments and institutions was supportive of Mulkay's (1972) claim that 'intellectual migration seems to occur very frequently . . . in most if not all scientific disciplines'; of Hagstrom's (1974) observation that 'scientists typically work in more than one specialty and change specialties often' (more than one-quarter of his sample, he claimed, had changed primary specialties in the preceding 5 years); and of Whitley's (1984) reference to the findings of the US National Academy of Sciences 1972 survey, that 'physicists do indeed "migrate" to a considerable degree between sub-fields with one-third of PhDs changing their major interests in 1968–70'.[7] The number of my respondents who reported some significant change in career direction was much higher in actuality than in expectation, and the extent of the changes was in some cases quite striking.

There were, among the apparently substantial shifts from one discipline to another, a number of physicists who had turned to chemistry and engineering; a chemist who had migrated to biology (as well as a number who had, more predictably, become pharmacists); a biologist about to take up a post in experimental psychology; an anthropologist in a history department (and, again more predictably, an archaeologist in another); a historian who had become a sociologist; and an economist who had changed allegiance to political science. Outside my sample, there are many other well-known cases of intellectual pluralism, including three singled out by those I interviewed: Herbert Simon, whose contributions to political science and economics were complemented by those he made to mathematics and psychology; Michael Polanyi, who abandoned a distinguished career in chemistry to become a philosopher of science; and Thomas Kuhn, who started his career as a physicist before establishing himself as a historian.

Movements across specialisms within the same discipline may also at times be quite radical. Examples among my respondents included a physicist who had switched from elementary particles to astrophysics to radioisotope dating to applied energy research; a plant pathologist who had made a new career in studying fish vision; an engineer who had moved on from research on missile structures to a study of machine tool vibration; and a French literature specialist whose interests had evolved from sixteenth-century poetry to modern drama. More limited changes were commonplace in almost every field, and perhaps especially in academic law, where 'there is a traditional notion that everyone should be able to teach every subject', and in those disciplines, such as engineering and history, whose members are similarly encouraged to take the view that they are 'jacks of all trades'.

Career mobility of this kind is among the most potent sources of innovation and development within a discipline. Immigrants bring fresh ways of looking at familiar issues, and perhaps relevant but hitherto unfamiliar techniques as well. Documenting a celebrated case in point, Mullins (1972) was able to show that 17 of the 41 scientists in the community working on phage research in molecular biology were physicists and chemists by training: the physicists in particular had come to the conclusion that their original specialisms 'would provide no interesting research for some time', and that 'biology had the greatest number of unsolved problems which appeared open to fruitful investigation by physical methods'.[8] Ben-David (1960), looking at the more general picture of 'roles and innovations in medicine' coined the term 'role-hybrids' (subsequently elaborated by Ben-David and Collins 1966) to encapsulate this process:

> the individual moving from one role to another, such as from one profession or academic field to another . . . may attempt to [fit] the methods and techniques of the old role to the materials of the new one, with the deliberate purpose of creating a new role.

The end-point of active research

For the many academics who manage to survive the challenges and traumas of a mid-career change of life, there are many who do not; and yet others, as we have already seen, who have never faced the necessity or felt the urge to move out of their initial specialisms. They may for our present purposes be grouped together under the category of those whose research careers are at, or nearing, their end; though there are, as often before, significant differences to be discerned among them.

Let us begin by looking at the case of the researchers who, for one reason or another, conclude that they have no more to contribute within their existing fields of expertise, but who lack the incentive to start as virtual novices over again. The biologists I interviewed were particularly informative about the problems which arose and the career possibilities which remained open at this point, so I will take their observations as illustrative of a wider generality.

There was common agreement that the moment of crisis, at least among botanists and zoologists, occurred somewhere around the late 30s or early 40s. A number of respondents ascribed its incidence to an increasing administrative load which drained energies away from empirical research, and a mature professionalism which encouraged an emphasis on the theoretical and synoptic aspects of one's field, where necessary using research associates for data collection. An alternative response was to 'escape into administration' or, for people who were good at teaching, to concentrate on that. There were those again who simply opted to 'rest on their laurels and plod along'. As against this developmental-cum-structural view, however, other respondents offered an account of the matter more directly linked with the cognitive dimension of the research enterprise. According to the second school of thought, the intellectual menopause had less to do with the obligations of seniority and the growth over time of a reflective approach than it had with the average life expectancy of a research topic or an experimental technique that is, with the problems discussed in the preceding section. The appropriate response, on this interpretation, must be to 'retool your lab and rethink your problems'; to 'pick up the pieces, and update your techniques or change the emphasis of your research'.

Some who favoured the latter view were strongly critical of their older colleagues who had taken up the role of synthesizing elder statesmen: 'It is simply a way of maintaining their self-justification – a cheap and easy way out' said one. 'Such people do damned little work for their syntheses'. Another saw those senior scientists who were content to move out of the laboratory and adopt a supervisory function as 'people who want to "be scientists" rather than to do science in any genuine sense'.

The role of a senior academic as a supervisor of others' work, a synthesizer or a philosopher about his or her discipline, is perhaps more common in hard pure subjects than in other fields – because, as we shall go on to argue, they show a more marked career hiatus. But it is fairly typical for those relinquishing an active research career in any subject to take on a sizeable administrative commitment, either in their own departments or at the institutional level. An added option is to seek office in a learned society or relevant professional association. A few people at this stage decide to leave academic life altogether. But the most common choice of all is to concentrate on undergraduate teaching at the expense of generating new knowledge or supervising the research of doctoral students.

It has already been suggested that the life-expectation of a specialist in a competitive urban field is relatively short. Reif and Strauss (1965) proffer two pertinent quotations: 'Young scientists . . . eat up old scientists. . . . Well, they beat them down . . . you don't remain a scientist in the active, progressive sense of the word for a great many years any more'; and '[I have the] feeling that I'm worn out or burned out, and this is the end of my career'. The phenomenon of 'burn out' is most widely recognized in pure mathematics, where the peak of performance is often said to occur in the 20s or early 30s.[9] The older mathematicians in my sample were sceptical about this claim, though some acknowledged that the subject called for lengthy periods of close concentration when working through an argument, and so tended to favour those with high intellectual energy and a capacity for prolonged introspection: 'You have to be able to concentrate intensely enough to see the whole solution to a problem in your head.' Some areas of physics too, particularly the more theoretical aspects closely akin to mathematics, were designated by my respondents as 'a young man's field'; though in many experimental specialisms experience was said to compensate for age, so that people tended to get better with increasing maturity. The testimony of engineers on this point was ambivalent – again, it may have been related to the level of theoretical content, though my sample was too small to lend confirmation to this suggestion. The majority view, however, was that 'the career profile is a straight gradient – experience counts for a lot'; 'some people remain productive well into their fifties'; 'no-one peters out completely – there are some very active oldsters'.

In soft pure and soft applied disciplines, burning out is not recognized at all as part of a typical career pattern. There is no discernible early peak in research productivity; an increase in age betokens a parallel increase in expertise. A respondent in the field of modern languages maintained that 'modern linguists probably do their best work after the age of 45'; another pointed out that 'late-blooming is partly a matter of the amount of material you have to assimilate and the amount of detail you have to master – but it's also partly a result of the need for emotional maturity, insightfulness and empathy'.

One source of the perceived difference between hard and soft may be traced to the contrast, noted by Hagstrom (1965) and mentioned in the previous section, between 'powerful and general theories' which can be rapidly assimilated and deployed by energetic newcomers, and 'relatively unsystematic factual material' or 'elaborate and ramified theories' which only long years of study can command. Another, as we have seen, lies in the differential importance of specialized apparatus and techniques, and the tendency for both to become outdated within a comparatively short period in cumulative knowledge areas. Research in the softer domains commonly demands no instrumentation, and such techniques as it calls upon are on the whole stable and relatively unchanging.

All that has been remarked so far about the relationship between career stage and research productivity has been based on the subjective impressions of the practitioners themselves. In principle, it should be possible to provide a more systematic, detached and impartial analysis, based on a correlation of published writings with chronological maturity. A number of researchers have in fact attempted such a task, though – with irritating perversity – the objective evidence is as confused and contradictory as the subjective is clear and unequivocal.

The pioneering work is that of Lehman (1953), who set himself the herculean challenge of relating age to achievement – subsequently translated as 'outstanding performances' – not only in academic subjects such as medicine, psychology, philosophy, mathematics and most of the natural sciences, but in music, art, creative literature, politics and 'public leadership positions' as well (though not, interestingly enough, in such fields as history, sociology, anthropology or literary studies). Most of those comprising his sample were deceased, some (e.g. Mozart and Beethoven) long so. He was thus able to compare individuals born in the 1700s with those born since 1850. In his analysis, peaking of productivity appears to occur mostly in the late 30s – the range for chemistry is given as 26–30,[10] for physics and mathematics as 30–34 and for geology and medical sciences as around 35–39. Philosophers, too, are quoted as peaking between 35 and 39, except for metaphysicians, who enjoy a relatively late maturity of 40–44.[11] Lehman stresses, however, that intellectual productivity continues, albeit at a reduced rate, after the peak is passed. Taken as a whole, people beyond the age of 40 make over half the total contributions in any field, but the greatest rate of achievement occurs between 30 and 39.

Critics of Lehman's methods and dissenters from his findings include Dennis (1956, 1958, 1966) and a number of others enumerated in the brief, workmanlike review of the research literature on the subject by Fox (1983). Dennis relies on ageing data in two senses of the phrase, since his sample covers 738 people, born between 1600 and 1820, living to the age of 79 and beyond. He maintains that:

> in many groups [but not among creative artists] the decade of the 20s was the least productive period. . . . The highest rate of output, in the case of nearly all groups, was reached in the 40s or soon after. From age 40 onwards the output of scholars suffered little decrement. After age 60 the productivity of scientists decreased appreciably.

His main contention, that 'productivity persists in the later years of life', is echoed in a number of subsequent writings; others discern a twin-peaked pattern, with a second efflorescence of creativity among those in their 50s.

A small group of studies have concentrated on the *crème de la crème* of academic researchers, in the form of Nobel prize winners. Manniche and Falk (1957) found the peaks to be in the late 30s and early 40s. Moulin (1955) gives somewhat higher mean ages for the Nobel prize winners from 1901 to 1950.[12] Reif and Strauss (1965) state that 'during the past half dozen years . . . mean ages at the time of the award have been between 45 and 50 years in physics, chemistry and medicine' but that 'some men were in their late twenties when they did the outstanding work leading to subsequent awards of the prizes; indeed, their work was done at an average age of less than 35 years'. Zuckerman (1977), in her comprehensive exploration of the subject, would appear to dissent from this view, concluding that: 'Among Nobel laureates at least, science is not exclusively a young person's game; evidently it is a game the middle-aged can play as well.'[13]

Future generations of numerologists will doubtless continue to crunch out statistics, culled from diverse databases and generated from mutually incompatible assumptions, in the hope of producing a final, definitive statement on the relationship between age and productivity. Those lacking such inclinations, however, may conclude that there are too many complexities in all this to allow for more than a brace of unequivocal claims: first, that whatever the realities of the situation, the legend will die hard that subject areas making strong demands on abstractly symbolic or heavily quantitative reasoning are the main province of younger intellects; and, secondly, that for the rest, if custom has the scope to stale, yet age must lack the power to wither the propensity for intellectual excellence.

Personal matters

One of the self-imposed limitations of my research was that it did not enquire into the lives of respondents as private individuals (and in particular that it eschewed the possibilities opened up by those egregious psychological studies whose design is to correlate academic with sexual characteristics). None the less, I did invite comment on issues relating to professional commitment and job satisfaction. The responses on these points, though they have no direct bearing on the shape and development of academic careers, deserve a brief resumé.

It was typical of the active researchers my sample comprised that they admitted to a strong sense of personal involvement in their work. However, the form that involvement took varied somewhat from one knowledge area to another. The academics who were subjected to the strong competitive pressures of urban research seemed to find it hardest to 'switch off'. In some areas of physics, to survive, you have to be 'dedicated and determined', 'monomaniac' and 'obsessed'. Several interviewees found it difficult to leave their work behind: 'I live my physics.' There are departments where the labs are seldom empty.

The patterns among engineers and biologists seem less consistent. A number of the former, especially in the hotter areas of the subject, spoke of their 'total absorption' in their research interests: 'It amazes me how much time people spend working – at least that's true if you're active; and if it's not true it means you've opted out.' One respondent went on to describe how his wife had instituted a customs-type search of the car to impound all contraband work from the holiday baggage. Others, however, had schooled themselves against 'getting overwound and overdoing things'.

Again, while some biologists admitted that their professional concerns took up a large part of their lives ('you can't help carting your work round with you'),[14] others considered it essential to 'know when you have to stop working', and to avoid too much emotional intensity by the deliberate cultivation of other interests. By comparison, one respondent observed, 'physicists are more motivated and involved'.

There were fewer comments along these lines from those in the softer knowledge fields, though there remained a clear tendency to view the world from one's own disciplinary perspective. Much as a physicist might 'see everything from a physics point of view, 24 hours a day', or a biologist could discern 'a biological analogy in almost every situation', a number of historians claimed that their subject gave them a special understanding of life, 'a better feel for what is going on'; and a human geographer remarked that 'geography gives you a way of looking at the world: I can't imagine how I could stop being a geographer, especially when I'm in the countryside – seeing is an important part of geography to me'. But those who worked in disciplines concerned with human affairs were not perhaps as conscious of the dividing line between their occupational and their everyday lives, and seemed to adopt a more relaxed attitude towards their intellectual commitments.

The sense of personal pleasure to be derived from research activities was widely acknowledged, and there was not a single interviewee who confessed to being 'turned off' by, or uninvolved in, even its more routine aspects (it may be that, as one respondent suggested, most academics seem to end up in a field in which they find even the 'busy work' enjoyable, where others might consider it tedious). This is not to say that there are no boring or unsatisfactory facets of an academic life. The most common candidates under this heading were administration, committee work and marking undergraduate essays and exam scripts (the actual process of teaching was generally held to be enjoyable and worth while, and could sometimes be found to have a broadening effect on one's research).[15] Many of the younger academics felt frustrated by the lack of career prospects, especially when compared with the expansionist opportunities enjoyed by their predecessors a generation before; and some of the more senior ones expressed concern that increasing professionalization, along with other forces pressing for uniformity, would rule out the making of imaginative or risky appointments, and so reward safe mediocrity at the expense of wayward brilliance.

Few of those with some years of professional experience would have wanted to live their lives differently. Among the special virtues of their own disciplines – the ability, say, to immerse oneself in and come to appreciate another culture in modern language studies, history or anthropology; the engineer's pride in 'knowing how to do things'; the physicist's sense of command in knowing how things work – most of the academics I interviewed would affirm the enjoyment that one expressed of 'a vivid intellectual life, full of satisfaction and exhilaration', and share with another the claim that 'I can't imagine doing anything else, or any other job where I would be paid to talk to lots of bright people and do what I want to do.'

This last point – the special opportunity which academia affords 'to exercise your own creative instincts – to be your own boss' – was a leitmotif of the testimony from virtually every discipline. There is no contesting the importance given by respondents to freedom of choice and freedom of action in their research. How far that freedom is a real one, or how far it persists only as a romantic illusion, must be a topic for the next chapter to consider.

Addendum: A note on gender

More than one reader of this chapter in its draft form pointed out that it had nothing specific to say about the careers of women academics. The reason is straightforward enough: I made no conscious effort to control the sample for gender representation. Accordingly, out of the 221 academics I interviewed, only 22 were women.[16] This very small subsample failed to bring to light any systematic differences between male and female career patterns, particularly as there were no women in my groups of about a dozen respondents from mathematics, chemistry, geography and economics, and only two each from modern languages and pharmacy; there were a mere three in each larger group of some two dozen from biology, law, physics and sociology; none in engineering; and a significant proportion (6 out of 22) only in history.[17]

There is, however, a fairly substantial research literature, based mainly on US higher education. Apart from Bernard's (1964) influential study, much of this was published in the 1970s, when the topic would seem to have been in fashion. Both British and American findings suggest that women in academia have been marginalized in a number of respects. Not only are there far fewer of them: women PhDs tend to get posts in less prestigious institutions than do men PhDs from the same doctoral university level (Bernard 1964, Williams *et al.* 1974, Rendel 1984); they 'are more likely to receive initial appointments at lower ranks or in non-rank positions; they are promoted more slowly and receive tenure at a later age, if at all; they are less involved in administration' (Morlock 1973). Their salaries are lower (Morlock 1973, Carnegie Commission 1973, Williams *et al.* 1974), and more of them have part-time jobs (Carnegie Commission 1973, Williams *et al.* 1974). Their academic profiles also tend not to be as high; they are less well qualified (Williams *et al.* 1974); a smaller proportion than men have doctoral degrees from leading institutions (Carnegie Commission 1973); and they are less productive of research publications (Bernard 1964, Williams *et al.* 1974, Blackstone and Fulton 1975, Cole 1979). American findings suggest that women academics are more oriented to teaching and are given heavier teaching loads (Bernard

1964), though the British evidence suggests that the differences here are not significant (Williams *et al.* 1974).

It is widely remarked that there are different patterns between different subject fields.[18] As Bernard notes, 'it has been in languages and literature . . . that women have traditionally made their major contribution'. They are significantly under-represented in physical and social science, but they appear in sizeable numbers in female-oriented subject areas such as women's studies and home economics, and in relatively low-status fields such as library science and education (Bernard 1964, Carnegie Commission 1973, Blackstone and Fulton 1975). But, perhaps surprisingly, women's proportional share of professorial appointments is much higher in physics than it is in, for example, sociology; women physicists publish 'at rates equivalent with their male colleagues'; 'fare better in terms of rank'; and seem to be treated more closely on a par with men (Morlock 1973). The effects of differences in marital status are similarly unexpected. Married women with children are 'as likely to have a senior post as those without children', though both compare unfavourably in this respect with their unmarried women colleagues (Williams *et al.* 1974). However, married women in general appear to publish more than single women (Morlock 1973, Williams *et al.* 1974), as do married women scientists in particular, or at least those with small families (Cole 1979). Williams *et al.* offer a possible explanation: such women 'have to break existing social norms . . . they have to be women of exceptional drive and confidence . . . the pressures on them to achieve are greater than for other women'.

None of these studies is able to show much evidence of overt gender discrimination in the academic context. Bernard (1964) suggests that though some differentials are 'doubtless due to discrimination . . . it cannot be argued that all [academic women] were being seriously discriminated against'. Williams *et al.* (1974) state more categorically that 'it is impossible to demonstrate discrimination against women by the universities', while Cole (1979) remarks that 'the belief . . . that there is patterned and systematic bias and discrimination in hiring female PhDs is simply unsupported by data' and speculates that there could well be some measure of 'reverse discrimination in hiring'. The reasons postulated for the evident inequalities between men and women are various. They are generally agreed to reflect more subtle and pervasive considerations than a deliberate bias against women: 'a reflection of larger social differentiation'; the outcome of 'intermittent, mild, largely unconscious prejudice' (Blackstone and Fulton 1975); a consequence of 'accumulative disadvantage' (Cole 1979); or perhaps a matter of 'self-imposed' discrimination (Brown 1967, quoted in Williams *et al.* 1974), 'low self-evaluation' (Blackstone and Fulton 1975), or non-competitiveness among the female sex (Bernard 1964).

More specifically, it is suggested that there are psychological reasons (a lack of drive, low administrative ability) and socially induced expectations (role identities, a pressure to marry, and subsequent domestic commitments) to account for these differences between men's and women's career opportunities (Williams *et al.* 1974). Familiar considerations include careers interrupted for childbirth or hampered by other family obligations, together with the relative immobility of married women tied to husbands' workplaces (Bernard 1964). In relation to scientific fields in particular, Zuckerman and Cole (1975) identify a 'triple penalty' for women: the definition of science as an inappropriate female career (reducing recruitment); the belief that women are less competent at quantitative reasoning than men (reducing motivation); and 'some evidence for actual discrimination against women in the scientific community'.

There are signs that the discrepancies are gradually diminishing over time (Rendel 1984, University Grants Committee 1987). But even allowing for changing social attitudes and values, for equal opportunities legislation and (less probably) for a requirement of positive discrimination, it will clearly be many years before anything approaching parity of career chances between the sexes is likely to be established.

Notes

1 In this connection, Mulkay (1977) observes that 'graduate students, who naturally find it difficult to compete with mature scientists, are often given research topics which are somewhat peripheral and which are, therefore unlikely to attract the attention of older and more experienced researchers.'
2 Knorr-Cetina (1982) argues that the exploitation here, as in the case of research students, is mutual. She cites the case of a postdoctoral researcher who complained that he was 'being used' by the head of his laboratory:

> The post-doc conducted all the research in a project [acted as overseer to] students and technicians, and came up with ideas. . . . His name appeared on papers but not on patents which resulted from the research, and it was the head of the laboratory who decided when and where to publish, and who presented the work at conferences. However, while the head of the laboratory was using the post-doc to 'run' the project, the post-doc was using the head of the laboratory to promote his own career. He came to the laboratory to get access to journals, research money and 'hot' research topics; and he thought that his affiliation with a prestigious institute would enable him to get a high-paying, high-prestige position.

3 'A scientist rarely makes a career decision more consequential than the selection of a problem for research' (Gieryn 1978).
4 Thagaard (1987), by way of illustration, writes: 'According to my interviews with physicists and chemists it was emphasized that 10 years (including the graduate study) was necessary in order to qualify for work at the research frontier.'
5 As one biologist in my sample observed, 'it can be traumatic to go back to being a student when you've earned a reputation in your field'. Another remarked, 'if you invest a lot of effort in learning a difficult technique, you naturally want to use it to the maximum advantage – you have to think twice about picking up a different one'.

6 It is interesting to note how closely these (epistemologically based) comments echo the (sociologically based) assertion by Griffith and Mullins (1972), quoted on p. 68, that the typical lifespan of a successful 'coherent social group' in science is 10–15 years.

7 In his study of 'specialization and change in academic careers', Ziman (1987) argues that 'most scientists do in fact change their research specialties substantially in the course of their lives', but adds that they 'actually change . . . quite gradually. . . . Again and again, scientists described the evolution of their research interests as an unplanned process of *gradual* drift.' His sample was, however, wider than that of most writers on the topic, in that it included career scientists in freestanding research establishments, government laboratories and private industry, along with a small minority holding academic posts.

8 A history of the key role played by physicists in the phage group, and more generally in 'the biological revolution' which led up to the Watson-Crick model of DNA, is narrated in Fleming (1969). Among its other virtues it throws an interesting light on the epistemological contrasts between the two disciplines in question.

9 A view which received authoritative endorsement from G. H. Hardy in his well-known and widely-read *Mathematician's Apology* (1941). The claim is directly contradicted, on the basis of citation analysis, by Stern (1978): 'no clearcut relationship exists between age and productivity, or between age and quality of work. The claim that younger mathematicians (whether for physiological or sociological reasons) are more apt to create important work is, then, unsubstantiated.' Stern attributes an apparent dip in productivity in the 45–49 age group to increased administrative responsibilities at that career point.

10 This is surprising, in so far as the chemists among my respondents tended to the view that chemical physicists reached the end of their useful lives earlier than natural product chemists, but that in the case of the latter (to mix a metaphor) 'people usually blossom by their mid-thirties and then reach a plateau'. Comments were that 'there is no very obvious mid-career crisis – some people do allow themselves to become a bit out of date and old-fashioned but there is always new stuff to assimilate and nothing to keep you from doing research', and that 'some people are productive to incredible ages'.

11 Lehman claims that these 'early maxima' are steadily decreasing. The peaks in most fields tend to occur at younger ages in the twentieth century than they did in the eighteenth or nineteenth centuries.

12 More specifically, he quotes the average age for physicists as 45–46 and for chemists as about 50. The youngest prize winner in physics was 25, and the youngest in chemistry 35. A total of 31 per cent of the physicists were under 40; the corresponding figure for chemists was only 13 per cent.

13 This is not altogether consistent with her earlier acquiescence with Lehman that the highest productivity is to be found in the 30s (see the chapter on 'Age, ageing and age structure in science' in Merton 1973).

14 Terman (1954) notes that the physical scientists who formed part of his study frequently cited their work as their greatest source of life satisfaction. Mitroff (1974) concurs with Roe (1953) that all eminent scientists seem to have a strong devotion to their work, and that this spills into their weekends, holidays and all the time available.

15 A typical comment was that of a physicist I interviewed: 'Teaching is one of the

best ways to familiarise yourself with a new area of science which you aren't currently researching.'

16 The proportion is roughly comparable with recent statistics for the UK universities as a whole, which show the percentage of women full-time staff on academic and related grades as some 17 per cent of the total, and the percentage 'wholly university financed' as about 10 per cent (University Grant Committee 1987). Historically, the comparable US figures have been much higher, fluctuating between 20 and 28 per cent for the higher education system as a whole between 1889 and 1959 (Bernard 1964).

17 The UK statistics (University Grants Committee 1987) are not for individual subjects but for groupings of roughly cognate disciplines. The absence of a single female engineer in my sample of 22 is not out of keeping with the low UK representation (6.4 per cent) of women in 'Engineering and Technology' in 1984–5; physics is somewhat over-represented by 3 out of 23 as against a national total of 12.4 per cent for 'Biology, Mathematics and Physics', as is history by 6 out of 22 as against 14.5 per cent for 'Other Arts'; and sociology is under-represented by 3 out of 22 as against some 19 per cent for 'Administrative, Business and Social Studies'. But taken all in all, I am satisfied that there are no gross discrepancies between my sample and the national figures for the UK.

18 McDowell (1984) advances an ingenious argument suggesting that women may be attracted into disciplines in which the obsolesence of knowledge is relatively low, and which therefore exact fewer penalties on interrupted careers.

7

The Wider Context

The academy in the marketplace

So far, the considerations which have been advanced have rested on a particular, restricted view of the world of learning. I have set out to explore a problem which lies at the margins of the sociology of knowledge and the study of higher education; namely, how the nature of knowledge is related to the cultures of those who explore it. To make sense of the complexities which beset this issue, I have pushed into the background those contextual factors which, however intrinsically important, seem to bear on it only indirectly. In attempting at this point to set my findings into a wider framework, I shall again pose a deliberately limited ambition, invoking the broader questions of knowledge and society only in so far as they seem relevant to the themes already addressed. The question of how individual academics relate to the larger society they inhabit offers a suitable point of departure for the *tour d'horizon*.

One hackneyed image of the world of learning – for a variety of reasons less in vogue now than it was in bygone times – is that of the ivory tower. There is of course some comfort as well as some scholarly benefit to be drawn from a cloistered withdrawal from the everyday world. Though dons might be written off as 'remote and ineffectual' – as Hilaire Belloc once scathingly dubbed them – they would on this view wisely choose to spare themselves from mundane distractions, from the marketplace and the political arena, the better to concentrate on their prime task. But the comforts can have their negative aspects, as Kenneth Boulding (1956) reminded an earlier generation:

> As long as a subculture is isolated from the rest of the world, with all its lines of communication lying within, its image tends to be self-supporting and self-perpetuating. All the messages which are received by the individuals participating confirm the images which they have, because to a large extent the messages originate in these images. A

mutual admiration society is a fine way of persuading us that we are all fine fellows for nobody ever contradicts us.

But on another reading, any such sense of isolation has always been more illusory than real. As Barnett (1988) maintains, 'higher eduction in the modern world is inescapably bound into its host society'. Rothblatt (1985) is equally unequivocal in repudiating the notion of academics:

> as busily pursuing their work with no other consideration but the intrinisic pleasure of the intellectual task itself. That there is an intrinsic pleasure I will not deny, but that the pursuit of knowledge can be discussed apart from all the other pressures that affect human activity even of the most cerebral sort no one, I am certain, would defend. In this the economists have a point. Intellectual work must be supported by an economic surplus. How that surplus is sought and allocated is of great significance in discussing the autonomy of intellectual work.

We shall come back to the latter point. However, what needs to be established first is that, while academic activity cannot in practice be neatly separated from secular concerns, there is an inevitable conflict between the two. Rothblatt (1985) goes on to refer to:

> two different sets of pressures. . . . The first . . . consists of outside demands for a wide range of scientific services [originating] in government, in the military, in industry, or more vaguely from the public. . . . The second set of pressures . . . derive[s] from the internal constitution of science, from its cultural or value system and from the institutions that scientists themselves have built or have cooperated in building in order to maximise the conditions under which their work is performed.

Gibbons (1985), in his approach to the same issue, writes of:

> the tension between the way science (or knowledge) is *used* in our societies and the way in which it is supposed to be *generated*. The tension arises because it is not clear whether the knowledge that is generated is being used properly or whether if it were to be generated properly it would be usable.

Something of this tension between intrinsic and extrinsic considerations was touched on by J. D. Bernal as long ago as 1939. But it has come more sharply into view among sociologists of science in recent years, 'at a time when science has become more capital intensive while economic policies call for constraints and cutbacks in various sectors in society' (Elzinga 1987b).

The increasingly political and commercial orientation of science is not, however, in Elzinga's (1987b) view, a purely one-way process. He rejects the notion advanced by Weingart (1974) and others that ' "external" social influences are translated into cognitive developments and these, in turn, are translated into society' in favour of a more strongly reciprocal 'process of mutual accommodation and "mediation" '. The view he favours is of 'a complex interrelation of deinstitutionalisation or reinstitutionalisation of science on the one hand, and a scientification of society on the other'. As Elzinga (1987b) goes on to argue:

> social and cognitive regulative structures interplay with each other. In practice it is often impossible to draw a clear-cut line between the two. Truth-claiming activities are at one and the same time social power claiming activities in the real world of science in society. . . . As power- and knowledge-claiming structures in society change and become more reliant on basic research, knowledge- and power-claiming activities in science become at the same time selectively facilitated and constrained.

The symbiotic relationship between cognitive developments and social influences is perhaps at its most evident in the domains of the natural sciences and the science-based professions. Certainly, a major part of what has been written on the topic has been couched in terms of scientific and technological issues. It is the more easy, therefore, to overlook the rather different sets of considerations which relate to the humanities and social sciences on the one hand and the social professions on the other. I shall attempt where possible in the ensuing discussion to take them into account. However, I am not in a position to give more than a passing mention to the equally important but distinctive interplay between undergraduate teaching and external demands, both because it lay outside the scope of my background enquiry and because relatively little attention has been given to it in the research literature.[1]

Academics as social animals

Rothblatt's (1985) contention that 'Intellectual work must be supported by an economic surplus' applies in a direct and obvious way to the individual academic. The general economic climate is one of the main factors conditioning whether higher education is in a period of growth, stasis or contraction. In the boom years of the 1960s, higher education in many countries expanded: academic jobs were plentiful and there were good prospects of early advancement and promotion. In the recession of the 1970s and the relative stasis of the 1980s, the opposite has been the case: tenured posts have been hard to come by, the competition for them fierce and the waiting period in some disciplines long; senior positions have not always been replaced after their incumbents retire; and career opportunities have been relatively limited.

There are other less immediately evident but none the less important ways in which an academic's professional life may affect, and be affected by, the wider social environment in which he or she works. In some cases, the research an academic does may have significant implications for the world outside the scholarly cloister. Many of the now taken-for-granted improvements in the quality of human life, and many of the benefits of technological advance, can be traced back to their origins in academic enquiry and exploration. On the darker side, physicists may share a particular sense of responsibility for the creation of atomic and nuclear weapons, and engineers for the dubious blessings of nuclear power. Chemistry has given rise to its own forms of weaponry; biology to the possibility of bacteriological warfare and, along another pathway, to the ethical uncertainties of genetic engineering. The pure and applied sciences are not alone in their openness to such accusations. The appeal to history lies behind some of the most bitter territorial and racial disputes; sociological theorizing has given birth to powerful and sometimes destructive ideological movements; economics shares some of the blame for disastrous financial policies as well as some of the credit for successful ones. All in all, the outcome of research must be rated as a mixed blessing to humanity.

But this kind of argument allows for two possible responses, and which one is adopted remains a matter of individual conscience. Some academics may be ready to go along with the general concern that their research has real or potential negative effects; others will wish to dissociate themselves from the implications of their work, arguing that whether and how it is exploited is a matter for collective social responsibility. Thus, while there are those among the older generation of physicists who seek expiation in the wake of Hiroshima by what one of my respondents dubbed as 'indulging their social consciences', the engineers – in keeping with their pragmatic tradition – tend to stand aside from the politics of protest about Chernobyl and its counterparts, their natural line of argument being that if a thing works it must be good, and that one day it will be rendered foolproof. 'Engineers', remarked one of them, 'have no social conscience, though some pay lip service to the idea that they should'. Again, the ancestral philosophers to whose ideologies the Nazi movement appealed might well, had they been alive at the time, have denied responsibility for the particular ways in which their views were interpreted and put into effect.

The decision to engage in social action or to avoid it extends also to those problem areas to which research may seem to offer some answer or amelioration, whether or not they were the original concern of academics. Not many of the UK biologists in my sample chose to involve themselves in ecological or other pressure groups, not only because they are generally seen as too time-consuming, and because their members are inclined to take an over-simple view of the issues, but also because such activity 'adds nothing to your professional prestige'. On the other side of the Atlantic, respondents commented on a growing interest in matters of social moment – but there, too, 'there are still plenty of biologists who don't give a damn'. On the whole, it is wiser simply to steer clear of controversial issues.

Again, academic pharmacists are not often in the front line of those engaged in tackling drug abuse. The more ambitious and successful economists, one of my informants noted, are attracted by intellectual rather than by social and political issues – they take the view that ethical considerations are 'not my problem'. Historians commonly prefer to avoid relating their scholarly concerns to contemporary affairs, on the grounds that generalization from one situation to another is highly suspect. Sociologists, in contrast, have fewer inhibitions in connecting their academic stances with their attitudes towards wider political issues, though they may prefer to do so from the comfort of the armchair than in the rough-and-tumble of the hustings or the demonstration rally.[2]

Alongside the cases we have considered so far, of research which has helped to generate a particular set of social issues, or which may have a relevant response to a particular set of social demands, there are instances in which academic work may in its turn be affected by external factors. The values, causes and philosophies that academics as individuals espouse will often have their biographical origins outside the library or laboratory. Their most obvious manifestations are likely to be in knowledge areas which are themselves value-laden. The findings of my study confirm that economics and sociology are disciplines in which a practitioner's value position may show up in his work: right-wing economists tend to espouse one set of theories and left-wing economists another, and quite a few sociologists would regard themselves as 'being on the side of the under-dog'. Historians, in common with sociologists, would seldom contemplate using 'biassed' as a term of criticism, because 'it is taken for granted that every historian is biassed in one way or another'. Nevertheless, a distinction may be drawn here between being committed to a set of values (and perhaps allowing them to influence one's choice of specialism), and letting them 'impose a pattern on the past', or 'distorting evidence to fit preconceptions'. The position of academic lawyers is more complex. According to my informants, there is 'a craft tradition of constructing arguments from different sets of values', in a profession in which a well-formulated legal argument is considered as being independent of the side of the case it takes. Traditionalists 'pretend to be practising a Weberian, value-free science', and 'would regard the use of the law as a left-wing or right-wing weapon with total horror'. Reformists, on the other hand, see room for a critical function within legal studies: 'there can certainly be bad ideological law, but there can also be good'. Other social professions, such as education, social work and community nursing, allow a more direct, and sometimes painful, relationship between personal belief and occupational practice.

Some fields of enquiry would appear less open than others to the influence of external ideology and less hospitable to imported values. It may be over-simplistic to equate this difference to the distinction between disciplines concerned with things and disciplines concerned with people. In a sense, engineering is concerned with both, but academic engineers as a group tend to portray their work as value-free and apolitical. Even so, none of the mathematicians, physicists or chemists I interviewed could identify any part of their practice as subject to outside doctrinal influence, except in the very general sense that someone's world-view might influence his or her professional judgement – though a predilection for one theory against another was not, it was pointed out, immune to the subsequent demonstration of falsity. And although, among many others, Rose and Rose (1974) argue in convincing terms against the supposed neutrality of science, it is perhaps significant that they choose neurobiology as their subject, and show its rival approaches to reflect particular views about human beings.

The relationships here may sometimes be as profound and elusive as the workings of the Zeitgeist itself. As Foucault's (1970) influential study of *The Order of Things* implies, what people see and understand is conditioned by the contemporary intellectual climate.[3] Values may be unconsciously as well as consciously assimilated: academics 'may find themselves subject to "sea changes in social thought" running through society', as Henkel (1987) observes. Perhaps it is this phenomenon which lies behind her suggestion that 'academic values are being transformed . . . an inevitable process as academics are exposed to more external norms and influences'. More specifically, in relation to history, Wesseling (1985) remarks on the 'vague and unconscious' response of researchers to 'what actually goes on in society', adding that 'rather more unconsciously than consciously, society has an influence on what kind of historical research tends to be undertaken'.

However, the process of internalization of values may in some instances be calculated rather than inadvertent. Henkel (1987) remarks that:

> Academics are not, for the most part, helpless pawns in others' games. They are reading the changes and adapting in order to sustain their positions. Where they can, they are coopting external funders and strengthening their currency in the institutional and student market place.

Writing about the same study ('the responsiveness of higher education to external influences'), Kogan (1987) makes a related point, quoting one academic as saying 'we often work not with direct knowledge of what the external pressures are but with our own constructions and myths of what they are and what they might be'; and 'the important thing is the internal perception of what the exogenous pressures are'. But there is evidence also of resistance, of a reluctance or refusal to go along with external trends. Another of those interviewed saw it as possible for academics to remain as 'specialists not much touched by pressure from outside influences', and a third claimed that 'The threats from the environment are translated into justifications for what they are already doing.' Kogan (1987) concludes:

> managerial, centralising and instrumental rhetoric [has] had some effects on structure and on the disposition and content of courses. It is

not evident, however, that the underlying knowledge rules or intellectual ambitions . . . have changed. Teaching in this respect may change whilst research and scholarship continue to change less in response to system demands. . . . It is fair to assume that when change is imposed from the outside for reasons which the academy may not always share, the rhetoric of change will overreach its actuality.

Faced with this somewhat bewildering multiplicity of considerations, only two general points may confidently be made. The first is that certain significant differences continue to manifest themselves between different knowledge fields (though, as an aside, the picture is complicated here as elsewhere by the fact that a particular subject area may embrace not only topics which are discernibly of social relevance and ones which are not, but also both relatively value-free and heavily value-laden elements – plant taxonomy alongside human physiology, palaeography alongside the history of modern Europe). The second is that the pattern of involvement of academics with political and social issues outside academe can be seen to stem in part from their personal or professional concerns, but in comparably large part from extraneous considerations.

Outside influences on specialist groups

New considerations arise in turning from an assessment of how the outside world impinges on the aspirations and values of individual academics to a review of its effects on specialist groups, and in particular on the structure of their communication networks and the organization of their research activities.

Viewed in collective terms, research on a given topic may be enhanced by intellectual and technological developments outside its confines. As we have already seen, theories and techniques generated in one milieu may turn out to be productively applied elsewhere; instrumentation developed in one setting may be the occasion of significant advances in another. Computing provides a clear example of a facility which has affected the shape of many research fields. Contributions of this kind, while external from the perspective of a particular specialism, remain for the most part internal to the academic world as a whole.

The availability in practice of expensive equipment, and of the technical support that goes with it, must however be a reflection of economic circumstance. As Henkel (1987) notes, 'the capacity . . . to attract [research contracts] is an important criterion of evaluation . . . particularly where the acquisition of modern equipment, often essential even for keeping pace with a fast developing subject, depends upon it'. Thagaard (1987), in turn, emphasizes the importance of underpinning of this kind in many areas of pure and applied science, reminding us that 'Research instruments do not only influence the choice of research problems but also the organisation of research. Advanced and expensive machinery requires large-scale organisation of scientific work' – thus depriving the individual academic of some measure of freedom of choice (Ravetz 1971; Ziman 1981).

Economic constraints bear more harshly on the urban, capital-intensive areas of 'big science' than on the rural, labour-intensive pastures of the humanities and social sciences. But other types of sanction may affect hard and soft, pure and applied areas alike. Lay questioning of, or even in some cases formal legislation against, academic practice may be manifest in such ethically sensitive areas as genetic experimentation, the treatment of laboratory animals, the study of sexual behaviour, the critical acknowledgement of pornographic literature, or mental testing research which appears to contravene the requirements of racial equality. Political hostilities may be aroused outside as well as within academia at the promulgation of what may be labelled as seditious or blasphemous views, or at the apparent endorsement of socially – or morally – subversive writings. Demands may be made for greater relevance in research to external requirements. Pressure for increased academic accountability may arise from political, social and ethical considerations of this kind as much as from purely economic concerns about organizational efficiency and the ability of higher education to offer the taxpayer good value for money.

We shall need to return later to the call for relevance, since this poses a fundamental problem in relation to the autonomy of research communities. It may be useful first, however, to look at another less clearly visible form of inhibition on research activity, namely the way in which academia is itself predominantly organized. One of the physicists I interviewed expressed a concern, on the basis of his personal experience, at the way in which a promising research topic could 'fall into the cracks' of the specialist areas recognized as legitimate by the established academic peer groups and the funding agencies acting on the basis of their expert advice. Crane (1972) echoes the views of Ben-David (1964) and Campbell (1969) that 'if interdisciplinary specialization is required in order to develop an innovation, the organisation of university departments often inhibits it'. One effective way round this difficulty, Geiger (1987) suggests, has been the development of 'organised research units' (ORUs) set up within universities to accommodate forms of research which 'did not fit into the departmental structure, usually for reasons of size, duration and/or purpose'. He shows ORUs to be an important component in the recent development of academic research:

> the American university department, despite its considerable flexibility, is an inherently conservative institution when it comes to assimilating new forms of knowledge, particularly when this depends upon making additional appointments. In terms of conducting research . . . ORUs exist to do what departments cannot do: i.e. to expand into interdisciplinary, applied, or capital intensive areas in response to social demands for new knowledge.

In the course of the same discussion, Geiger introduces the distinction between interested and disinterested research: the 'concern of the investigator' in the latter being 'with the validity of the knowledge contribution, not with whatever use might be made of it', and the former being typically initiated by a sponsor whose financial support would be 'predicated on the probability that the investigator's knowledge contribution would, at least in the long run, have utility'. Geiger emphasizes that 'the basic–applied axis of research [is] by no means coextensive with the interested–disinterested axis': funding agencies may have an interest in basic research in the expectation that it could ultimately have some practical pay-off, and some applied research activities may be undertaken for their own sakes and not with an ulterior end in view.[4]

Elzinga (1987b) provides a detailed exploration of the way in which fundamental research may be supported for extrinsic reasons:

> Support to basic research has become selective, and the criteria of selection are ultimately tied to an industrial economic policy or social policy agenda in society. Basic research that can rapidly be exploited or which holds potential for future technological markets tends to be favoured. Thus demands of societal relevance are transferred from the field of applied science into fundamental research. . . . Legitimations of decisions in academic research are increasingly involving such "externalist" considerations as social relevance, utility and appropriateness that were traditionally reserved for mission-oriented and sectoral research projects and programs.

Accordingly, Elzinga suggests, 'it has become difficult to separate basic science from applied science, because the political goal-setting and prioritising perspective has come into the picture so centrally'. What this amounts to is a process of 'epistemic drift', which he defines variously as 'a shift from a traditional reputational control system associated with disciplinary science to one that is disengaged from disciplinary science and, thus, more open to external regulation by governmental and managerial policy impositions' (Elzinga 1985); and 'the tendency whereby knowledge structures and social structures within the university system tend to become reorganised into dysfunctional patterns when research communities come under strong external pressures of relevance and accountability' (Elzinga 1987a).

There are, as Elzinga (1987a) sees it, two distinct causes of epistemic drift:

> a continuing pressure of mandating science in line with political and bureaucratic decision-making institutions, and via the pressure of market forces at a time when emerging technology clusters like microelectronics, biotechnology and advanced industrial materials have to be based on strategic reserves of basic research.

The former tends to push research towards 'politicization' or 'socialization' – 'state dirigism or orientation deriving from government'. The resulting 'externally based regulatives and controls ... may crystallise around sectoral functions of knowledge utilisation (housing, defence, development aid, health care, social problems, etc.) ... or it may be around social and political movements (environment, women, black studies, etc)'. The latter cause, i.e. market forces, tends to pull research towards 'commercialization' or 'privatization'; hence the phenomenon of 'science and technology parks, ... little "Silicon valleys", cropping up around ... universities' (Elzinga 1987a) – 'a case of multi-national capital buying itself a ringside seat in the arena of Big Science' (Elzinga 1987b).[5]

The vulnerability to epistemic drift is not of course confined to hard pure areas. Among soft pure academic communities, those in the social sciences are also susceptible to industrial sponsorship and consultancy, although the direction their research takes is in general more likely to be dominated by state agencies and government-funded research councils with a bias towards enquiry which can be represented as socially useful. Research in the humanities, however, is relatively immune, both because the contribution it is able to make to the wider society is less directly utilitarian, and because – for the reasons explored in earlier chapters – scholarly enquiry of this kind is neither readily amenable to large-scale collective activity nor for the most part financially demanding. But *ipso facto* its comparative freedom from the fetters of government and commerce is won at the expense of a philistine perception that it is marginal and irrelevant as well as small-scale and trivial. The notion of epistemic drift is also less obviously relevant to research in the technological or social professions, though for a very different reason. They, it is commonly assumed, have nowhere left to drift to, being in part beholden to the larger professional groups whose research and training interests they represent, and for the rest under the sway of private and governmental industry (including defence) in the case of hard applied research groups and of the relevant ministries and social welfare agencies in the case of soft applied ones.

Organized research units, as Geiger (1987) shows, can play an important part as intermediaries between sponsors and the specialist communities whose know-how they seek to commandeer: 'the utilization of ORUs has allowed American universities to expand selected parts of their research commitments without significantly affecting their fundamental instructional mission as represented in academic departments'. In more abstract terms, van den Daele *et al.* (1977) refer to 'new forms of institutionalization and new communication structures', adding that 'The external problems set by science policy programs become foci for the formation of new communities.' They dub these 'hybrid communities', because they typically comprise researchers from a variety of different specialisms, together with non-scientists. Hybrid communities, they go on to assert, develop their own 'evaluation standards, reputation structures and career patterns'. Whitley (1982) takes up the argument, noting that 'scientific ideals and goals become altered to accommodate themselves to these new relations [with the medical, business and political establishments], as new reputational communities have established themselves around non-academic or quasi-academic goals'. The contrast is sharpened by Elzinga (1987a):[6] 'Traditional systems are ones where reputation accrues through internal recognition and peer review; in the new reputational systems reputation may be linked to recognition of services to an external economic or political elite.'

Elzinga here returns to his earlier contention that the relationship between 'social and cognitive regulative structures' is by no means unidirectional: 'External processes of stimulation, professionalization, sectoralization, etc. do not effect organizational and epistemic structural changes directly in higher educational systems, but rather by mediation, for example by hybrid communities and broker communities'; and at the same time 'a good "hybrid research community" that is associated with a particular field of research is one that is also successful in representing the interests of the research community and getting money, positions and resources'. Rip (1981), in his critique of the earlier account of hybrid communities by van den Daele *et al.* (1977), agrees that 'the appearance of hybrid communities is an indicator for an attempt at political direction of science, while its success depends on the institutionalization of the external regulatives in a manner compatible with the internal regulatives'. He also endorses a further important point:

> the cognitive state of a discipline and the nature of its internal regulatives are independent variables determining the attitudes of scientists towards external orientation. This implies that resistance of scientists cannot always be reduced by the institutional measures that administrators can take (e.g. money, opportunities, career structure), and that science policy has to take the cognitive aspects of its policy object into account (Rip 1981).

In other words, too exclusive a concentration on the (admittedly intriguing) processes of negotiation between specialist research communities on the one hand and the paymasters who wish to harness them to secular goals on the other plays down two fundamental points: first, that it is knowledge, viewed as a commodity, that forms the object of their shared concern; but, secondly, that knowledge is more than a *mere* commodity, subject to paper transactions. Much of the previous discussion has been concerned to establish that its development cannot be represented simply as a by-product of, or (as the relativists would have it) a chimera created by, social, economic and political considerations within and outside academia.

Disciplinary status and power

We shall next consider disciplines as a whole, rather than as conglomerates of individuals or specialist groups. One useful approach to their relationship with their environment is to consider how they are brought into being, the conditions for their survival, and what happens to them in decline.

There seems to be agreement on two distinct modes of genesis, though the variations on both modes are presented in a plurality of guises (compare Becher and Kogan 1980; Blume 1985; Elzinga 1987a). In the most basic terms, there are those disciplines which owe their origins to internal causes, and those which come into being for reasons which lie outside the sphere of purely academic influence. Disciplines which are internally generated need not concern us here. It may nevertheless be remarked in passing that Becher and Kogan see them as stemming either from fission, the process by which a large and increasingly independent specialism breaks away from the parent discipline to establish an autonomous existence (as in the secession of computing from mathematics), or from fusion, the mechanism that governs the amalgamation of two overlapping specialisms from different disciplines and their subsequent emergence as a new field (as in the birth of biochemistry from a fertile liaison between biology and chemistry). Blume refers instead to differentiation (a concept close to, if not identical with, fission) and extension, which he describes as 'the attempt to extend the scope of science to cover areas of experience, phenomena, where previously there was no science', giving as instances psychoanalysis as developed by Freud and the origination by I. A. Richards of practical criticism in literature.

Externally generated disciplines provide a clear example of the interaction between academia and the world which lies beyond its confines. Becher and Kogan draw attention to a single pattern of origination, namely that stemming from potential market demand. They characterize the responsiveness to market considerations as 'particularly marked in relation to vocational courses', such as accountancy and nursing, whose establishment depends on their being seen both as 'academically acceptable and as viable in terms of student numbers'. The same process is identified by Blume as professionalization. He gives engineering education as an example, drawing attention to the 'intellectualising dynamic' which leads to 'greater autonomy, more theoretical instruction, and higher entry requirements . . . the movement to a gradually more theoretically-based curriculum at the expense of earlier practical emphases'. But Blume adds a further 'mode by which new fields of research become established in the university', which he calls external stimulation: 'the development of a technical field [which] begins when someone perceives the potential utility of a particular phenomenon (a natural process or an effect) for serving a particular social function'. Examples of this process would include aeronautical engineering, biotechnology and medical physics, all of which involve 'the reorganisation of existing knowledge and the generation of new problem hierarchies . . . around a technical concept or set of such . . . concepts'.

Elzinga (1987a) adopts a more eclectic approach to the emergence and establishment of new disciplines, allowing both for internalist and externalist, and sociological and epistemological accounts of the same phenomenon. His main concern is with external factors of change. Taking up Blume's categories, he argues that external stimulation should include 'the non-technological sciences and varieties of learning', in that the social sciences have administrative uses and the humanities may serve ideological ends: 'Indeed it is not unusual to find new fields of investigation crystallising around . . . new administrative practices, welfare needs or an ideological discourse in society.' The last of these may be exemplified by peace and conflict research, environmental research and women's studies, though Elzinga notes that 'as movements' demands are taken up and translated into researchable problems . . . the research may become encapsulated and lose its radical sting', as a result of its having 'to suit the definitions of corporativist funding bodies'. His general conclusion is that:

> we find in the emergence of some new disciplines a confluence of various different, sometimes contradictory interests and stakes: popular grass root movements, academic disciplines or rather their traditional knowledge 'bearers' with their own disciplines to defend; professionalization of specific groups of highly qualified or skilled persons in society; and a variety of corporativist interests. Many of the new disciplines that emerged in the seventies . . . did so on the basis of external corporativist or professional stimulation, or else thanks to pressures from below, from popular movements. In both instances it is thus more a question of external motive factors than internal ones (Elzinga 1987a).

These comments are reminiscent of Elzinga's previously quoted account of the process of epistemic drift at the level of research specialisms. The comparison is underlined in a further reference (Elzinga 1985) to Blume's four sources of disciplinary origination:

> Blume's conceptual framework allows the successive policy shifts from the 1960s onwards to be interpreted as shifts in focus from cognitive to social factors as central for policy considerations; from having been largely based on or involving a consideration of internalist regulatives, science policy doctrines have come to reflect more strongly the factors belonging to the two externalist processes: socio-economic stimulation and professionalization.

Whatever their origins may be, emergent disciplines must face the competitive demands of those which are already established. Crane (1972) observes that, in the development of a new field, 'the existing academic system must be capable of expansion, of creating new positions and new departments in order to absorb the innovation and permit it to develop'. If the newcomer is seen as a threat to established interests, or as a rival claimant for the available resources, its development is likely to be inhibited (Spiegel-Rösing 1974).

From a particular sociological perspective, disciplines may be viewed as engaging in a constant Darwinian struggle for power and status, in which the hardiest and most adaptable flourish while the weakest go to the wall. Henkel (1987) is not alone in discerning the attractions of 'the evolutionary analogy and the concept of the survival of the fittest'. But it has also to be recognized that the competitiveness here is in large measure occasioned by the dependence, noted earlier, of intellectual work on external economic support and on the means by which that support is acquired and distributed. Freedom of research is in general limited by the need to persuade others that the necessary resources should be provided. Unless, as rarely happens, money is available in sufficient abundance to dispense with any competition for it, disciplines are forced into the position of rival interest groups. Their quest for status, which one might see as in some respects analogous with the individual academic's concern with reputation, is stimulated not merely by an intrinsic tribal pride but by an extrinsic need to justify their existence and maintain their collective livelihood. Or as Spiegel-Rösing (1974) puts it, the subjective attribution of status can have objective consequences: status brings the resources essential for the cognitive development of a discipline.

Henkel (1987) points out that disciplines 'may find themselves having to select and adapt strategies on the organisational, normative and political front in order to deal with their changing environment and to compete successfully with rival interests'. The nature of such 'disciplinary strategies of status maintenance' is examined closely in Spiegel-Rösing's discussion of the subject: here, we shall concern ourselves only with a selected few.

One common approach has already been identified in the earlier examination of epistemic drift: the establishment of a claim to external utility. In the exploration by Kogan, Henkel and others of 'the responsiveness of higher education to external influences', Henkel (1987) observes that, with certain important exceptions, 'the power of individual disciplines . . . increasingly depended on their perceived contribution to the economy'. When that contribution must – in the very nature of the subject in question – be indirect at best, the issue can only be argued in more or less far-fetched terms. Thus, a justification may be sought for apparently disinterested research, such as that in particle physics into the ultimate constitution of matter, in terms of the eventual possibility that it will yield applicable results. Such claims are so manifestly implausible in the case of many humanities subjects that the attempt is rarely made to advance them: though Kogan (1987) notes the case of a history department – not, it must be said, in an élite institution – whose continued survival depended on the modest contribution it was able to establish to the study of tourism.

But even in the most crassly utilitarian social climate, the external standing of a discipline is at least in some measure independent of its proven economic worth. It was contended, in the discussion of disciplinary pecking orders in Chapter 4, that within the academic world itself hard knowledge domains are regarded more highly than soft ones, and pure than applied. This perception is to a certain extent shared by outside

observers of the academic scene, who will tend, independently of calcula-
tions of utility, to show a greater sense of awe towards research in biochemistry and physics at the one extreme than to studies related to
education or social work at the other. The establishment of a strong
academic image is therefore by no means irrelevant as a move in the game
for external credibility and status.

Spiegel-Rösing (1974) distinguishes in this connection between strategies
for image improvement as such and those which are also directed towards
more fundamental changes in substance. The former may rest on careful
reinterpretations of a discipline's history or on modified claims about the
nature of its prevailing mission. Changes of nomenclature may themselves
prove significant. One of my biology respondents noted that a number of
botany departments had judged it worth relabelling themselves as departments of plant science; another suggested that analogously, at the specialist
level, functional morphology had acquired a more vigorous image when it
was renamed biomechanics. In mathematics, too, one informant remarked, 'people play word games to improve their status. For instance, the
group that originally called themselves analysts then took on the name
classical analysts, then became functional analysts, and now call themselves
hard analysts'. Elzinga (1987a) notes that the establishment of nursing
studies as a field of applied research has been characterized by 'quibbles
about whether to call part of the new subject "nursing care" generally, or
"health care research", or again "ward oriented research" '. However, what
is at stake here is more than a mere choice of name: 'the quibble about the
terminology . . . is not neutral. Rather it reflects strong vested interests on
the parts of different actors' and underlying disagreements about what
form of knowledge is to occupy the prime focus of attention. The change of
nomenclature in an established discipline can in its turn stem from more
than a social concern with 'impression management'; it may, as suggested
above, involve a cognitive change in substance, signalled by an identifiable
shift in paradigm, the viewing of familiar phenomena through new eyes.

The viability of a discipline is also closely bound up with its capacity to
attract students, which is not necessarily commensurate with its ability to
guarantee them subsequent employment. The recruitment market is as
unpredictable and as subject to the capriciousness of fashion as the market
for graduate labour, as can be seen by the substantial variations over time in
the power and resources which a particular discipline can command. In its
heyday, the study of the classics stood at the pinnacle of scholarly prestige
among the non-vocational disciplines, as did divinity among those predominantly concerned with training for a profession. Now, both struggle
for survival in the absence of any substantial student demand for places in
even the most long-established and well-regarded departments. More recently, analytical philosophy has seemed to purvey a more faded glory than
it did in the post-war generation; and linguistics, perhaps an overpriced
stock a decade or two ago, seems to have fallen back to reflect a more
modest market valuation,

The most apparently self-confident and respected disciplines are not immune to external influences of this kind. Many of my economist respondents reported a decline in morale within their intellectual community, largely related to the failure of economic measures to cope with the world recession of the early 1970s. Henkel (1987) reports that:

Both history and physics were found in our study to be under threat in different ways. . . . Physics is suffering from poor school teaching of the subject, retraction of research funding for big science and competition with engineering for students and for institutional support. Historians were being forced to make statements about the relevance and value of their subject to employers.

The vagaries of disciplinary fortune can, then, be seen as a further manifestation of the complex relationship between academia and its wider environment. One much-quoted thesis, which passes under the name of finalization theory, links the vulnerability to external influence of scientific disciplines with the stages of their evolutionary cycle. Böhme *et al.* (1976), following Kuhn (1962), argue that any science must pass through a three-phase sequence: from pre-paradigmatic to having provisional paradigms, and thence to the establishment of clear, mature paradigms. In the second of these phases, when the preoccupation is with theoretical development, a discipline is more or less impervious to attempts at outside interference. In the first, however, it is vulnerable to invasion by extraneous considerations because there are no strong internal regulatives that can contest them. And in the third, also sometimes referred to as the post-paradigmatic phase, there is no further theoretical expansion; internal regulatives cease to operate as the prime motor of research; and thus the mature science becomes again open to political and economic intervention. As Rip (1981) explicates: 'The river of science has, as it were, reached its delta and can now be made to change its course very easily. The internalization of external goals is called *finalization*,[7] and the resulting specialized developments are called finalized specialties or disciplines.'

This attractively simple account of the disciplinary equivalent of epistemic drift at the specialist level, though it made a considerable impact on the sociology of science when it was first advanced, has subsequently been questioned on a number of counts. Besides the vagueness of the notion of maturity, as Rip points out, it involves a strongly reductionist assumption that all science follows the model of physics (in the context of which the theory was evolved). It also shares the deterministic overtones for which Kuhn's work has been criticized, implying an inevitability of evolutionary pattern for which counterexamples can readily be found. Elzinga (1987a) adds two further indictments. First, 'the case studies that have been carried out have not succeeded in demonstrating how social factors influence "truth" in fields of knowledge. Indeed this very thesis has helped to fan the flames of relativism.' His second objection is perhaps more fundamental:

Even if we were to agree that certain fields of research become mature in the sense that no further theoretical developments are needed or possible, it does not follow that the researchers' right and responsibility ceases regarding the need to translate practitioner problems into research problems. This is not an automatic process. Also the researchers' responsibility for maintaining high standards and choosing methodologies or basic concepts, accepting or rejecting hypotheses, or publishing their results for scrutiny in the scientific community, all this does not cease to hold.

Whatever the merits or demerits of the doctrine of finalization, its applicability outside the field of hard science in however modified a form remains to be argued. But enough has perhaps already been said about the ways in which non-scientific subjects in their turn cannot escape the necessity to interact with the outside world and to accommodate to its demands. The case seems unarguable against any extreme form of disciplinary isolationism: even an ivory tower is not immune from environmental influences, be they the gales of natural happenstance or the man-made depredations of atmospheric pollution.

Knowledge domains and social relevance

A map of the world meets a purpose different from, and in some respects more useful than, a one-inch survey map of a limited piece of terrain. In a somewhat similar fashion, the four contrasting knowledge domains identified in Chapter 1 (hard pure, soft pure, hard applied and soft applied) serve at a macroscopic level to consolidate the diverse features identified at the microscopic levels of the individual and the specialism and at the intermediate level of the discipline. This process of consolidation, though it inevitably blurs the subtle variations that can be observed in close perspective, has the advantages of simplifying, and hence to some extent clarifying and underlining, the salient features of the map of knowledge.

With much of the detail already explored, relatively little remains to be said about the interplay between knowledge domains, viewed as aggregates, and the socioeconomic climate in which they have to justify their existence. This section will accordingly serve as a brief resumé of what has gone before, while also attempting to draw out its main implications.

Hard pure knowledge tends to carry high prestige, involving as it does the search for the general laws governing the areas of human understanding with which it is concerned. It is commonly held to be intellectually demanding, and is seen as attracting individuals of high ability. The purity and élitism are, however, mitigated by the promise that it may, in possibly unexpected ways, have beneficial application. These features help to explain the substantial sums which society seems prepared to invest in problem-centred enquiry concerned with causal explanation of a general kind. The funding of 'big science' calls for a particularly effective professional-political lobby, which is fostered by strong, well-organized and closely knit specialist associations. Even in less costly areas of investigation, grantsmanship is an art to be cultivated by the successful careerist: the earning of outside funds is a positive influence in the process of professional recognition and advancement. Overall, the substantial dependence of hard pure research on external sponsorship opens the way to political and commercial intervention, and may lead in some situations to a heavy emphasis on work considered to be socially applicable, at the expense of those areas of enquiry whose direction is determined by predominantly epistemological considerations.

In hard applied areas, where the prime function of knowledge is the generation of product-oriented techniques, and more directly of products as such, the profile is different. Effort tends to be spread across a wide front rather than clustered round a limited number of problems. It is therefore less easy for a single interest group to coalesce and to present a coherent, united case for funding. The difficulty may be compounded by the utilitarian criteria invoked in assessing research promise. In particular, the views of non-academic, professional practitioners in the field of application are likely to have some influence, clouding the simpler, more domestic processes of peer group judgement. The value attached to directly useful knowledge is related to broader cultural considerations, and varies over time and place. In Western and Central Europe there has been a tradition of according social esteem to practice-related enquiry, as may be seen in the strong infrastructure of technological and applied institutes within their educational systems as a whole. In Britain, on the other hand, less positive social attitudes have been fostered by the equation of élitism and theoretical purity with the gentry, and practical application with the working classes (see Wiener 1981; Barnett 1986). It has taken unremitting political insistence on promoting contract-based, utilitarian research to shift the balance in the direction of favouring application. But there are countervailing tendencies among élite applied scientists towards achieving independence from external influence by favouring the more theoretical, less instrumental aspects of the domain – a particular form of 'academic drift' (Neave 1979; Clark 1983) which is the alter ego to the epistemic drift already identified in hard pure enquiry.

Both hard pure and hard applied knowledge involve their champions in active competition for research funds and a corresponding dependence on the goodwill of both the public and private sectors of the economy. Pressure of this kind is noticeably less intense at that end of the soft pure domain which deals with inapplicable, largely atheoretical knowledge, involving the study of the particular rather than the general and the search for empathetic understanding rather than causal explanation. The view from the external world of this form of knowledge is ambivalent. On the one hand, scholarship is a respected attribute and activity; on the other, it is open to the hostile accusation of being arcane, inbred and largely pointless.

What has at times been proudly designated by academics as the pursuit of learning for its own sake may understandably be written down by the laity as not possessing any wider social justification, and hence as having little if any call on the public purse. It seems too personal and specific to merit large investment, and is in any case too cheap to need it, involving as it typically does one or at most two people rather than a substantial research team, and demanding no more than access to source material, modest funds for books and the cost of occasional travel. Because fund-raising is not a significant activity, the specialisms concerned have no pressing need for strong promotional public relations. This, coupled with the individualism which is one of the inherent features of soft pure research, means that their professional organizations, viewed as groups representative of their interests to the outside world, are relatively weak.

But the soft pure knowledge domain is perhaps even more heterogeneous than its counterparts, in that it also embodies areas of enquiry that aspire to something of the generality of hard pure research and that may offer some potentiality of application. Economics is a discipline which straddles the boundaries of hard and soft, pure and applied: 'What is, or is not, an economic problem is largely determined by the analytical framework of neoclassical economics but external influences do affect the range of issues tackled and policy demands lead to extensions of that framework to the new areas which were not previously considered appropriate' (Whitley 1984); 'The claim is . . . for unifying as well as more sophisticated theories. [The] preoccupations are largely internalist, although the externalist influences upon a subject so enmeshed in society are powerful' (Henkel 1987). Sociology, too, displays elements of a quest for grand, over-arching theories in awkward conjunction with a tendency towards policy-oriented enquiry: though here, the influence of research on practice is seldom a very direct one, and may be argued to take the form of a general enlightenment – a modification of commonly held concepts – rather than of effective prescription for social amelioration or improvement (Weiss 1977; Thomas 1985). In the social sciences generally, the role of outside political agencies would appear to be stronger than it is in the humanities, the natural sciences or the technical professions.

The predominant feature of soft applied knowledge is the susceptibility of its research agenda to dictation by non-academic interests. Because of their close links and overlapping membership with the academic community, the relevant professional practitioners' associations will often have a strong say in identifying issues and approving strategies of enquiry, as in the cases of nursing and social work. Government ministries will tend, by their control of sectoral research budgets, to promote developmental activities alongside investigation into 'useful' topics (Kogan and Henkel 1983). Client groups may also seek to exert their influence. As Whitley (1984) observes, 'where the central phenomenon of a field is largely defined by powerful non-scientific [i.e. non-academic] groups . . . its autonomy is very limited and subject to invasion in the name of "relevance"'.

The implication of this analysis is that even when aggregated at a broad general level, different epistemological categories can be seen to be associated with distinctive sets of relationships between the academic communities concerned and the wider contexts in which they subsist. No part of the world of learning is immune from interaction with its environment, but the form that interaction takes will clearly reflect the nature of the knowledge domain in question.

Notes

1 The only significant exception of which I am aware is the large-scale study of higher education and the labour market conducted in the mid-1980s by Maurice Kogan and others (see Boys *et al.* 1988).
2 The issue is perhaps more complicated than this makes it seem. One sociologist I interviewed remarked that 'many sociologists have strong feelings of social justice, but most sublimate them into research rather than translating them into action'. But the comment of another that 'the kind of sociology one practices is seen as a political and an existential statement', allows a different interpretation. In true dissenting tradition, Nicolaus (1972) accuses 'the ruling elite' among his colleagues of being in the business of giving 'information and advice to the ruling class . . . about ways and means to keep the people down':

> The honoured sociologist, the big-status sociologist, the fat-contract sociologist, the jet-set sociologist, the book-a-year sociologist, the socio-logist who wears the livery, the suit and tie, of his masters – this is the type of sociologist who is nothing more nor less than a house servant in the corporate establishment, a white intellectual Uncle Tom . . . for any government and ruling class. . . . Sociology has worked to create and increase the inequitable distribution of knowledge; it has worked to make the subject population relatively more impotent and ignorant.

3 Elzinga (1987b) gives a nice illustration, depicting the way in which intellectual fashions have changed in the sociology of science. He argues that 'Merton's sociological scheme and Popper's philosophical one' (see Merton 1973, on the norms of science, and Popper 1979, on the principle of falsification) sought to portray science as functionally autonomous and cognitively authoritative, and hence as 'relatively immune and independent of societal influences'. In 'some of the newer trends . . . facts are sometimes seen not to be formed primarily or at all by confrontations with objective realities, but by the social mediation and cultural weave in which researchers work . . . the boundaries between science and non-science are said to be dependent on negotiation and power struggles, both at the micro and macro levels.' Accordingly, 'contrasting the newer imagery with the traditional one that has legitimated traditional academic science, the defrocking of the priesthood of science may serve to legitimate pragmatic science policy doctrines . . . which form the basis of mission orientation and politicization of science'.
4 This claim perhaps amounts to no more than a further indication of the diversity within superficially homogeneous disciplinary areas. The phrase 'disinterested applied research' could reasonably be used to refer to predominantly theoretical

work in such fields as pharmacy and mechanical engineering. A contrast might be noted here with what is sometimes called 'applicable mathematics', i.e. research topics within the disciplinary confines of pure mathematics which promise to be capable of exploitation in applied subject fields.

5 The dependency can cut both ways. Henkel (1987) observes that:

> There are fields in which industry is at the leading edge of knowledge. Examples in physics are digital electronics and opto-electronics . . . some teachers in higher education were using their links with industry to gain knowledge of current developments in opto-electronics for transmission to students.

6 And blunted again by Knorr-Cetina (1982), who argues that even in apparently disinterested pure science 'the arenas of action within which . . . inquiry proceeds are *transepistemic* – that is, they in principle include scientists and non-scientists, and encompass arguments and concerns of . . . a "non-technical" nature'. These transepistemic arenas are 'the locus in which the establishment, definition, renewal or expansion of resource-relationships is effectively negotiated'.

7 ' "Finalization" is a process through which external goals for science become the guide-lines of the development of the scientific theory itself' (Böhme *et al.* 1976).

8

Implications for Theory and Practice

Tidying up the categories

The research on which my exposition has been based was shaped and directed by one underlying assumption: namely, that there are identifiable patterns to be found within the relationship between knowledge forms and their associated knowledge communities. However, inside the limits of this defining framework, I have attempted to avoid any firm preconceptions about the nature of the information to be sought, allowing the data themselves to yield up consistencies and to dominate the forms of explanation offered to account for them. A grounded approach of this kind (Glaser and Strauss 1967) offers more assurance than does a theoretical stance based on a particular set of axioms that the range of evidence taken into consideration will not be intentionally or subliminally restricted (see Pantin 1968): that the resulting theoretical account will be faithful to a wide spectrum of data, and not merely one which is preselected by the theorist's own assumptions. But as against that, it is less likely, except where the phenomena under review are themselves very simple and straightforward in character, to generate a powerful and apparently all-embracing explanatory structure.[1]

There are other reasons why the emergence is not to be expected of a single theory which could account for all the considerations which have so far been advanced. Leaving aside the contention that human affairs – allowing as they do for intentionality – are too complex to be amenable to the law-like regularities to be discerned among natural phenomena, it has already been acknowledged that academic communities are subject to influences from the wider society as well as from the inherent nature of the epistemological issues on which they are engaged. It therefore seems highly improbable that a neat one-to-one correspondence can be found between forms of knowledge and the characteristic cultures of those who engage in them.

None the less, there remains scope for a tidying-up operation of the kind

I shall now attempt. In seeking identifiable patterns in the data and advancing recognizably related explanations for them, I shall begin by looking again at some of the main categories employed in the course of my exposition and attempting to clarify and systematize the connections between them.

Much of the preceding discussion has been conducted in terms of disciplines and specialisms, seen as marking two different levels of specificity. Each of these concepts has the property of combining, in ways which are not easily separable, both cognitive and social characteristics. Thus, when we speak of a discipline, or of a specialism, we tend to run together the notions of a particular field of knowledge and an associated group of academics: people belong to a discipline, or embrace a specialism, but that discipline or specialism is defined in terms of its intellectual content as much as by its adoptive community.

When it becomes necessary, for the purposes of conceptual clarification, to distinguish the two aspects – epistemological and sociological – we are forced into a somewhat artificial form of categorization, in that a natural one is not readily to hand. For my present purposes, I shall use the term 'subject' to refer to the cognitive component of a discipline, and the term 'segment' to designate the corresponding component of a specialism. Their social counterparts will be labelled 'disciplinary community' and 'network', respectively. These ascriptions are not reflected in the looseness of general parlance, and have not indeed been consistently deployed in the preceding pages, but they are perhaps near enough to commonsense usage to serve as a temporary expedient for the requirements of closer analysis.

Subjects and segments, then, are to be seen as cognitive entities, and disciplinary communities and networks as social ones, formed by the logical dissection of disciplines and specialisms. These entities possess certain important attributes which have formed the topic of previous discussion. Segments, as well as subjects, may be hard or soft, pure or applied. Both sets of dualities in practice allow for gradation; neither hardness nor softness, purity nor application, should be seen as absolutes, but as end-points of continua. So too, networks and disciplinary communities may be characterized as highly urban or preeminently rural in their patterns of interaction, or as lying somewhere between the two extremes. Disciplinary communities may in varying degrees be seen as convergent, i.e. manifesting a sense of collectivity and mutual identity, or divergent, i.e. schismatic and ideologically fragmented.[2]

It is important to observe the asymmetry in this exercise in conceptual mapping. Subjects and segments share both sets of their cognitive attributes; disciplinary communities and networks do not. That is to say, the notion of convergence, which is roughly analogous with the sense of nationhood attributable to sovereign countries (but not to their member states, counties or departments), can be applied at the level of a disciplinary community but not at the level of a network. Both networks and disciplinary communities may be more or less tightly knit, but the sense in which this epithet is applied differs between the two, and the distinction helps to highlight the contrast between the convergent/divergent spectrum on the one hand and the urban/rural spectrum on the other.

Networks are at least in certain respects homogeneous and coherent by definition, where communities may or may not be so as a matter of contingency. To say that a disciplinary community is tightly knit is to say something about the *Weltanschauung* (compounded by folklore, mythology and hero-worship) which binds its constituent networks to one another; to say that it is loosely knit is to imply a collectivity held together not by a strong sentiment of cultural affinity but by the weaker bonds of historical or social circumstance.[3] But to say that a network is tightly knit is not to say anything new about the mutuality of its members' scholarly interests and concerns, since all networks, whether tight or loose, owe their very existence to such characteristics; rather, it is to say something about its predominantly urban mode of existence, about the intensity and nature of the interaction between the individuals who comprise it. Putting it differently, tightly knit convergent disciplinary communities are characterized normatively, in terms of a commonality of intellectual values and a coherence of cultural assumptions among the networks and individuals within their jurisdiction; tightly knit urban networks are identifiable operationally, in terms of the types of activities and practices in which those who belong to them engage.

We may wish for certain purposes (as in Chapter 1) to denote subjects as hard or soft, pure or applied, while recognizing that they are in reality an admixture of segments with different combinations of characteristics. The amalgam may be predominantly pure (as in chemistry) while some parts of it are clearly applied, or predominantly hard (as in mechanical engineering) while some parts of it are clearly soft. Similarly, when we choose to designate disciplinary communities as urban or rural, we are in practice identifying a predominance among what is often a heterogeneity of urban and rural networks. But to say of a disciplinary community that it is convergent or divergent is to refer to the nature of the relationships between its networks, not to the predominance of one type of network over another (since degrees of convergence are not, within the meaning of the term, accorded to networks as such).

The basic dimensions

Some further issues need to be clarified before we turn to consider the implications of applying this taxonomy to the knowledge forms and knowledge communities which have been the subject of the enquiry. In the first place, Pantin's (1968) distinction (see Chapter 1) between the restricted and unrestricted sciences has been subsumed in passing under that between hard and soft knowledge areas. The correspondence deserves now to be underlined, so that it is clear that we are not required to deal with a further distinct set of categories.

Briefly, restricted knowledge has clearly defined boundaries; the problems with which it is concerned tend to be relatively narrow and circumscribed. It focuses on quantitative issues, and tends to have a well-developed theoretical structure embracing causal propositions, generalizable findings and universal laws. It is cumulative, in that new findings tend to be linear developments of the existing state of knowledge. That is to say, it shares the defining properties of hard pure knowledge identified in Chapter 1. Unrestricted knowledge has the opposite characteristics: unclear boundaries, problems which are broad in scope and loose in definition, a relatively unspecific theoretical structure, a concern with the qualitative and particular, and a reiterative pattern of enquiry. It is thus cognate with soft pure knowledge as also characterized in Chapter 1.

We have already established the sense in which convergent disciplinary communities are equivalent to tightly knit ones, and the different sense in which urban networks may also be said to be tightly knit, thus disposing of another analytically redundant set of terms. This leaves us with four basic sets of properties: hard/soft and pure/applied in the cognitive realm; convergent/divergent and urban/rural in the social. It should be noted that these properties are not only relative rather than absolute, but that their attributions may change over time and space. To give some instances, a subject which at one stage appears predominantly soft (as economics did before it became more strongly theory-orientated and mathematically sophisticated) may at a later stage seem noticeably harder; one which takes a strongly applied form in one kind of situation ('mechanical engineering' in a polytechnic) may emerge as comparatively pure elsewhere ('engineering science' in an élite research university); a disciplinary community which is identifiable at a particular moment as convergent (e.g. linguists in the 1950s) may subsequently diverge; and another (comprising, say, physicists) which looks predominantly urban in one country (the USA) may have a more rural profile in another (Latin America).

The characteristics of the four basic dimensions have been explored at various points in previous chapters. However, it may be helpful here to bring together and underline a few points of substance which have arisen in the course of the discussion, without any pretence at offering a comprehensive review. On the cognitive side, the notions of contextual imperatives and contextual associations, the first a feature of hard knowledge areas and the second of soft, proved useful in Chapters 5 and 6 in showing how the cumulative, sequential nature of hard pure knowledge limits the range of currently relevant topics and reduces the degree of explanatory preamble necessary in setting out an argument. Another way of indicating the difference is to note that in hard, restricted fields, the available methods tend to determine the choice of problems; in soft, unrestricted ones, it seems rather that the problems determine the methods.[4] A further important dichotomy, this time between the two ends of the pure/applied continuum, was identified in Chapter 7, where it was noted that pure knowledge, though increasingly vulnerable to epistemic drift, is essentially self-regulating, and that applied knowledge, though occasionally prone to academic drift, is in its nature open to external influence.

As far as social distinctions are concerned, convergence can be related to the maintenance of reasonably uniform standards and procedures, and the existence of 'intellectual control' and a 'stable elite' (Mulkay 1977; see Chapter 4). Divergent communities lack these features, tolerating a greater measure of intellectual deviance and in some cases degenerating into self-destructive disputation. In contrast, the defining feature of the rural/urban dimension, as delineated in Chapter 5, is the people-to-problem ratio: the number of researchers engaged at any one time on a particular problem or constellation of problems. Urban researchers tend to occupy a narrow area of intellectual territory and to cluster round a limited number of discrete topics which appear amenable to short-term solutions. Their rural counterparts span a broader area, across which problems are thinly scattered and within which they are not sharply distinguished: articulating the solutions to such problems is often a lengthy business.

The purpose of elaborating these distinctions is two-fold. First, it draws attention to the range and variety of academic activity and to certain systematic differences relating to that activity. Secondly, it provides an analytical framework for exploring the connections between the epistemological attributes of subjects and segments and the sociological properties of disciplinary communities and networks.

Applying the taxonomy

The conceptual scaffolding which was earlier put in place has served its purpose, and may therefore be dispensed with. Having made the necessary theoretical distinctions between hardness and softness, and purity and application, as related to the cognitive aspects of disciplines and specialisms, and convergence and divergence, and urban and rural research styles, as related to their social aspects, it is no longer necessary to preserve the figurative boundary, erected as an expository device, between subjects and segments on the one hand and disciplinary communities and networks on the other. Now that the two sets of entities have been shown as logically separable in analysis, their factual interconnections can be more rigorously explored in synthesis.

From this point onwards, therefore, we shall refer directly (and quite properly) to disciplines and specialisms as combining within their essential natures both epistemological and sociological aspects, and will use the conjunction to identify the nature of the links between the two. The first move towards this end will be to apply our four-dimensional taxonomy to the 12 individual disciplines which have formed the main subject of our investigation and to some of their component specialisms (the exercise has of course to be seen as one conducted within the context of leading research departments, related to a particular point in history, and carried out at a fairly high level of generality).

Along the hard/soft dimension, physics, chemistry, pharmacy and mathematics are predominantly hard; biology and mechanical engineering less evidently so. Economics and geography may be classed as borderline disciplines on the other side of the divide; history, modern languages, sociology and law lie firmly at the soft end of the scale. But we have noted, in passing, that there are also physicists who study the more complex and far from clear-cut areas of the subject such as meteorology and cosmology, and a number of applied branches which lack the conceptual sharpness and mathematical underpinning that would characterize them as unequivocally hard knowledge areas. Demographic and economic history are relatively hard branches of their discipline; modern languages embraces the harder areas of textual analysis and classical philology alongside critical theory and other soft specialisms. Within those disciplines which occupy the middle ground – biology and economics among them – one similarly finds a mixture of hard and soft elements (microbiology as against ecology; macroeconomics as against developmental economics).

At the disciplinary level, only 3 of our 12 disciplines (engineering, pharmacy and law) can readily be classed as applied: the other 9 are predominantly pure. But a number of the latter include areas of application, just as certain applied subjects contain relatively pure elements. Chemistry, for example, comprises not only the pure field of physical chemistry but also synthetic organic chemistry, which has numerous commercial applications. Economics is concerned not only with mathematical theory but also with industrial organization. Similarly, mechanical engineering has areas of overlap with physics, especially in its more theoretical aspects. And in academic law, the study of jurisprudence represents a pure component, whereas family law is nothing if not applied.

Turning to the social aspects, it is evident that some disciplines enjoy a high level of convergence. The most obvious perhaps is physics, where the sense of commonality is powerful in spite of the existence of numerous and sometimes mutually incomprehensible specialisms. My respondents in the subject commented on an overriding sense of collective kinship, a mutuality of interests, a shared intellectual style, a consensual understanding of 'profound simplicities', and even 'a quasi-religious belief in the unity of nature'. It is not easy to doubt that physicists share a particular way of approaching problems, a collective ideology and even a common world view.

History, for very different reasons, may also be classed as a convergent discipline. Its diversity of coverage is much greater than that of physics, in that its subject matter knows few restrictions. It is not characterized by any dominating conceptual structure, nor by any strongly developed techniques or methods of enquiry (indeed, historians tend to describe their discipline as a craft, to assert that it is 'rooted in evidence, not based on theories', and to comment that 'history has sources but no methods'). None the less, there is, as among physicists, a sense of inhabiting 'a particular and definable world', a sharing of 'common assumptions and styles of thought', and a strong tradition of intellectual kinship. 'Most historians', said one, 'see themselves as part of the same fraternity'; more historians used the phrase 'community of scholars' than did respondents in any other discipline.

Two other strong candidates for convergence among the 12 disciplines which formed the basis of this study are mathematics and economics. The former is characterized by its practitioners as having 'common modes of discourse'; universal agreement on 'the notions of proof and definition, and on the criteria for acceptability'; and 'the need for a special talent'. The latter, economics, embodies 'a clear consensus about method and judgement', 'a common basic training', and a sharing of 'the same fundamental principles'.

There are 3 of our 12 areas of enquiry which can be seen as occupying the intermediate ground between the convergent and the divergent. One of these is law, another chemistry, and the third biology. What disables academic lawyers from unequivocally convergent status is a continuing dispute about the nature of the subject. Although they have 'the same basic intellectual knowhow', 'a common core of technique', 'a shared data base', and 'the same forms of thought and rules in formulating arguments', they are none the less divided in their views about whether law departments ought to concentrate on the content of their subject (black letter law), or should aim to place it in its social context (the socio-legal approach), or indeed to view it from a predominantly sociological perspective (the sociology of law movement).[5] This uncertainty over what the discipline is or ought to be makes it inappropriate to categorize academic law as a highly convergent field. Biologists convey a similar ambiguity. They are 'very heterogeneous'; in particular, there is 'a mutual antagonism' between those who study structures and processes and those whose concern is with organisms or communities. But the subject is not prone to 'deep and permanent divisions'; there is 'more intellectual unity than the structural diversity of the subject suggests'. Again, chemists have 'many shared assumptions, and a common basis in the study of molecules', but it is 'hard to think of it as a unified discipline'. Chemists 'tend to cut each other down', and 'slanging is more common among chemists than among other scientists': 'When under attack, chemists draw their wagons into a circle, and then start firing into the middle. People tend to be highly critical of each other, rather than supportive. They don't hang together, because the field itself is so fragmented.' So chemistry too has to be located some way towards the divergent end of the scale.

This categorization leaves 5 divergent disciplines among the original 12. The collective identity of mechanical engineers suffers from their being diffused across a wide field and lacking a central core of theory. On their own testimony, 'We don't have a corporate image or a collective view, and we don't close our ranks'; and 'there is envy and a competition among engineers which physicists don't have'. In applications for grant funds, mechanical engineers 'can't get their act together in the way the physicists do'. Sociology is seen as fissiparous and fragmented: 'in so far as it is a family, it is a fractious family'. It is 'a discipline with not much unity or much agreement on perspectives and problems': one might even say, as two sociologists I interviewed (one English, one American) did: 'it is not really a discipline'. Its lack of candidature for convergent status is borne out by references in the literature: 'Sociology is a multiple paradigm science' (Ritzer 1975, 1979, 1980); 'The attempts to order sociology by ideology and by paradigm compound its confusions' (Martindale 1979). Modern languages might be designated as a cluster of related disciplines, rather than a single unity, but it is arguable that each of its constituent communities is split, not only between literary critics and linguistic scholars, but also within the former between advocates of conflicting theories – the psychoanalytic approach, deconstruction, structuralism, and the like. Against this background, no sense emerged from the interviews of any commonality of intellectual perspective or any closely shared set of disciplinary values. Finally, geographers and pharmacists identify themselves as 'highly multidisciplinary', having numerous overlaps with neighbouring subject groups and a heterogeneous set of professional concerns. Papers in these two fields frequently appear in the journals of other disciplines, with the result that the journals dedicated to their own disciplines tend to be weakly supported and lacking in prestige. Accordingly, it seems reasonable to categorize geography and pharmacy, alongside mechanical engineering, sociology and modern languages, as instances of divergence.

We come, finally, to the urban/rural dimension. It is a curiosity that, although much of the writing in the sociology of science has focused on urban research activity, its actual incidence in the academic workplace is quite limited. The only discipline in my sample which could be designated as substantially urban in research style is physics. Outside that sample, biochemistry may offer another case in point. Chemistry, contrary perhaps to its external image, must be classified as rural in its aggregate make-up: it is uncommon for researchers to compete in 'a fight for the finish'; publication delays can be quite lengthy in most subdisciplines, and the circulation of preprints is noticeably less prevalent than in physics; laboratory investigation 'doesn't involve expensive machines, experiments on a large scale, or collaboration in a global sense'; and the community 'thinks small – it is a cottage industry'. Some groups of mathematicians meet the criteria of general gregariousness and occasional disputes over priority, but the pressure for publication is not high, the choice of problems at any given time usually rather wide, and the people-to-problem ratio is normally rather low. Across the landscape as a whole, urban research can be seen to take place only in scattered pockets, engaging a few networks within the confines of a limited number of disciplinary communities (microbiologists; control engineers; a number of specialties in pharmacy and more generally in biomedical science). There are few if any urban groupings to be found in history, modern languages, economics, sociology, geography or academic law.

Connections between categories

This venture in labelling need not be seen as an end in itself. It can be put to good purpose in helping us to identify some of the significant, if only partial, interconnections between cognitive and social characteristics. To take a fairly evident trend revealed in the course of the exercise, it would appear that instances of urban research are to be found exclusively in hard – and predominantly in hard pure – knowledge fields. This is not surprising, in that it is in such fields that the research front is sufficiently narrow and the problems sharply defined enough to encourage academics to cluster round a limited area of intellectual territory.[6] As we have noted, however, only a subsection of hard specialisms generates an urban style of research; others are rural, or at best suburban, because the possible themes of enquiry are numerous, the extent of overlap between individual research interests is small and the publication delays are long.

One might expect this link at the level of segments and networks to be reflected in a similar relationship between the degree of convergence of disciplinary communities and the cognitive attributes of academic subjects. It would seem probable that tightly knit, cohesive academic clans would be promoted by the shared study of a restricted, densely structured and clearly bounded area of knowledge; equally, one might regard subject areas with these characteristics as reflecting the shared definitions imposed by tightly knit academic groups. By the same reasoning, loosely knit communities would seem to be the likeliest products – or producers – of an unrestricted, incohate and relatively permeable disciplinary field. However, the correspondence here is not as close in practice as it might promise to be in principle. As we have seen, some predominantly hard disciplines (physics, mathematics) enjoy a high degree of convergence, and most soft ones (modern languages, sociology, law) a low one; biology occupies an intermediate position on both scales; and the match for geography and economics is perhaps near enough. But the two hard applied disciplines in the sample (mechanical engineering and pharmacy) are misfits. So, noticeably, are chemistry and history; the former as a hard pure but relatively divergent subject and the second as a soft pure but convergent one.

Two possible reasons for these anomalies are that external influences operate, especially in areas with numerous applications, to loosen the ties between communities and the forms of knowledge they study; and that the cognitive properties of disciplines are in any case no more than aggregations of their epistemologically heterogeneous specialisms. Applied subjects, both hard and soft, are, as we have noted in Chapter 7, particularly amenable to outside intervention, and appear liable accordingly to lack the sense of collectivity that convergence requires.[7] Further special considerations apply to chemistry and history. In the case of the former, the coherence of its disciplinary community may be weakened both by its sizeable dependence on industrial sponsorship and by the highly atomistic and fragmentary character of its subject matter. History, though epistemologically soft, seems in an apparently paradoxical way to have achieved its convergent status by virtue of its very open-endedness, all-embracing catholicity of coverage and relative absence of theoretical divisions (in that it manages to remain largely atheoretical).

The visceral, complex connections at a very general level between knowledge forms and knowledge communities are reinforced by many linkages of a more limited and specific kind. Previous chapters have identified two main types of association: those which bear on the collective activities of academics and those which affect them as individuals. Among the first, we have noted differences in the validation process associated with particular knowledge areas, together with variations in the degree of importance attached to refereeing and citation; diversities in the ways in which reputations are established, disciplinary élites are identified, eminence recognized and power exploited; contrasts in the sources of, and shapes taken by, intellectual fashion in different domains of enquiry; and distinctions in the impact made by radically new ideas. We have also observed systematic deviations in language and style, modes of competitiveness, the nature and incidence of collaboration and the consequences of controversy. In terms of individual experience, as against group behaviour, we have been able to identify characteristic divergences in recruitment and initiation, choice of specialisms, form of doctoral supervision, mobility between research fields, peaking in productivity and achievement, and intensity of involvement in work. In Chapter 7, it was suggested that the interplay between academic communities and their external environment also follows disparate patterns in one cognitive context as against another.

Such considerations, taken together, seem to offer a fair degree of support to the thesis that fields of enquiry and academic cultures are closely interconnected. A study of the research literature suggests that the significance of the bonding between the two has been underplayed in previous investigations of epistemological and social issues in academia.

A further note on status

Even if it is conceded that there are more densely woven and more systematically patterned ligaments connecting forms and communities of knowledge that has hitherto been supposed, and that a closer examination of them may help to enhance our understanding of the physiology of the academic enterprise, there remains a legitimate question to be answered. What, it may be asked, follows from all this? Does the investigation analysis and argument which has gone into the attempt to establish the nature and extent of such relationships amount to anything other than an elaborate intellectual exercise; is it any better than a mere conceptual crossword puzzle whose solution has no consequences of real consequence? I can do no more than sketch an answer here, beginning with a further consideration of the issue of intellectual status and going on briefly to explore some of the implications of diversity.

The disparities which have been identified within subjects and segments, disciplinary communities and networks have significant effects on judgements of academic quality, and in particular on the standing accorded to disciplines and specialisms in virtue of their epistemological and sociological attributes. This is a matter of some practical concern. Higher education is suffused with considerations of value and almost obsessively taken up with the identification of excellence; grading of a more or less rarified kind is endemic. The placing of both knowledge fields and those that profess them in a finely tuned order of merit has to be recognized as contributing to a much wider process of appraisal, a process which stretches all the way from the ranking of academic institutions to the classification of students' work.

The degree of convergence of a discipline, for example, has evident political implications. Convergent communities are favourably placed to advance their collective interests (since they know what their collective interests are, and enjoy a clear sense of unity in promoting them), if necessary at the expense of other, less fortunately endowed groups of colleagues.[8] They also tend to command the respect, admiration and envy of divergent disciplinary communities, and thus to be identified as members of the academic élite. To reinforce their advantages, they are further liable to be regarded by viewers outside the academic world as having privileged status. Thus physicists, historians, mathematicians and economists (among other élite groups, such as medical academics, outside the present sample) are in a position to enjoy considerable power both within the intellectual sphere and beyond its boundaries. Conversely, disciplines at the opposite end of the convergent/divergent spectrum are seen internally as politically weak and externally as lacking in good intellectual standing. This perception is heightened if one of the disciplines in question allows a domestic quarrel to erupt into public view (as happened in Britain in the early 1980s in relation to English literature): at that point, there may well be a damaging loss of both academic and public credibility.

At the level of individual specialisms, there is a finer set of distinctions to be made. As noted in Chapters 4, and 7, the most favoured specialisms are those that are pure; not only pure but hard, and not only hard but urban. In other words, good standing accrues on each scale at the end which emphasizes the theoretical, the quantitative and the sharply defined. This of course leaves a wide scatter of areas of enquiry which have a reasonably high reputation because they meet a significant proportion of such requirements. Examples from different fields might include theoretical welfare economics, demographic history, fluid dynamics and physical chemistry. Other areas, because of their particular constellation of properties, seem doomed to a place relatively far down the academic pecking order. Thus food chemistry, plant physiology, regional geography, social psychology, literary history, alongside many other specialisms in the chemical, biological and social sciences and the humanities, tend to be given a lower intellectual rating than their practitioners might find acceptable, because they do not meet sufficiently the favoured criteria: hardness, purity and an urban research style.

As with many exercises in social discrimination, this one is to some degree dependent on wider national values. Britain (see Chapter 7) is held to be peculiarly subject to anti-utilitarian snobbery, to the extent that the British intelligentsia has traditionally downgraded socially relevant technologies such as pharmacy and engineering – though medical science, perhaps because of its apparently convergent status, enjoys considerable prestige. The general climate in Continental Europe and the United States seems more favourable to hard applied subjects at least, but there remains a common tendency for practitioners in fields which are academically well-entrenched and established to look sideways at soft applied researchers (those in public administration, social work, education and the like) because their disciplines are viewed as lacking in proper rigour.[9]

It would seem in some respects unfair that – in large part because of the intrinsic nature of their subject matter – certain academic communities are able to exploit their social and cognitive advantages while others – perhaps through no fault of their own – are not. After all, even the stigmas associated with factionalism and family disputes often appear to be a consequence of what the underlying knowledge base is like (for instance, biology is perhaps necessarily divided between the study of systems and a concern with whole organisms, modern languages between linguistic research and literary scholarship, and geography between investigations of physical and social phenomena). To those denied it, the ascription of privilege may seem like that of class in England or of caste in India – simply a characteristic feature of the academic scene, having no necessary connection with either merit or worth, but none the less enabling the chosen groups to enjoy superiority and command deference. Those who are so privileged would doubtless reply that their subjects are intellectually more than usually demanding, call for a particular clarity of thought and expression and, because they impose clear and unequivocal criteria of merit, exercise a firm control on quality. (In contrast, as one mechanical engineer remarked, 'engineering is more pedestrian and there are less breakthroughs – the signs of brilliance are less pronounced and less evident'.)

It is not surprising in the circumstances that groups of academics in disciplines lacking high prestige have occasionally initiated reforms designed to increase the degree of hardness of certain specialisms and (it may be hoped), in association with this, the degree of convergence of their community as a whole. To take a few cases in point, a coterie of behavioural psychologists, in the early decades after the Second World War, set out to develop highly quantitative techniques in an effort to create a science of behaviour based on mathematical models. Similarly, advocates of the 'new geography' in the early 1960s argued that the adoption of numerical approaches would help to push the subject 'back into the mainstream of scientific method' (Slaymaker 1968, quoted in Goodson 1983). At one stage in the development of political science, 'The use of statistical methods became more complex and sophisticated, mathematical and quasi-mathematical formulations were frequently used, and vocabularies became increasingly technical and esoteric' (Waldo 1975, quoted in Ruscio 1986). In none of these instances did the revolution take hold sufficiently to create a new disciplinary image, because, it could be argued, the knowledge domain in question was not in essence sufficiently amenable to the imposition of the techniques and methods of hard science. 'Academic drift' (see Chapter 7) none the less continues to exercise a strong attraction for those who are too low in the pecking order for their own comfort.

Diversity and its consequences

Although one of the central purposes of my research has been to emphasize the existence and to begin to identify the nature of the connections between fields of study and those who work in them, it has (like many such investigations) had other incidental outcomes. In particular, the examination of both the cognitive and social aspects of intellectual enquiry has highlighted a remarkable diversity in the activities that go to make up the academic enterprise. Knowledge areas, professional networks and individual career patterns can be classified, and operationally distinguished one from another, in a multiplicity of different ways. On this reading, it would seem that variety is not merely the spice but the very essence of scholarly life.

In so far as the distinctions are accepted as observational realities rather than theoretical artefacts, they can be argued to have significant implications for the management of higher education and the policies of individual institutions within it. The current political trends within many, if not most, national systems reflect a concern to tidy up and rationalize – to render both more efficient and more economical – what is seen, in organizational terms, as a ramshackle and unnecessarily Byzantine structure. These sentiments are understandable in the light of the massive growth of post-secondary provision witnessed in most countries inside a single generation, the accompanying escalation in costs, and the coincidental pressures of worldwide economic recession. They have, however, tended to be given expression through the adoption of a somewhat naïve view of higher education itself. It appears to have been derived from the conventional stereotype of an urban research community whose activities are conducted on a sizeable scale, based on well-organized teams, highly competitive one with another, and heavily dependent on external funding from industry and government. It is consequent on this interpretation that any academic department that does not measure up to such requirements is too small to be viable, managed in an amateurish fashion, insufficiently motivated to earn its keep within the ranks of the intellectual élite, and undeserving of resources for anything other than undergraduate teaching.

The implications of such a perspective sit uneasily with the actualities of current practice, as a number of previous studies have emphasized. For example, Lodahl and Gordon (1972) noted that their findings:

> strongly argue against some current tendencies to view university problems in terms that are too simple to match the demands of technology and the associated realities of attitudes and activities found within scientific disciplines. Our results seem to indicate that there are differences between disciplines that go to the heart of teaching, research, and student–faculty relationships.

Biglan (1973b), in similar vein, issued a warning that:

> any attempt at universal standards for academia will impose a uniformity of activity and output which is inconsistent with the particular subject matter requirements of specific areas.

To pursue these considerations in the light of the present study, it must first be remarked that a large majority of academic departments are expected to maintain teaching programmes across a wide spectrum of the subject areas they represent. This means that, unless they are relatively large, their staffing policies have to be geared to the provision of several different specialisms, and hence that their academic membership can usually include no more than one or two people within any given specialism. There is, in other words, seldom a critical mass of researchers with cognate interests, such as would make it easy for departmentally based research teams to be established, let alone to make an identifiable impact.[10] There are some obvious exceptions to this generalization. Some departments, for instance, manage to build up viable (if unstable) research groups through the recruitment, on grant funds, of doctoral students and postdoctoral fellows. Others consciously narrow their undergraduate programmes, cutting out whole areas of the subject concerned, in order to concentrate research as well as teaching effort within a limited number of fields. And quite large departments are able to operate on a generous enough scale to build up areas of research specialization within their tenured faculty while still maintaining a broad teaching provision. The difficulty is also ameliorated by the fact that some academics are involved in more than one research field at any given time and many teach in more than one topic area.

Even so, the overall picture is of academic institutions made up of basic organizational units whose constituent faculty members have relatively little mutuality of research interest. Given that different categories of specialism (pure and applied, hard and soft, urban and rural) may well coexist within the confines of a single small department, it also follows that there must be several distinct career patterns, reputation-building strategies, forms of external relationship, and the like. From this perspective, departments have indeed a noticeable resemblance to holding companies for their members, much as institutions can be portrayed as holding companies for their basic units (Halsey and Trow 1971; Becher and Kogan 1980).[11]

The absence of internal research communities has more direct implications for those working in urban contexts than for their opposite numbers engaged in rural enquiries. As we have seen, they gain clear professional advantages by establishing collaborative research programmes. Accordingly, they often find it necessary to link up with colleagues who are geographically scattered (one striking example, cited in Becher 1987b, was of a co-publication by authors in Kansas, Aarhus and Calcutta). Those who are highly active will tend to identify more strongly with external colleagues in their professional networks than with internal colleagues with whom they may have much less in common. They are, in Gouldner's terms, cosmopolitans, as against the locals who remain committed to rural specialisms (Gouldner 1957).

Such observations have a bearing on the comparisons between different departments in the same institution and similar departments in different institutions. Some, as we have seen, may enjoy a higher status than their competitors for no better reason than that they are affiliated to disciplines which manifest a high degree of convergence; others, in contrast, are marked down for their lack of intellectual coherence because their parent disciplines are divergent and fragmented. Academics in convergent departments with predominantly urban characteristics are likely to accumulate more prestigious honours and awards, and a larger volume of grant funding, than those in divergent disciplines with predominantly rural research patterns. Departments with a preponderance of urban researchers will often enjoy a reputation for higher productivity than departments in the same field with a majority of rural researchers, even though the output of the latter may be well above average for their particular spread of specialisms, and the output of the former may in their context be substantially below average. There is no *intrinsic* scholarly merit in hard as opposed to soft, urban as opposed to rural, or pure as opposed to applied, research: yet 'objective' criteria – at least those of a strictly academic, rather than an entrepreneurial kind – will tend to favour the first of each of these categories because they seem to lend themselves to simple and uncontentious measurement as against complex and contestable judgement.

Individual academics differ in comparable ways, according to their type of specialization. Those in urban networks, because of the greater intensity of their involvement in their research, may appear to be more hard working and more dedicated than their colleagues with rural life-styles. They are also likely to be well placed in their ability to earn outside funds and in the frequency of their publication. These are basic criteria for determining academic worth and eligibility for promotion: as in a number of other respects, urban researchers are liable to be favoured at the expense of rural ones if such yardsticks are too literally and crudely applied.

These arguments suggest that it is unjust and inappropriate to lump together for administrative purposes different institutions, different subject departments and different individuals, taking little or no account of the variety of characteristics which they may between them quite reasonably display. Bureaucratically inspired measures of performance, which may be seen as one by-product of a demand for efficiency and accountability in higher education, offer a striking instance of this tendency. They are typically designed for imposition with equally blind impartiality across the whole range of academic endeavour. But however carefully chosen the individual criteria which make up such composite instruments may be, it is not difficult to demonstrate the unevenness of their application and their varying relevance to different subject fields. An example may serve to illustrate the point.

Consider an agency for academic management which chooses to allocate resources to departments on the basis of the following mixture of internalist and externalist requirements: the annual level of outside research funding; the volume of refereed research publications (which, together with research funding, is likely to have some correlation with postgraduate student numbers); the ability – suitably quantified – to recruit good undergraduate students (which is likely to be linked to the staff–student ratio); and the subsequent employment statistics of those who have graduated. Each of these seems a perfectly reasonable measure of departmental competence. It may be useful to see what ratings, taken together, they are likely to yield for departments commonly held to be of good academic standing in four different disciplinary areas – physics, history, engineering and law.

Even the best physics departments, in the present context, have a relatively poor undergraduate recruitment (and a correspondingly low staff–student ratio), related, it is often said, to deficiencies in secondary schooling. The employment prospects for their graduates, according to recent statistics, are not particularly outstanding. They promise to come out well, however, on research grants and on refereed publications. Prestigious history departments will almost certainly do well on undergraduate recruitment (and on staff–student ratios), relatively poorly on graduate employment, only moderately well on publication (at least, in comparison with physics; see Chapter 5) and very poorly on grant earnings. The profiles of leading engineering departments are likely to be different again: a reasonably high level of outside funding, a modest publication record (coupled with a dearth of postgraduates), a comparatively weak calibre of undergraduate student, but excellent employment prospects. Law departments of high standing are destined to offer an equally patchy performance, doing well only in those areas in which physics departments do badly, and badly in areas in which they do well: healthy recruitment, good employment statistics, negligible grant funding and a poor publication record (together with few postgraduate students).

There are bound to be inherent limitations in any attempt to apply such quasi-objective 'performance indicators' to an organization as complex and diverse as a university. The persistence with which central funding bodies, and sometimes university bureaucracies themselves, espouse such simplistic devices may arise as much from a desire to appear to be fair and unbiased as from a less scrupulous wish to make managerial life easier. But once any recognition is allowed to the need to disaggregate the component elements in the organization, and to consider them in their particularity, rules of thumb of this kind must none the less be seen as totally inappropriate.

Nor do the considerations advanced earlier make it seem any more reasonable, despite its evident administrative attractions, to attempt to simplify and streamline the criteria for career progress within the institution as a whole: the distinctions between individuals' activities are sufficiently diverse to require some degree of subtlety, flexibility and openness alike in initial appointment, granting of tenure and promotion to higher rank.

A more fitting strategy for the assessment of academic worth would call for the detailed and reasonably sensitive case-by-case approach adopted in English common law, as against the rule-bound features generally held to be more appropriate in criminal proceedings. That is to say, it would almost certainly be the wisest policy to make do with the familiar system of peer group judgement whose inadequacies (see Chapter 4) are well acknowledged, but whose overwhelming advantage lies in its responsiveness to the variety and idiosyncrasy of all that counts as a legitimate form of intellectual endeavour.

In summary, it can be argued that a horticultural analogy is more appropriate than an industrial one in the advancement of learning. A market garden is successful in so far as it cultivates a variety of produce to meet its clients' disparate needs. To drive a bulldozer through it in the interests of greater efficiency and higher productivity makes sense only if one wishes to transform it into a cornfield. Corn grows easily, but too assiduous a concentration on producing it will – as we now know to our cost – create a massive and useless surplus of one particular commodity, and a corresponding scarcity of those whose cultivation, though beneficial in its own right, happens to be more demanding, more labour-intensive, and generally less easy to govern.

The case for autonomy

The imposition of managerialist values is not the only threat which academia faces. The discussion in Chapter 7 highlighted the extent to which research communities form part of a wider social environment upon whose support they depend and to whose interests they are accordingly required to subscribe. Such obligations pose a problem whose resolution can differ in practice between one country and another and between one historical period and the next. The problem, however, is perennial, and the tension to which it gives rise inevitable. 'This tension in the political or policy sphere', Elzinga (1987b) writes, 'between utility and freedom, between steering and serendipity, runs parallel to the tension in the economic sphere between bounded resources and unbounded needs in research and development.'

Many commentators agree that the inroads on academic autonomy have increased significantly in recent years: but from a historical perspective (as Rothblatt 1985 demonstrates), the scope for outside intervention has been there from the earliest establishment of the academic profession. The role of those from whom the wherewithal comes – the direct agencies of government, the quasi-independent research councils, the independent grant-awarding foundations and the commercial and industrial sponsors concerned to buy knowledge and know-how – is crucial, and can be argued to carry certain moral obligations to preserve the integrity of the intellectual enterprise. Gibbons (1985) refers to 'the fear that, as a commodity, science will be manipulated for their own ends by those who allocate resources for research', adding that 'Given the economic and military potential of contemporary scientific knowledge, such manipulation cannot be regarded with equanimity.'

Leaving aside the issues which bear with particular insistence on hard pure knowledge, many other aspects of academic life have been affected by 'the trend towards more centralized bureaucratic control . . . accompanied by greater emphasis on socially determined research objectives' (Geiger 1985). The considerations advanced in the previous chapter suggest, moreover, that 'grassroots movements' and professional lobbies may also attempt to shape the direction, and sometimes to censor or suppress the outcomes, of research: government and 'the military–industrial complex' are not alone in their concern to harness academic activity to suit their sectional interests.

The more narrowly functional the intellectual climate becomes, the greater the danger that 'The less seemingly applicable sciences, zoology, animal behaviour, plant physiology, or entomology – all fields which have made significant contributions to knowledge – could be permanently shrunk with little likelihood of attracting gifted young scientists' (Zinberg 1985). The relatively inexpensive disciplines outside science, however well they are regarded, may run the risk of similar impoverishment, as Kogan's (1987) study of history departments in contemporary British higher education underlines.

Developments of this kind lead inevitably to a defensive concern that something must be allowed to survive in the way of enquiry which is not blatantly the creature of outside circumstance. But the more emotive arguments – the appeals to the time-worn principles of academic freedom, the dire warnings of a crisis of civilized values – are unlikely to cut much ice among those enemies of an enlightened culture who were long ago pilloried by Matthew Arnold as barbarians and philistines. As Rothblatt (1985) realistically acknowledges, even 'the historic argument on behalf of pure science, namely, that it will one day result in applied science and technology, is largely unproven'.

How, then, can the case for preserving some necessary measure of academic autonomy be most effectively deployed? One of the physicists I interviewed was emphatic in his acknowledgement that society, acting through the government funding agencies, had an absolute right to channel research in the directions it considered most appropriate. He was equally clear that it was counterproductive for this right to be exercised, in that to do so could eventually undermine the very foundations from which intellectual enquiry drew its stability and strength. The government, he contended, would best serve the interests of the public by facilitating basic research while minimizing attempts to direct it.

Geiger (1985) argues in essentially similar vein:

> reliance upon the internal mechanisms of science and the scientific community would ultimately be more conducive to furthering constructive types of adaptation. The essential work of science – hypothesising, testing, challenging, and reinterpreting knowledge – imports an inherent dynamic to its cognitive foundations. The basic institutional resources for the organization and funding of university research, then, ought to be designed insofar as possible to complement and facilitate the natural processes of adaptation and change that are continually at work in science. In the final analysis only such an approach seems capable of coping with the inescapable uncertainties that the future most certainly holds.

The argument from unpredictability is one cogent line of attack on instrumentalism, since even applied research is not immune from an uncertainty of means, if not of ends in view. However well-formulated its goals, the intellectual understanding that may be needed before those goals can be achieved is not so easily legislated in advance.

Another powerful rationale can be developed in terms of the inherent authority of specialized knowledge. As Rothblatt (1985) reminds us, too liberal a degree of outside involvement in the determination of research activity serves to undermine academics' professional expertise, posing:

> challenges in the way in which they govern themselves, ask questions, decide the research agenda, identify and reward success. . . . Once the authority of the expert is rejected, standards are difficult to establish. There is no arbiter to distinguish the degree of scientific achievement.

A different, if equally dangerous, limitation may be imposed by outside interests on those areas of knowledge predominantly concerned with human affairs. The freedom to question established values is not the sole prerogative of centres of learning, though that may be strongly implied in some of the more high-minded discussions of the role of the university.[12] A spirit of free intellectual enquiry would none the less seem an essential ingredient of any society which aspires to the virtues of democracy, and needs for that reason to be judiciously preserved. Social and political pressures, if allowed too easily to exert themselves, can have the effect of stifling critical discussion, especially in those areas of the humanities and social sciences which lend themselves to challenging received orthodoxy. For politicians in power to be able readily to command that particular academic departments should be open to external inspection, because they have been alleged to display 'Marxist bias', is not an unimaginably long step away from giving sanction to the infamous purges associated with Senator McCarthy in the early postwar years in the USA; nor, of course, to those of a different colour, but an even more devastating kind, perpetrated by the Stalinist regime in the USSR.

Elzinga (1987a) succinctly sums up the position in relation to academic knowledge as a whole: 'The principle of autonomy cannot be ditched; on the contrary, strong relevance and accountability pressures . . . must be met with increased consciousness concerning the internalist mechanisms for quality control in the knowledge process.' He goes on to remark that:

> Arguments for autonomy may be based on (a) moral principles such as the need for critical research potential; (b) pragmatic principles that stipulate how good research results are only forthcoming if quality control criteria are upheld; and (c) epistemological claims concerning internal regulatives and their characteristic status of independent variables determining the attitudes . . . towards external orientation, be it under pressure of sectoral policies, commercialisation or medial penetration. The third type of argument if it can be developed is a very strong argument for autonomy.

It is the establishment of this 'third type of argument' which I would take to be one of the main outcomes of my enquiries. Much as it can be shown that ecological environments establish a homeostasis which may be disrupted in quite unanticipated ways by external intervention, so too it can be argued that cultural systems depend on a delicate mutual adjustment of interests which, if insensitively encroached upon, can result in their disintegration. I have sought to show that the ideals and the practices of academic communities are intimately bound up with the nature of the knowledge they pursue. On the social dimension, too forceful a super-imposition of the extrinsic values of accountability and relevance on the intrinsic values of reputation-seeking and quality control by peer group judgement can only lead to intellectual subservience, and thence to academic sterility. On the cognitive side of the equation, knowledge itself, viewed as a cultural resource, demands good husbandry and steady replenishment. It cannot, except in the short term, be constantly subjected to the stripping of its more marketable assets or the repression of the more challenging insights that it yields.

Mutual understandings and common causes

In an effort to preserve even a modest degree of intellectual integrity the enemy within should not remain unnoticed. Barnett (1988) underlines the danger of internal rivalry and dissension, pointing to 'a fairly unprincipled struggle' between competing interest groups, 'particularly evident at times of institutional threat but present all the time nevertheless'. In consequence, because the professional identity of academics 'lies with their own discipline, there is a general failure to notice those larger threats to academic freedom which affect the academic community as a whole'.

Barnett goes on to suggest that it is 'the fragmentation of the academic community into discrete disciplinary sub-cultures' which is to blame for 'reducing the internal sense of community across academic fields'. If he is right in his diagnosis, the condition would seem to have no easy remedy. The argument in the preceding pages has implied that knowledge has its own internal dynamic, and one which seems to demand an increasing level of specificity and specialization as enquiry proceeds. It is not so much an ingrained wilfulness that drives academics into exploring the deep and narrow parts of the territory they inhabit, but rather that – even if its boundaries are always subject to change, and new perspectives on it may occasionally be discerned – the broader, more open landscape is already well mapped.

It was suggested in Chapter 1 that knowledge is itself diverse and disparate, and in Chapter 3 that its piecemeal character gives rise to the very fragmentation of which Barnett complains. Clark (1983) rounds off his notable conspectus of the world of learning with a similar conclusion:

> It is around the formidable array of specific subjects and their self-generating and autonomous tendencies that higher education becomes something unique, to be first understood in its own terms. . . . Knowledge will remain a divided and imperfect substance. In its fissions and faults we come closest to a root cause of the many odd ways of the higher education system.

But Clark also remarks, in the course of his account, that all academics 'are part of a single "community of scholars", sharing an interest that sets them apart from others'. And Bailey (1977) reminds us that, from an anthropological perspective, the notion of group identity is context-dependent: what looks from one standpoint to be 'an arena of disputing factions' can be seen from another as 'a single culture which directs interactions between the many distinct and often mutually hostile groups'. He writes, too, of 'that sense of likeness with other members of the [academic] community and difference from outsiders, empirically present and not to be ignored', and of the 'community of culture . . . the whole set of tribes possess in common'.

The problem remains of how to bridge the evident divisions and thus to promote that recognition of commonality which seems essential to the maintenance of some measure of collective independence. Another anthropologist, in advocating 'an ethnography of the disciplines', has sketched the outlines of a possible solution:

> The problem of the integration of cultural life becomes one of making it possible for people inhabiting different worlds to have a genuine, and reciprocal, impact upon one another . . . the first step is surely to accept the depth of the differences; the second to understand what these differences are; and the third to construct some sort of vocabulary in which they can be publicly formulated (Geertz 1983).

It is primarily towards taking the first and second of those steps that the present enquiry has been directed. Paradoxically, the more it becomes necessary to recognize the academic scene as disjointed and compartmentalized, the more essential it becomes to turn towards an apprehension of that scene in its entirety. The tribes, after all, share the same ethnicity; the territories they occupy are part of the same land mass.

If this, and other studies of its kind, can begin to succeed in constructing 'some sort of vocabulary' which enables academics in different fields better to understand each other – and hence perhaps to enhance their appreciation of their own particular share of the enterprise – it may be hoped that further benefits would ensue. An enhanced recognition of mutuality could serve as a better defence against the intrusive managerialism which seeks to impose a crude form of accountability, based on false assumptions about the nature of intellectual endeavour, and bolstered by insensitive and often spurious 'indicators of performance'. It might even help to persuade the wider society, on whose patronage the pursuit of knowledge ultimately depends, to maintain for academics a reasonable liberty – if one which remains well short of license – in their choice of what to study and how to study it.

Notes

1 It might be added that (as Khun's 1962 analysis has shown) the more universal a theory appears to be, the more vulnerable it is in the long run to contradictory evidence. Explanations which are generated from, and are firmly grounded in, a broad span of empirical data are less likely to be toppled; but only at the expense, in Kuhn's terms, of failing to present a sufficiently clear paradigm to allow for revolutionary conflict.

2 The convergent–divergent distinction is comparable along the social dimension (as is the hard–soft distinction along the cognitive dimension) with Kuhn's (1962, 1970) contrast between paradigmatic and pre-paradigmatic disciplines; and, following him, the dichotomy marked by Lodahl and Gordon (1972)

between high and low levels of paradigm development. However, since these authors elide the social and cognitive aspects, their analysis implies that all hard disciplines are necessarily convergent (and vice versa) and all soft disciplines necessarily divergent (and vice versa). And this, as will shortly be argued, is a misleading simplification, since it allows no scope for convergent communities to be associated with soft knowledge and divergent with hard. Hence the avoidance, in this chapter, of references to paradigmatic status.

3 The point is not an easy one to make with clarity, and perhaps deserves elaboration. There are some countries which possess a unified national ideology, or at least a sentiment of shared identity of a kind which others do not. This is sometimes the case even when there are strongly marked internal divisions (linguistic, tribal, ethnic, political, religious, or a mixture of these) within the population as a whole. To take some examples, among the countries with a marked sense of nationhood, one might include Israel (with its multiplicity of political schisms) and the USA (with its polyglot population), alongside such more apparently homogeneous nations as Japan, Sweden, France, Libya or Iran. Countries which are visibly fragmented would include the Lebanon, Sri Lanka, Northern Ireland, Nicaragua, Mozambique and South Africa, together with currently peaceable countries such as Belgium, Nigeria or Cyprus (in each of which two or more historically and culturally separate groups now happen more or less successfully to coexist). In similar ways, some disciplinary communities, such as physicists and economists, may have diverse constituent networks while clearly subscribing to the same overall cultural norms; others, such as sociologists or scholars of English Literature, may seem no more internally differentiated but may none the less be lacking in collective coherence.

4 Closely comparable problems would seem a less pervasive phenomenon across epistemological boundaries than mutually applicable techniques. This leads on to the speculation that disciplinary imperialism – the invasion and attempted colonization of others' territories – is typically a product of the transferability of methods from one set of problems to another, and therefore more commonly originates from a hard than a soft knowledge base.

5 The distinctions between the latter two perspectives are neatly delineated by Campbell and Wiles (1976). Their article also provides some useful insights into the development of the social sciences in Britain in the 1960s and 1970s.

6 This observation parallels the relationship hinted at in Chapters 3 and 4 between well-defined, closed segments and cohesive networks on the one hand, and between segments with permeable boundaries and loosely knit networks on the other.

7 The suggestion here may however be an artefact of the limited representation in the sample of hard applied disciplines. Further investigation might, I suspect, accord convergence to academic medicine, accountancy, and perhaps to others among the technical professions.

8 In a remark tinged with envy, one of the botanists I interviewed commented, 'The unity of biochemistry is a useful slogan, which has helped the subject to advance.'

9 As an interesting sidelight on the issue of socio-academic status, it would seem that lower-ranking and applied disciplines accord more recognition to consultancy activities than do higher-ranking and predominantly pure ones. Thus, my informants in economics and physics, a number of whom undertook private

work for outside contractors for a fee, were adamant that such work would not be mentioned in any application for career advancement (unless perhaps, one or two conceded, it was done for a prestigious agency of national or international government); but the geographers, lawyers, engineers and pharmacists I interviewed assured me that consultancies were in their communities regarded as a proper, and indeed significant, feature of any *curriculum vitae*.

10 'The department *qua* department is less significant for the furtherance of its members' research than it is as a centre of graduate training and the academic career. . . . The true research communities are the "invisible colleges" – the handful of people around the world working in some subdiscipline or line or inquiry' (Trow 1976b).

11 One might indeed wonder how the average basic unit manages to be kept together, given that almost every constituent member has his or her individual profile of activities and concerns. Two answers, among other possible ones, may be noted. The first invokes disciplinary loyalties, which, particularly in convergent communities, can be counted upon to override the more temporary affiliations to specialized research areas. The second draws on the analysis by Trow (1976b) in which, in the related conflict of interests between teaching and research, he argues that an emphasis on:

> . the dominant norms and functions of university academic departments simplifies and distorts reality by implying that all the members of a department are oriented primarily . . . to research, and fill their departmental functions in similar ways. In fact, there is a very considerable division of academic labour, both within and between departments. But this arises *informally*, and not through a formal assignment of roles and functions to different departmental members. Thus, the formal characteristics (and the equality) of departments and their members are preserved, while a considerable variability in individual talent, preference and disposition allows people actually to distribute their time and energy very differently among the various functions of the department. . . . The academic division of labour . . . allows the academic department . . . to perform in actuality a wider range of functions than would be possible if its members were more homogeneous in orientation and personal preference.

12 To the contrary, a sceptical observer might conclude that the majority of academics are depressingly ready to conform to current social expectations.

Appendix: Research Issues

Sources of data

This enquiry is based both on a scrutiny of the relevant research literature (see Bibliography) and on the material derived from interviews with practising academics in a dozen disciplines. The discussion which follows concentrates on the latter. In alphabetical order (with numbers in parentheses of those contributing) the disciplines covered are:

Biology: botany and zoology (27)*

Chemistry (15)

Economics (13)

Geography (12)

History (22)*

Law (24)*

Mathematics (13)

Mechanical engineering (22)*

Modern languages: French, German, Spanish, Italian (12)

Pharmacy (16)

Physics (23)*

Sociology (22)*

The asterisks indicate the subjects which provided the central body of data; those without asterisks were tackled in less depth, and could in that sense be classified as subsidiary. Altogether I conducted 221 interviews across the 12 disciplines. The shortest lasted half an hour and the longest nearly 2 hours. The average length was somewhere between an hour and an hour and a quarter.

Methods of data collection

The interviews were of a type characterized in the social sciences as semi-structured and in-depth. The first term means that the interviewer has a general checklist of points to be raised, but allows the respondent's interests and the resulting shape of the discussion to dictate the order and form in which these points are introduced. The second implies that the duration of the interview should be extensive enough and the degree of rapport strong enough for respondents to discuss complex and perhaps sensitive issues if they are so inclined.

A particular variant on standard interviewing techniques was adopted. Because the emphasis was on exploring as many aspects of disciplinary communities as possible, as against collecting statistically based information on a narrower range of topics, it was not considered essential for every interview to span the complete agenda: some respondents could take the opportunity to focus in detail on particular issues, while others could be invited to concentrate on the items which had hitherto been neglected. Moreover, since unforeseen points of a kind worth exploring further might be expected to crop up in the course of any given set of interviews, room would need to be provided for topics to be added between one interview and another. They might also of course be deleted if sufficient clarification had already been achieved.

Rather than being conceived of as a small-scale social survey, therefore, the study should be seen as analogous with a detective investigation, in which significant clues could be followed up and interesting testimony corroborated with (or contradicted by) other witnesses. It was nearly always possible, as the interviews in any particular field proceeded, to find corroboration from at least one other respondent – often more – about key aspects of the disciplinary culture.

In practice, the basic checklist did not change very significantly from the start of the first interview cycle in January 1980 to its completion in April 1987. That is to say, the main categories – the structure of the discipline, the pattern of academic careers in the field, the nature of professional life, forms of communication and publication, and relevant value issues – remained more or less constant, even though a number of subsidiary themes needed to be modified systematically between one discipline and another as well as individually between one respondent and another.

Wherever it proved feasible, those who agreed to make themselves available for interviewing were sent a brief note in advance explaining the purpose of the study and outlining the topics with which it was concerned. The note, in the form in which it had evolved by 1986/7, read as follows:

A study of the cultures of disciplines

Introduction

This note is meant to set the background for a series of open-ended interviews with practitioners in various academic disciplines. It is assumed that those who have agreed to participate are interested in a reflective discussion of their own subject specialism, and are willing to make their views known to an interested, but uninitiated, enquirer.

Context

The enquiry – of which it is hoped that the proposed discussion with you would form a part – is directed towards substantiating, or repudiating, the hunch that the members of different disciplines differ from one another in systematic and discernible ways. It is the nature rather than the causes of these differences which provides the immediate focus: but it could well turn out that some of the more significant contrasts relate to epistemological issues – that is, to the forms of knowledge characteristic of particular areas of intellectual investigation.

It is not intended to elicit any information about the personal, as opposed to the professional, lives of those interviewed. (Whether, e.g. biologists drive faster cars than historians may be an interesting issue, but it is no concern of the present proposal.)

Content and format

There are likely to be six main areas for discussion (see below) though I am anxious not to be rigid about these, and would like to leave scope for others to be raised according to individual interest. Whether or not all six are covered will be a matter for individual informants to decide.

I would hope, in the normal course of events, to interview each informant in his or her own room, at a mutually convenient time. The length of the session would again be a matter of the informant's own choice, but – on the basis of experience – I would expect the timespan to lie somewhere between an upper limit of an hour and a half and a lower limit of half an hour. The normal conventions of anonymity and confidentiality would of course be strictly observed.

Some possible themes for discussion

The structure of the subject

External and internal boundaries; extent of overall cohesion/ fragmentation; relationships with neighbouring fields, etc.

Epistemological issues

Nature of evidence; forms of controversy; scope for ideology; verification/confirmation procedures, etc.

Career patterns

Modes of recruitment; initial barriers to tenure; choice of speciali- zation; mobility between specialisms; extent of emigration from/ immigration to other disciplines, etc.

Reputation and rewards

Criteria for professional recognition; terms of praise and blame; nature and existence of disciplinary heroes; marks of distinction, etc.

Aspects of professional practice

Individual scholarship *vs* teamwork; types of professional association; varieties of communication; publishing patterns; purposes of citation; availability of outside funds; characteristics of competition, etc.

Costs and benefits of disciplinary membership

Pros and cons of professional career; qualities fostered; predominant values; enjoyment, frustration and boredom in work, etc.

In almost every case, recipients commented that this note had given them a reasonable idea of what kind of discussion to expect; although they were offered a specific opportunity to raise any preliminary queries, very few wanted to do so. The implication is that the academics concerned felt generally at ease with the themes of the interviews. As might have been expected from their professional skills and background, they were invariably both articulate and lucid in their responses, to an extent which made interviewing them pleasurable as well as not too demanding (see Platt 1981 for some detailed comments on academics as interview subjects). A sizeable proportion of respondents remarked at the end of the session that they had enjoyed the opportunity to talk about their work; some went on to voice their regret that opportunities of this kind were so rare.

Variables in the research design

At the outset, a careful attempt was made to span the full range from senior to junior members of any department visited. That is to say, doctoral students and untenured research fellows were sought out as well as mid-career academics and those approaching retirement. However, no systematic difference was discernible in the responses of any of these categories: though views within a given community might differ, they did not appear significantly to do so in terms of age and experience. Accordingly, though the later interviews continued to involve academics of varying degrees of seniority, this was less a matter of deliberate design than had been the case earlier on.

Two of my concerns in drawing up the sample were, first, to be able to offset the particular characteristics of individual departments, and, secondly, to see how far national idiosyncrasies might play a part in the picture which emerged of one discipline or another. Together, they implied the need not only to widen the enquiry beyond a single department but also to extend it if possible outside Britain. The one requirement was taken into account by ensuring that every main discipline at least should be represented by two or more departments in British universities; and the other by adding a modest-sized US dimension to the enquiry. A list of the institutions visited in relation to each discipline is set out in Table 1. Their choice was determined partly by geographical considerations. All those in the UK were within relatively easy reach of my academic base; in the US, I conducted most of the interviews at Berkeley (where I was a Visiting Fellow for 3 months in 1980 and a further 3 months in 1986) and the remainder in universities reasonably accessible to it.

Table 1   Institutions visited in relation to the disciplines in the study

Discipline	UK	USA
Biology	Bristol, Reading	California (Berkeley)
Chemistry	Southampton	California (Berkeley, Santa Barbara, Los Angeles), Stanford
Economics	Cambridge	California (Berkeley, Santa Barbara, Los Angeles), Stanford
Geography	Cambridge	California (Berkeley, Santa Barbara, Los Angeles)
History	Exeter, London (University College)	California (Berkeley)
Law	Kent, London (LSE), Southampton	California (Berkeley)
Mathematics	Southampton	California (Berkeley, Santa Barbara, Los Angeles), Stanford
Mechanical Engineering	Birmingham, London (Imperial)	California (Berkeley)
Modern Languages	Cambridge	California (Berkeley, Santa Barbara, Los Angeles), Stanford
Pharmacy	Brighton Polytechnic, London (Chelsea)	California (San Francisco)
Physics	Bristol, London (Imperial)	California (Berkeley)
Sociology	Essex, London (LSE), Kent	California (Berkeley)

Note: Pilot interviews for biology, history, law, mechanical engineering, physics and sociology were carried out in Sussex

As already remarked, the interviews in California were intended mainly to gain some impression of how British academics might differ from their American counterparts. It transpired that the differences were, save in a few cases, negligible: it seemed that I was talking to more of the very community whose members I had already interviewed. I persisted with the transatlantic study partly because I thought I might succeed in catching more contrasts, but also because it provided an opportunity for me to extend my data base. The increase in spread of US universities (from one for the six main disciplines to four for the subsidiary ones) again made little difference: the chemists, the modern linguists and so on in one institution were very much like those in another.

Some lessons learned

In retrospect, it has emerged that a number of elements in the research design which initially seemed important – the need for respondents to span the full range of age and experience, the need for cross-institutional and even cross-national comparisons – have proved relatively insignificant when subjected to more detailed analysis. There were no particularly revealing discontinuities in perception or response across such categories. However, when it came to the question of academic careers, I had insufficient first-hand material to draw any meaningful distinction between men and women, and my addendum to the text on this issue had therefore to rely entirely on the research findings of others. If I were to start again, I would want to build in some more systematic allowance for gender differences. Because the existing research base appears to be so weak in relation to applied fields, I would also with the wisdom of hindsight have concentrated my own enquiries more heavily in their direction.

What now seem to me the most important dimensions of analysis – namely the similarities between specialisms located within different disciplines and the contrasts between specialisms located within the same disciplines – were not foreseen, and therefore not systematically taken into account in the initial planning of the research. Any future investigation along the lines of the one attempted here would, I suggest, do well to build them in as an integral part of its plans.

Unfinished business

Much more remains to be done in the way of a systematic study of the nature of knowledge fields and the cultural aspects of the communities engaged in their exploration. In the first place, it could be useful to undertake further case studies of some of the disciplines not included in the current sample. As already suggested, a concentration on such applied fields as medicine, accountancy, management studies, education and social work should yield new insights into a relatively neglected but none the less substantial sector of academic activity. The understanding of each of the 12 disciplines could also be given greater dimensionality and depth by pursuing the type of close observation suggested by Geertz (1976) in his prospectus for 'an ethnography of the disciplines', and adopted by Evans (1988) in his study of modern linguists.

Different but perhaps equally significant benefits could accrue from taking further the investigation by a number of sociologists and historians of science of how academic specialisms evolve, and relating them to the socio-political studies of school subjects by writers such as Ball (1982), Cooper (1985) and Goodson (1983). One possible outcome of such work might be to identify more fully the commonalities between problems, methods and theories in specialisms scattered across a number of disciplinary fields, and hence to throw additional light on the nature of knowledge itself.

The relatively decentralized higher education structures characteristic of Britain and the USA may well underplay certain features of the more centralized systems in, for example, France, Sweden and the USSR. Powerful free-standing research institutes such as those in France and Germany, and national academies such as those in Russia, seem likely to affect the way in which disciplinary cultures are defined and the form of their relationships with their associated knowledge fields. The understanding of these matters could also be enriched by a further study, along the lines initiated by Geiger (1987), of organized research units (see Chapter 7) and of industrial and government research establishments, following Ziman (1987).

Some useful gaps in the exploration of non-élite institutions have been filled by Ruscio (1987), but his work still remains at the pioneering stage. The study of comparable issues in the very different settings of Third World countries has not, as far as I am aware, even begun. Moves in both these directions ought to clarify links between teaching and research, thus (it might be hoped) connecting studies such as my own with those which focus mainly on aspects of undergraduate education.

In these and perhaps other ways, the findings recorded, the hypotheses developed, the explanations advanced in the course of this book might be put to the test, extended in a number of new directions, and elaborated in a number of different respects. What has been offered here is after all a prolegomenon, not an epilogue: a naming ceremony for a new and untried set of ideas, rather than the obituary on an inquiry whose course is fully run.

Bibliography

Allison, P. D. (1980) Inequalities in scientific productivity. *Social Studies of Science*, **10**, pp. 163–79.

Anthony, L. J., East, H. and Slater, M. J. (1969) The growth of the literature of physics. *Reports on Progress in Physics*, **32**, pp. 709–67.

Arnold, M. (1894) *Culture and Anarchy*. Uniform edition. London, Smith and Elder.

Bailey, F. G. (1977) *Morality and Expediency*. Oxford: Blackwell.

Ball, S. J. (1982) Competition and conflict in the teaching of English. *Journal of Curriculum Studies*, **14**, 1, pp. 1–28.

Barber, B. (1961) Resistance by scientists to scientific discovery. *Science*, **134**, pp. 596–602.

Barber, B. (1968) The functions and dysfunctions of fashion in science. *Mens en Maatschappij*, **43**, 6, pp. 501–514.

Barnes, B. and Dolby, R. G. A. (1970) The scientific ethos. *European Journal of Sociology*, **2**, pp. 3–25.

Barnett, C. (1986) *The Audit of War*. London, Macmillan.

Barnett, R. (1988) Limits to academic freedom. In Tight, M. (ed.) *Academic Freedom and Responsibility*. Milton Keynes, Open University Press.

Barry, B. (1981) Do neighbours make good fences? *Political Theory*, **9**, 3, pp. 293–301.

Baruch, J. (1984) The cultures of science and technology. *Science*, **244**, p. 7.

Bazerman, C. (1981) What written knowledge does. *Philosophy of the Social Sciences*, **2**, pp. 361–87.

Bazerman, C. (1987) Literate acts and the emergent social structure of science. *Social Epistemology*, **1**, 4, pp. 295–310.

Becher, T. (1987a) The disciplinary shaping of the profession. In Clark, B. R. (ed.) *The Academic Profession*. Berkeley, University of California Press.

Becher, T. (1987b) Disciplinary discourse. *Studies in Higher Education*, **12**, 3, pp. 261–74.

Becher, T. and Kogan, M. (1980) *Process and Structure in Higher Education*. London, Heinemann.

Becker, H. S. (1982) *Art Worlds*. Berkeley, University of California Press.

Becker, H. S., Geer, B. and Hughes, E. C. (1961) *Boys in White*. Chicago, University of Chicago Press.

Ben-David, J. (1960) Roles and innovations in medicine. *American Journal of Sociology*, **65**, pp. 557–68.

Ben-David, J. (1964) Scientific growth: A sociological view. *Minerva*, **2**, pp. 455–76.

Ben-David, J. and Collins, R. (1966) Social factors in the origin of a new science. *American Sociological Review*, **31**, pp. 451–65.

Bereiter, C. and Freedman, M. B. (1962) Fields of study and the people in them. In Sanford, N. (ed.) *The American College*. New York, John Wiley.

Bernal, J. D. (1939) *The Social Function of Science*. London, Routledge.

Bernard, J. (1964) *Academic Women*. University Park, Penn., Pennsylvania State University Press.

Biglan, A. (1973a) The characteristics of subject matter in different scientific areas. *Journal of Applied Psychology*, **57**, 3, pp. 195–203.

Biglan, A. (1973b) Relationships between subject matter characteristics and the structure and output of university departments. *Journal of Applied Psychology*, **57**, 3, pp. 204–213.

Blackstone, T. and Fulton, O. (1975) Sex discrimination among women university teachers. *British Journal of Sociology*, **26**, 3, pp. 261–75.

Blaug, M. (1985) *Great Economists since Keynes*. Brighton, Wheatsheaf.

Blaug, M. (1986) *Great Economists before Keynes*. Brighton, Wheatsheaf.

Blume, S. (1985) After the darkest hour . . . integrity and engagement in the development of university research. In Wittrock, B. and Elzinga, A. (eds) *The University Research System*. Stockholm, Almqvist and Wiksell.

Böhme, G., van den Dael, W. and Krohn, W. (1976) Finalization in science. *Social Science Information*, **15**, pp. 307–330.

Boissevain, J. (1974) Towards a sociology of social anthropology. *Theory and Society*, **1**, pp. 211–30.

Boulding, K. (1956) *The Image*. Ann Arbor, University of Michigan Press.

Bourdieu, P. (1979) Les trois etats du capital culturel. *Actes de la Recherche en Sciences Sociales*, **30**, pp. 3–6.

Bourdieu, P. (1981) The specificity of the scientific field. In Lemert, C. C. (ed.) *French Sociology*. New York, Columbia University Press.

Boys, C., Brennan, J., Henkel, M., Kirkland, J., Kogan, M. and Youll, P. (1988) *Higher Education and the Preparation for Work*. London, Jessica Kingsley.

Brown, D. G. (1967) *The Mobile Professors*. Washington, D.C., American Council on Education.

Buchanan, J. M. (1966) Economics and its scientific neighbours. In Krupp, S. R. (ed.) *The Structure of Economic Science*. Engelwood Cliffs, N.J., Prentice-Hall.

Bucher, R. and Strauss, A. (1961) Professions in process. *American Journal of Sociology*, **66**, pp. 325–34.

Bulik, S. (1982) *Structure and Subject Interaction*. New York, Marcel Dekker.

Burke, P. (1980) *Sociology and History*. London, Allen and Unwin.

Burton, R. E. and Kebler, R. W. (1960) The 'half-life' of some scientific and technical literatures. *American Documentation*, **11**, pp. 18–22.

Campbell, C. M. and Wiles, P. (1976) The study of law in society in Britain. *Law and Society Review*, **10**, pp. 547–78.

Campbell, D. T. (1969) Ethnocentrism of disciplines and the fish-scale model of omniscience. In Sherif, M. and Sherif, C. (eds) *Interdisciplinary Relationships in the Social Sciences*. Chicago, Aldine.

Carnegie Commission on Higher Education (1973) *Opportunities for Women in Higher Education*. New York, McGraw-Hill.

Carter, J. (ed.) (1961) *A.E. Housman: Selected Prose*. Cambridge, Cambridge University Press.

Chubin, D. E. (1976) The conceptualisation of scientific specialties. *Sociological Quarterly*, **17**, pp. 448–76.

Chubin, D. E. and Moitra, S. (1975) Content analysis of references. *Social Studies of Science*, **5**, pp. 423–41.

Church, C. H. (1973) The professional pale. In Taylor, G. P. (ed.) *History in Higher Education*. Sheffield, Sheffield Polytechnic.

Church, C. H. (1976) Disciplinary dynamics. *Studies in Higher Education*, **1**, 2, pp. 101–118.

Church, C. H. (1978) Constraints on the historian. *Studies in Higher Education*, **3**, 2, pp. 127–38.

Clark, B. R. (1963) Faculty culture. In Lunsford, T. F. (ed.) *The Study of Campus Cultures*. Boulder, Col., Western Interstate Commission for Higher Education.

Clark, B. R. (1980) Academic Culture. Working Paper No. 42. New Haven, Conn., Yale University Higher Education Research Group.

Clark, B. R. (1983) *The Higher Education System*. Berkeley, University of California Press.

Clark, B. R. (1987a) *The Academic Life*. Princeton, Princeton University Press.

Clark, B. R. (ed.) (1987b) *The Academic Profession*. Berkeley, University of California Press.

Clarke, B. L. (1964) Multiple authorship trends in scientific papers. *Science*, **143**, pp. 822–4.

Cohn, B. S. (1962) An anthropologist among the historians. *South Atlantic Quarterly*, **61**, Winter, pp. 13–28.

Cole, J. R. (1979) *Fair Science: Women in the Scientific Community*. New York, Free Press.

Cole, J. R. and Cole, S. (1973) *Social Stratification in Science*. Chicago, Chicago University Press.

Cole, S. (1970) Professional standing and the reception of scientific discoveries. *American Journal of Sociology*, **76**, pp. 286–306.

Cole, S. (1978) Scientific reward systems: A comparative analysis. In Jones, R. A. (ed.) *Research in Sociology of Knowledge, Sciences and Art*, **1**. Greenwich, Conn.: JAI.

Cole, S. (1983) The hierarchy of the sciences. *American Journal of Sociology*, **89**, 1, pp. 111–39.

Cole, S. and Cole, J. (1967) Scientific output and recognition. *American Sociological Review*, **32**, pp. 377–90.

Cole, S., Cole, J. R. and Simon, G. A. (1981) Chance and consensus in peer review. *Science*, **214**, pp. 881–6.

Cole, S., Rubin, L. and Cole, J. R. (1977) Peer review and the support of science. *Scientific American*, **237**, October, pp. 34–41.

Collins, R. (1975) *Conflict Sociology*. London and San Diego, Academic Press.

Cooper, B. (1985) *Renegotiating Secondary School Mathematics*. Lewes, Falmer Press.

Crane, D. (1965) Scientists at major and minor universities. *American Sociological Review*, **30**, pp. 699–714.

Crane, D. (1967) The gatekeepers of science. *American Sociologist*, **2**, pp. 195–201.

Crane, D. (1969a) Social structure in a group of scientists. *American Sociological Review*, **34**, pp. 335–52.

Crane, D. (1969b) Fashion in science. *Social Problems*, **16**, pp. 433–40.

Crane, D. (1972) *Invisible Colleges*. Chicago, University of Chicago Press.

Crick, M. (1976) *Explorations in Language and Meaning*. London, Malaby Press.

Cronin, B. (1984) *The Citation Process*. London, Taylor Graham.

Darnton, R. (1968) *Mesmerism and the End of the Enlightenment in France*. Cambridge, Mass., Harvard University Press.

Dasgupta, P. and David, P. A. (1985) *Information Disclosure and the Economics of Science and Technology*. Publication No. 48. Stanford, Stanford University Centre for Economic Policy Research.

Dennis, W. (1956) Age and productivity among scientists. *Science*, **123**, pp. 724–5.

Dennis, W. (1958) The age decrement in outstanding scientific contributions. *American Psychologist*, **13**, pp. 457–60.

Dennis, W. (1966) Creative productivity between the ages of 20 and 80 years. *Journal of Gerontology*, **21**, pp. 1–8.

Dill, D. D. (1982) The management of academic culture. *Higher Education*, **11**, pp. 303–320.

Duncan, S. S. (1974) The isolation of scientific discovery. *Science Studies*, **4**, pp. 109–134.

Elzinga, A. (1985) Research bureaucracy and the drift of epistemic criteria. In Wittrock, B. and Elzinga, A. (eds) *The University Research System*. Stockholm, Almqvist and Wiksell.

Elzinga, A. (1987a) Internal and external regulatives in research and higher education systems. In Premfors, R. (ed.) *Disciplinary Perspectives on Higher Education and Research*. Report No. 37. Stockholm, University of Stockholm GSHR.

Elzinga, A. (1987b) Politicization of science and epistemic drift. Mimeo: Dalarö 1987 International Conference, Swedish National Board of Universities and Colleges, Research on Higher Education Program.

Erikson, K. T. (1970) Sociology and the historical perspective. *American Sociologist*, **5**, pp. 331–8.

Evans, C. (1983) EFCOM versus PHILIT: The politics of modern languages. Mimeo: Zeitschrift fur Hochschuldidaktic, Klagenfurt.

Evans, C. (1988) *Language People*. Milton Keynes, Open University Press.

Evans-Pritchard, E. E. (1951) *Social Anthropology*. London, Routledge.

Fell, H. B. (1960) Fashion in cell biology. *Science*, **132**, pp. 1625–7.

Fisher, C. S. (1973) Some social characteristics of mathematicians and their work. *American Journal of Sociology*, **75**, 5, pp. 1094–1118.

Fleming, D. (1969) Emigré physicists and the biological revolution. In Fleming, D. and Bailyn, B. (eds) *The Intellectual Migration*. Cambridge, Mass., Harvard University Press.

Foucault, M. (1970) *The Order of Things*. London, Tavistock.

Fox, M. F. (1983) Publication productivity among scientists. *Social Studies of Science*, **13**, 2, pp. 285–305.

Fox, M. F. and Faver, C. A. (1982) The process of collaboration in scholarly research. *Scholarly Publishing*, **13**, pp. 327–39.

Gaff, J. G. and Wilson, R. C. (1971) Faculty cultures and interdisciplinary studies. *Journal of Higher Education*, **43**, 3, pp. 186–201.

Galtung, J. (1981) Structure, culture and intellectual style. *Social Science Information*, **20**, pp. 817–56.

Gaston, J. (1970) The reward system in British science. *American Sociological Review*, **35**, pp. 718–32.

Gaston, J. (1971) Secretiveness and competition for priority in physics. *Minerva* **9**, pp. 472–92.

Gaston, J. (1972) Communication and the reward system of science. In Halmos, P. (ed.) Sociology of science. *Sociological Review Monograph*, **18**, pp. 25–41.

Gaston, J. (1973) *Originality and Competition in Science*. Chicago, University of Chicago Press.

Geertz, C. (1976) Toward an ethnography of the disciplines. Mimeo: Princeton Institute for Advanced Study.

Geertz, C. (1980) Blurred genres. *The American Scholar*, **49**, pp. 165–78.

Geertz, C. (1983) *Local Knowledge*. New York, Basic Books.

Geiger, R. (1985) The home of scientists: A perspective on university research. In Wittrock, B. and Elzinga, A. (eds) *The University Research System*. Stockholm, Almqvist and Wiksell.

Geiger, R. (1987) Organized research and American universities. Mimeo: Dalarö 1987 International Conference, Swedish National Board of Universities and Colleges, Research on Higher Education Progam.

Gerholm, T. (1985) On tacit knowledge in academia. In Gustavson, L. (ed.) *On Communication: No. 3*. Linköping, University of Linköping Department of Communication Studies.

Gerstl, J. E. and Hutton, S. P. (1966) *Engineers*. London, Tavistock.

Gibbons, M. (1985) Introduction. In Gibbons, M. and Wittrock, B. (eds) *Science as a Commodity*. Harlow, Longman.

Gieryn, T. F. (1978) Problem retention and problem change in science. In Gaston, J. (ed.) *Sociology of Science (Sociological Inquiry*, **48**, 3–4). San Francisco, Jossey Bass.

Gilbert, G. N. (1977a) Competition, differentiation and careers in science. *Social Science Information*, **16**, pp. 103–123.

Gilbert, G. (1977b) Referencing as persuasion. *Social Studies of Science*, **7**, pp. 113–22.

Glaser, B. G. and Strauss, A. (1967) *The Discovery of Grounded Theory*. New York, Aldine.

Goodson, I. (1983) *School Subjects and Curriculum Change*. London, Croom Helm.

Gouldner, A. W. (1957) Cosmopolitans and locals. *Administrative Science Quarterly*, **2**, pp. 281–306 and 444–80.

Graham, L. (1983) Introduction. In Graham, L., Lepenies, W. and Weingart, P. (eds) *Functions and Uses of Disciplinary Histories*. Dordrecht, Reidel.

Griffith, B. C. and Miller, A. J. (1970) Networks of informal communication among scientifically productive scientists. In Nelson, C. E. and Pollock, D. K. (eds) *Communication among Scientists and Engineers*. Lexington, Mass., Heath.

Griffith, B. C. and Mullins, N. C. (1972) Coherent groups in scientific change. *Science*, **177**, pp. 959–64.

Griffith, B. C. and Small, H. G. (1983) The structure of the social and behavioural sciences literature. Mimeo: Royal Institute of Technology Library, Stockholm.

Gustin, B. (1973) Charisma, recognition and the motivation of scientists. *American Journal of Sociology*, **78**, 5, pp. 1119–34.

Hagstrom, W. O. (1965) *The Scientific Community*. New York, Basic Books.

Hagstrom, W. O. (1974) Competition in science. *American Sociological Review*, **39**, pp. 1–18.

Halsey, A. H. and Trow, M. (1971) *The British Academics*. London, Faber.

Hardy, G. H. (1941) *A Mathematician's Apology.* Cambridge, Cambridge University Press.

Hargens, L. L. (1975) *Patterns of Scientific Research.* Washington, American Sociological Association.

Hargens, L. and Hagstrom, W. (1967) Sponsored and contest mobility of American scientists. *Sociology of Education,* **40,** pp. 24–8.

Henkel, M. (1987) The discipline: Still the dominant force in higher education? Mimeo: Dalarö 1987 International Conference, Swedish National Board of Universities and Colleges, Research on Higher Education Program.

Hirst, P. H. (1974) *Knowledge and the Curriculum.* London, Routledge.

Holloway, S. W. F., Jewson, N. D. and Mason, D. J. (1986) 'Professionalisation' or 'occupational imperialism'? Some reflections on pharmacy in Britain. *Social Science of Medicine,* **23,** 3, pp. 323–32.

Horton, R. (1967) African traditional thought and Western science: I. *Africa,* **37,** 1, pp. 50–71.

Jacobsen, B. (1981) Collection type and integration type curricula in systems of higher education. *Acta Sociologica,* **24,** 1–2, pp. 25–41.

Jamison, A. (1982) National components of scientific knowledge. Mimeo: University of Lund, Research Policy Institute.

Johnson, H. G. (1971) The Keynesian revolution and the monetarist counter-revolution. *American Economic Review,* **61,** 3 (supplement), pp. 1–14.

Jones, G. S. (1976) From historical sociology to theoretical history. *British Journal of Sociology,* **27,** pp. 295–305.

Jones, R. A. (1980) Myth and symbol among the Nacirema Tsigoloicos. *American Sociologist,* **15,** pp. 207–212.

Kemp, R. V. (1977) Controversy in scientific research and tactics of communication. *Sociological Review,* **25,** pp. 515–34.

King, A. R. and Brownell, J. (1966) *The Curriculum and the Disciplines of Knowledge.* New York, John Wiley.

Klamer, A. (1984) *The New Classical Macroeconomics.* Brighton, Wheatsheaf.

Kleinman, S. (1983) Collective matters as individual concerns. *Urban Life,* **12,** 2, pp. 203–225.

Knorr-Cetina, K. D. (1981) *The Manufacture of Knowledge.* Oxford, Pergamon.

Knorr-Cetina, K. D. (1982) Scientific communities or transepistemic arenas of research? *Social Studies of Science,* **12,** pp. 101–130.

Kogan, M. (1987) The responsiveness of higher education to external influences. Mimeo: Dalarö 1987 International Conference, Swedish National Board of Universities and Colleges, Research on Higher Education Program.

Kogan, M. and Henkel, M. (1983) *Government and Research.* London, Heinemann.

Kolb, D. A. (1981) Learning styles and disciplinary differences. In Chickering, A. (ed.) *The Modern American College.* San Francisco, Jossey Bass.

Kolb, D. A. (1984) *Experiential Learning.* Engelwood Cliffs, N.J., Prentice-Hall.

Kuhn, T. S. (1962). *The Structure of Scientific Revolutions.* Chicago, University of Chicago Press.

Kuhn, T. S. (1970). *The Structure of Scientific Revolutions,* 2nd edition. Chicago, University of Chicago Press.

Kuhn, T. (1977) *The Essential Tension.* Chicago, University of Chicago Press.

Kuper, A. (1975) *Anthropologists and Anthropology.* Harmondsworth, Penguin.

Law, J. (1976) X-ray protein crystallography. In Lemaine, G., Macleod, R., Mulkay,

M. and Weingart, P. (eds) *Perspectives on the Emergence of Scientific Disciplines*. The Hague, Mouton.

Lehman, H. C. (1953) *Age and Achievement*. Princeton, Princeton University Press.

Leijonhufvud, A. (1973) Life among the Econ. *Western Economic Journal*, **9**, 3, pp. 327–37.

Lewis, G. C. (1849) *An Essay on the Influence of Authority on Matters of Opinion*. Reprint edition 1974. New York, Arno Press.

Lightfield, E. T. (1971) Output and recognition of sociologists. *American Sociologist*, **6**, pp. 128–33.

Lodahl, J. B. and Gordon, G. (1972) The structure of scientific fields and the functioning of university graduate departments. *American Sociological Review*, **37**, pp. 57–72.

MacRoberts, M. H. and MacRoberts, B. R. (1984) The negational reference: Or the art of dissembling. *Social Studies of Science*, **14**, pp. 91–4.

Manniche, E. and Falk, G. (1957) Age and the Nobel Prize. *Behavioural Science*, **2**, pp. 301–307.

Marquis, D. and Allen, T. (1966) Communication patterns in applied technology. *American Psychologist*, **21**, pp. 1052–60.

Martindale, D. (1979) Ideologies, paradigms and theories. In Snizek, W. E., Fuhrman, E. R. and Miller, M. K. (eds) *Contemporary Issues in Theory and Research: A Sociological Perspective*. London, Aldwych Press.

Masterman, M. (1970) The nature of a paradigm. In Lakatos, I. and Musgrave, A. (eds) *Criticism and the Growth of Knowledge*. Cambridge, Cambridge University Press.

McDowell, J. M. (1984) Obsolescence of knowledge and career publication profiles. *American Economic Review*, **72**, 4, pp. 752–68.

Megill, A. (1987) Provocation on belief: Part 4. *Social Epistemology*, **1**, 1, pp. 106–108.

Merton, R. (1957) Priorities in scientific discovery. *American Sociological Review*, **22**, pp. 635–59.

Merton, R. K. (1973) *The Sociology of Science*. Chicago, University of Chicago Press.

Mikesell, M. W. (1969) The borderlands of geography as a social science. In Sherif, M. and Sherif, C. (eds) *Interdisciplinary Relationships in the Social Sciences*. Chicago, Aldine.

Mitroff, I. I. (1974) *The Subjective Side of Science*. Amsterdam, Elsevier.

Morlock, L. (1973) Discipline variation in the status of academic women. In Rossi, A. S. and Calderwood, A. (eds) *Academic Women on the Move*. New York, Russell Sage Foundation.

Moulin, L. (1955) The Nobel Prizes for the sciences from 1901–1950. *British Journal of Sociology*, **6**, pp. 246–63.

Mulkay, M. (1969) Some aspects of cultural growth in the natural sciences. *Social Research*, **36**, pp. 22–52.

Mulkay, M. (1972) *The Social Process of Innovation*. London, Macmillan.

Mulkay, M. (1974) Conceptual displacements and migration in science. *Science Studies*, **4**, pp. 205–234.

Mulkay, M. J. (1976) The mediating role of the scientific elite. *Social Studies of Science*, **6**, pp. 445–70.

Mulkay, M. (1977) The sociology of the scientific research community. In Spiegel-Rösing, I. and Price, D. de S. (eds) *Science, Technology and Society*. London, Sage.

Mulkay, M. J. and Edge, D. O. (1973) Cognitive, technical and social factors in the growth of radio astronomy. *Social Science Information*, **12**, pp. 25–61.

Mullins, N. (1968) The distribution of social and cultural properties in informal communication networks among biological scientists. *American Sociological Review*, **33**, p. 786–97.

Mullins, N. (1972) The development of a scientific specialty. *Minerva*, **10**, pp. 52–82.

Mullins, N. (1973a) *Theory and Theory Groups in American Sociology*. New York, Harper and Row.

Mullins, N. C. (1973b) The development of specialties in social science. *Science Studies*, **3**, pp. 245–73.

Murray, S. O. (1983) *Group Formation in Social Science*. Edmonton, Alberta, Linguistic Research Inc.

Nadel, E. (1980) Formal communication, journal concentration and the rise of a discipline in physics. *Sociology*, **14**, 3, pp. 401–416.

Neave, G. (1979) Academic drift: Some views from Europe. *Studies in Higher Education*, **4**, 2, pp. 143–59.

Nicolaus, M. (1972) Sociology liberation movement. In Pateman, T. (ed.) *Counter Course*. Harmondsworth, Penguin.

Oromaner, M. (1983) Professional standing and the reception of contributions to economics. *Research in Higher Education*, **19**, 3, pp. 351–62.

Pantin, C. F. A. (1968) *The Relations Between the Sciences*. Cambridge, Cambridge University Press.

Parlett, M. (1977) The department as a learning milieu. *Studies in Higher Education*, **2**, 2, pp. 173–81.

Patel, N. (1973) Collaboration in the professional growth of American sociology. *Social Science Information*, **12**, pp. 77–92.

Pickering, A. (1984) *Constructing Quarks*. Edinburgh, Edinburgh University Press.

Platt, J. (1976) *Realities in Social Research*. Brighton, Sussex University Press.

Platt, J. (1981) On interviewing one's peers. *British Journal of Sociology*, **32**, 1, pp. 75–91.

Polanyi, M. (1962) The republic of science. *Minerva*, **1**, 1, pp. 54–73.

Popper, K. (1979) *Objective Knowledge*. Oxford, Oxford University Press.

Porter, M. (1984) Saint George or the dragon. *Network*, **29**, May, pp. 1–2.

Price, D. (1963) *Big Science, Little Science*. New York, Columbia University Press.

Price, D. de S. (1965) Networks of scientific papers. *Science*, **149**, 3683, pp. 510–15.

Price, D. J. (1970) Citation measures of hard science, soft science, technology and non-science. In Nelson, C. E. and Pollock, D. K. (eds) *Communication among Scientists and Engineers*. Lexington, Mass., Heath.

Price, D. and Beaver, D. (1966) Collaboration in an invisible college. *American Psychologist*, **21**, pp. 1011–18.

Ravetz, J. R. (1971) *Scientific Knowledge and its Social Problems*. Oxford, Clarendon Press.

Reif, F. (1961) The competitive world of the pure scientist. *Science*, **134**, 3494, pp. 1957–62.

Reif, F. and Strauss, A. (1965) The impact of rapid discovery on the scientist's career. *Social Problems*, **12**, pp. 297–311.

Rendel, M. (1984) Women academics in the seventies. In Acker, S. and Warren Piper, D. (eds) *Is Higher Education Fair to Women?* Guildford, SRHE.

Reskin, B. F. (1977) Scientific productivity and the reward structure of science. *American Sociological Review*, **42**, pp. 491–504.

Rip, A. (1981) A cognitive approach to science policy. *Research Policy*, **10**, pp. 294–311.

Ritzer, G. (1975) Sociology: A multiple paradigm science. *American Sociologist*, **10**, pp. 156–67.
Ritzer, G. (1979) Toward an integrated sociological paradigm. In Snizek, W. E., Fuhrman, E. R. and Miller, M. K. (eds) *Contemporary Issues in Theory and Research*. London, Aldwych.
Ritzer, G. (1980) *Sociology: A Multiple Paradigm Science*. Revised edition. Boston, Allyn and Bacon.
Roberts, A. H. (1970) The system of communication in the language sciences. In Nelson, C. E. and Pollock, D. K. (eds) *Communication among Scientists and Engineers*. Lexington, Mass., Heath.
Roe, A. (1953) *The Making of a Scientist*. New York, Dodd, Mead.
Rorty, R. (1979) *Philosophy and the Mirror of Nature*. Princeton, Princeton University Press.
Rose, M. and Rose, S. (1974) Do not adjust your mind, there is a fault in reality. In Whitley, R. (ed.) *Social Processes of Scientific Development*. London, Routledge.
Rothblatt, S. (1968) *The Revolution of the Dons*. London, Faber.
Rothblatt, S. (1985) The notion of an open scientific community in scientific perspective. In Gibbons, M. and Wittrock, B. (eds) *Science as a Commodity*. Harlow, Longman.
Rothman, R. A. (1972) A dissenting view on the scientific ethos. *British Journal of Sociology*, **23**, pp. 102–108.
Ruscio, K. P. (1985) Specializations in academic disciplines. Mimeo: University of California, Los Angeles, Comparative Higher Education Research Group.
Ruscio, K. P. (1986) Bridging specialisations. *Review of Higher Education*, **10**, 1, pp. 29–45.
Ruscio, K. P. (1987) Many sectors, many professions. In Clark, B. R. (ed.) *The Academic Profession*. Berkeley, University of California Press.
Salmond, A. (1982) Theoretical landscapes: On cross-cultural conceptions of knowledge. In Parkin, D. (ed.) *Semantic Anthropology*. London and San Diego, Academic Press.
Sanford, N. (1971) Academic culture and the teacher's development. *Soundings*, Winter, pp. 357–71.
Schatzman, L. and Strauss, A. (1966) A sociology of psychiatry. *Social Problems*, **14**, pp. 3–16.
Shinn, T. (1982) Scientific disciplines and organizational specificity. In Elias, N., Martins, H. and Whitley, R. D. (eds) *Scientific Establishments and Hierarchies*. Dordrecht, Reidel.
Slaymaker, O. (1968) The new geography. *Geographical Journal*, **134**, 3, pp. 405–407.
Small, H. (1978) Cited documents as concept symbols. *Social Studies of Science*, **8**, pp. 327–40.
Smith, D. (1982) Social history and sociology – more than just good friends. *Sociological Review*, **30**, 2, pp. 286–308.
Snyder, B. R. (1971) *The Hidden Curriculum*. New York, Knopf.
Snow, C. P. (1959) *The Two Cultures and the Scientific Revolution*. Cambridge, Cambridge University Press.
Spiegel-Rösing, I. (1974) Disziplinare stratagien die statussichering. *Homo*, **25**, 1, pp. 11–37.
Startup, R. (1980) The sociology of mathematics. *Sociology and Social Research*, **64**, 2, pp. 151–67.

Steig, M. (1986) *The Origin and Development of Scholarly Historical Periodicals*. Alabama, University of Alabama Press.

Stern, N. (1978) Age and achievement in mathematics. *Social Studies of Science*, **8**, pp. 127–40.

Stevens, R. E. (1953) Characteristics of scientific literatures. *American Council of Learned Societies Monograph*, **6**.

Stoddart, D. R. (1967) Growth and structure of geography. *Transactions and Papers of the Institute of British Geographers*, **41**.

Storer, N. and Parsons, T. (1968) The disciplines as a differentiating force. In Montgomery, E. B. (ed.) *The Foundations of Access to Knowledge*. Syracuse, Syracuse University Press.

Strauss, A. and Rainwater, L. (1962) *The Professional Scientist*. Chicago, Aldine.

Swales, J. (1988) Discourse communities, genres and English as an international language. *World Englishes*, **7**, 2, pp. 211–20.

Taylor, P. J. (1976) An interpretation of the quantification debate in British geography. *Transactions of the Institute of British Geographers N.S.*, **1**, 2.

Terman, L. M. (1954) Scientists and nonscientists in a group of 800 gifted men. *Psychological Monographs*, **68**, 7.

Thagaard, T. (1987) Does the organization of research in universities further creativity? Mimeo: Dalarö 1987 International Conference, Swedish National Board of Universities and Colleges, Research on Higher Education Program.

Thomas, P. (1985) *The Aims and Outcomes of Social Policy Research*. London, Croom Helm.

Toulmin, S. (1972) *Human Understanding, Vol. 1*. Oxford, Clarendon Press.

Traweek, S. (1982) Uptime, downtime, spacetime and power. Unpublished PhD thesis, University of California Santa Cruz.

Trow, M. (1976a) The public and private lives of higher education. *Daedalus*, **104**, pp. 113–27.

Trow, M. (1976b) The American university department as a context for learning. *Studies in Higher Education*, **1**, 1, pp. 11–22.

University Grants Committee (1987) *University Statistics 1986–87, Vol. 1: Students and Staff*. Cheltenham, Universities Statistical Record.

van den Braembussche, A. (1979) The Annales paradigm. In Callebaut, W., Demey, M., Pinxten, R. and Vandamme, F. (eds) *Theory of Knowledge and Science Policy*. Ghent, Communication and Cognition.

van den Daele, W., Krohn, W. and Weingart, P. (1977) The political direction of scientific development. In Mendelsohn, E., Weingart, P. and Whitley, R. (eds) *The Social Production of Scientific Knowledge*. Dordrecht, Reidel.

Waldo, D. (1975) Political science: Tradition, discipline, profession, science, enterprise. In Greenstein, F. and Polsby, N. (eds) *Political Science: Scope and Theory*. Reading, Mass., Addison Wesley.

Waterman, A. T. (1966) Social influences and scientists. *Science*, **151**, pp. 61–4.

Watson, J. D. (1970) *The Double Helix*. Harmondsworth, Penguin.

Waugh, E. (1956) An open letter. In Mitford, N. (ed.) *Noblesse Oblige*. London, Hamish Hamilton.

Wax, M. L. (1969) Myth and interrelationship in social science. In Sherif, M. and Sherif, C. (eds) *Interdisciplinary Relationships in the Social Sciences*. Chicago, Aldine.

Weber, E. (1977) *Peasants into Frenchman*. London, Chatto and Windus.

Weingart, P. (1974) On a sociological theory of scientific change. In Whitley, R. (ed.) *Social Processes of Scientific Development*. London, Routledge.

Weinstock, M. (1971) Citation indexes. In *Encyclopaedia of Library Information Science*. New York, Marcel Dekker.

Weiss, C. H. (ed.) (1977) *Using Social Research in Public Policy Making*. Lexington, Mass., Lexington Books.

Wesseling, H. L. (1985) The identification of scientific advancement in history. In Hägerstrand, T. (ed.) *The Identification of Progress in Learning*. Cambridge, Cambridge University Press.

Whitley, R. (1969) Communication nets in science. *Sociological Review*, **17**, pp. 219–33.

Whitley, R. (1976) Umbrella and polytheistic scientific disciplines and their elites. *Social Studies of Science*, **6**, pp. 471–97.

Whitley, R. (1977) The sociology of scientific work and the history of scientific developments. In Blume, S. (ed.) *Perspectives in the Sociology of Science*. New York, John Wiley.

Whitley, R. (1982) The establishment and structure of the sciences as reputational organizations. In Elias, N., Martins, W. and Whitley, R. (eds) *Scientific Establishments and Hierarchies*. Dordrecht, Reidel.

Whitley, R. (1984) *The Intellectual and Social Organization of the Sciences*. Oxford, Clarendon Press.

Wiener, M. (1981) *English Culture and the Decline of the Industrial Spirit*. Cambridge, Cambridge University Press.

Wilder, R. L. (1981) *Mathematics as a Cultural System*. Oxford, Pergamon.

Williams, G., Blackstone, T. and Metcalf, D. (1974) *The Academic Labour Market*. Amsterdam, Elsevier.

Wolfe, D. M. and Kolb, D. A. (1979) Career development, personal growth and experiential learning. In Kolb, D., Rubin, I. and McIntyre, J. (eds) *Organizational Psychology*, 3rd edition. Engelwood Cliffs, N.J., Prentice-Hall.

Yates, P. D. (1985) Science and sensibility. Mimeo: University of Sussex.

Ziman, J. (1973) Foreword. In Gaston, G. (ed.), *Originality and Competition in Science*. Chicago, Chicago University Press.

Ziman, J. (1981) What are the options? Social determinants of personal research plans. *Minerva*, **19**, 1, pp. 1–42.

Ziman, J. (1987) *Knowing Everything about Nothing*. Cambridge, Cambridge University Press.

Zinberg, D. (1985) The legacy of success. In Gibbons, M. and Wittrock, B. (eds) *Science as a Commodity*. Harlow, Longman.

Zuckerman, H. (1968) Patterns of name ordering among authors of scientific papers. *American Journal of Sociology*, **74**, pp. 276–91.

Zuckerman, H. A. (1970) Stratification in American science. *Sociological Inquiry*, **40**, pp. 235–57.

Zuckerman, H. A. (1977) *Scientific Elite: Nobel Laureates in the United States*. New York, Free Press.

Zuckerman, H. and Cole, J. R. (1975) Women in American science. *Minerva*, **13**, 1, pp. 82–102.

Zuckerman, H. and Merton, R. K. (1971) Patterns of evaluation in science. *Minerva*, **9**, pp. 66–100.

Zuckerman, H. and Merton, R. K. (1973) Age, ageing and age structure in science. In Merton, R. K. (ed.) *The Sociology of Science*. Chicago, University of Chicago Press.

Index

The Society for Research into Higher Education

The Society exists both to encourage and co-ordinate research and development into all aspects of higher education, including academic, organizational and policy issues; and also to provide a forum for debate – verbal and printed.

The Society's income derives from subscriptions, book sales, conference fees, and grants. It receives no subsidies and is wholly independent. Its corporate members are institutions of higher education, research institutions and professional, industrial, and governmental bodies. Its individual members include teachers and researchers, administrators and students. Members are found in all parts of the world and the Society regards its international work as amongst its most important activities.

The Society discusses and comments on policy, organizes conferences, and encourages research. Under the imprint SRHE & OPEN UNIVERSITY PRESS, it is a specialist publisher of research, having some 40 titles in print. It also publishes *Studies in Higher Education* (three times a year) which is mainly concerned with academic issues; *Higher Education Quarterly* (formerly *Universities Quarterly*) mainly concerned with policy issues; *Abstracts* (three times a year); an *International Newsletter* (twice a year) and *SRHE News* (four times a year).

The Society's committees, study groups and branches are run by members (with help from a small secretariat at Guildford), and aim to provide a forum for discussion. The groups at present include a Teacher Education Study Group, a Staff Development Group, and a Continuing Education Group, each of which may have their own organization, subscriptions, or publications (e.g. the *Staff Development Newsletter*). A further Questions of Quality Group has organized a series of Anglo-American seminars in the USA and the UK.

The Governing Council, elected by members, comments on current issues; and discusses policies with leading figures, notably at its evening forums. The Society organizes seminars on current research, and is in touch with bodies in the UK such as the NAB, CVCP, UGC, CNAA and with sister-bodies overseas. It co-operates with the British Council on courses run in conjunction with its conferences.

The Society's conferences are often held jointly; and have considered 'Standards and Criteria' (1986, with Bulmershe College); 'Restructuring' (1987, with the City of Birmingham Polytechnic); 'Academic Freedom' (1988, with the University of Surrey). In 1989, 'Access and Institutional Change' (with the Polytechnic of North London). In 1990, the topic will be 'Industry and Higher Education' (with the

University of Surrey). In 1991, the topic will be 'Research in HE'. Other conferences have considered the DES 'Green Paper' (1985); 'HE After the Election' (1987) and 'After the Reform Act' (July 1988). An annual series on 'The First Year Experience' with the University of South Carolina and Teeside Polytechnic held two meetings in 1988 in Cambridge, and another in St Andrews in July 1989.

For some of the Society's conferences, special studies are commissioned in advance, as *Precedings*.

Members receive free of charge the Society's *Abstracts*, annual conference proceedings (or 'Precedings'), *SRHE News* and *International Newsletter*. They may buy SRHE & Open University Press books at discount, and *Higher Education Quarterly* on special terms. Corporate members also receive the Society's journal *Studies in Higher Education* free (individuals on special terms). Members may also obtain certain other journals at a discount, including the NFER *Register of Educational Research*. There is a substantial discount to members, and to staff of corporate members, on annual and some other conference fees.

Further information: SRHE at the University, Guildford. GU2 5XH UK (0483) 39003.